THE SECRETS
of the VAULTED SKY

ALSO BY DAVID BERLINSKI

DAVID BERLINSKI

THE SECRETS
of the VAULTED SKY

ASTROLOGY
AND THE ART OF
PREDICTION

HARCOURT, INC.

Orlando   Austin   New York   San Diego   Toronto   London

www.HarcourtBooks.com

Library of Congress Cataloging-in-Publication Data
Berlinski, David, 1942–
The secrets of the vaulted sky: astrology and the art of prediction/David Berlinski.
p.   cm
Includes bibliographical references and index.
ISBN 0-15-100527-3
1. Astrology—History.   I. Title.
BF1674.B47   2003
133.5—dc21   2003009789

Text set in Adobe Garamond
Designed by Linda Lockowitz

Printed in the United States of America

First U.S. edition
A C E G I K J H F D B

To
my mother
—unconquerable—

CONTENTS

Stand up and lift your hand and bless
A man that finds great bitterness
In thinking of his lost renown.
A Roman Caesar is held down
Under this hump.

—W. B. YEATS

THE SECRETS
of the VAULTED SKY

ASTROLOGICAL SYMBOLS

SIGNS	PLANETS	ASPECTS
♈ ARIES	☉ SUN	☌ CONJUNCTION
♉ TAURUS	☽ MOON	✶ SEXTILE
♊ GEMINI	☿ MERCURY	△ TRINE
♋ CANCER	♀ VENUS	□ SQUARE
♌ LEO	♂ MARS	☍ OPPOSITION
♍ VIRGO	♃ JUPITER	
♎ LIBRA	♄ SATURN	
♏ SCORPIO	♅ URANUS	
♐ SAGITTARIUS	♆ NEPTUNE	
♑ CAPRICORN	♇	
	OR	
♒ ACQUARIUS	♇ PLUTO	
♓ PISCES		

SIGNS AND CAUSES, ACTION AND FREEDOM

STROLOGY IS A failed science in the simple but inescapable sense that in this country and in Europe, it is no longer taken seriously by scientists. Whether it is a *failure* and whether it is a *science*—now these are other questions.

The earliest astrologers were Babylonian court officials or scribes, and some of what they wrote suggests the modern world seen through a desert haze. There are causes and their effects. Things happen as part of a regular pattern. The night sky is a great forward-looking panorama.

But there is another note, a darker kind of music, in their runes or ruins. The night sky is the place where the gods reveal their will. A shadow on the moon, an eclipse, or a planet that rises and then abruptly reverses its direction—these are not so much causes chasing their effects as signs, inscriptions in a universal code. The world of material objects exists only to express this perpetual drama, the everlasting theater in which intelligence and intention give rise to change.

So, you see, the distinction was there from the first, a doubled impulse. The stars are causes *or* they are signs.

But if the stars are causes of human action, how do they achieve their effects across the vastness of space? And if they are signs revealing the future, how does intelligence impose its will upon matter?

These questions endure, an ever-present intellectual torment.

The physical sciences have conquered time. They have penetrated the veil of the future. And they have domesticated, but not explained, action at a distance. But their conquest lies along an extraordinarily narrow dimension, and it is genuine only when material objects in ceaseless motion are under investigation.

In our ordinary lives we face the world that human beings have always faced, one in spirit with the astrologers. We plan, plot, scheme, and by a process we can barely describe, let alone explain, we, too, inscribe our will on matter. There is, perhaps, nothing god-like in this, but the mystery is the same.

The veil behind which we shelter and which hides the future from our eyes remains where it has always been, rent in part by the sciences, and rent in part by our desires. But rent in part and only partly rent.

The astrologers carried out a four-thousand-year-old conversation. They chattered and, like us, they plotted and they schemed. Some were charlatans, others men of great sensitivity and intelligence. They are a part now of the perpetual inventory of things carried in memory, but their questions, and their aspirations—these remain.

A WRITER
OF OBSCURE BOOKS

T HE HOTEL PIAZZA Armerina was dark and somber, in the Sicilian style. Dinner was served by the proprietor and his wife, the both of them ancient, wrinkled. He cooked and she served. Neither of them spoke anything but the local Sicilian dialect, as much Arabic as Italian.

I spent that evening reading the Roman astrologer Julius Firmicus Maternus in the hotel's library, the cushions giving off a deep camphor smell. His *Mathesos* is, among other things, an expression of Stoicism in philosophy, and paganism in life. Maternus was by training a lawyer, and there is some evidence that he served in Rome as a senator; his astrological works were written in his retirement in Sicily, and they reflect the considered opinions of a mature man, someone shrewd and knowledgeable about the world, intimate with what Sicilians still call the *sistema del potere,* the system of power.

Like many attorneys, he was persuaded that his training had allowed him to see to the heart of any problem. Ancient astrologers claimed to have discovered the birth chart of the universe itself—the *thema mundi.* Gravely, Maternus considers the question whether the universe had a birthday and, with the air of a man conveying a considerable secret, concludes "the universe did not have any certain day of origin." With the matter settled in lawyerly fashion, he lets slip the pose and poignantly adds what is, after all, the plain truth: "Human reason has not been able to conceive or explain the origin of the universe."

Whatever the origins of the universe, human actions, Maternus argues, "are caused by the movements of the planets and by [their] various patterns."

And then he adds three blunt and terrible words: "Fortune destroys us."

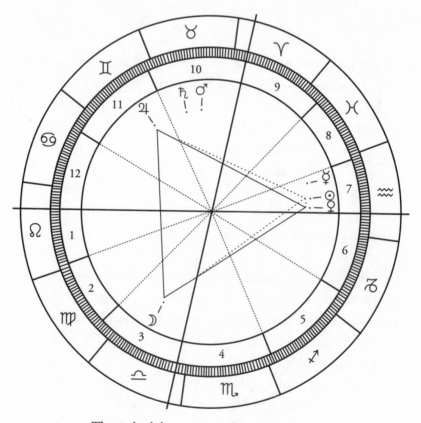

The author's horoscope indicates his destiny
as a writer of obscure books.

Using my laptop, an odd link to the modern world, and the Sicilian dial-up connection that I managed to access in Palermo, I got an American computer service to cast my own chart. I thought I had the sun, Saturn, and Mercury in the seventh house.

It was a configuration, Maternus had written, that "produces stone workers, corpse watchers, funeral organizers, or guardians of tombs."

The church clock at the center of the Piazza Armerina struck midnight.

Corpse watchers? And then I looked more closely at my chart. Saturn I could see was not quite in the seventh house.

I had instead Mercury together with the sun in the seventh house. Saturn was elsewhere. And of this configuration, Maternus had written that "this produces writers with great knowledge of literature." I felt vindicated.

But directly thereafter, he had added that "Saturn in Aspect to this combination makes evil, malicious characters and students or writers of obscure books."

Did I have Saturn in aspect to Mercury and the sun?

Oh, most definitely. I could see that now. Most definitely.

Fragments from Rawlinson's 1870 edition of the *Enuma Anu Enlil.*
The script is cuneiform, the language Akkadian.
(courtesy of the Bibliothèque Nationale de France)

CHAPTER ONE

ARIES

♈

RAWLINSON'S LEOPARD

L IKE EVERYONE ELSE, I wanted to see into the future, and if the future was blank and inscrutable, the past would have to do. For my kind of time travel, books are more revealing than stars. That morning I trudged down the banks of the Seine to visit the Bibliothèque Nationale, the great national library of France. The thing is like a Babylonian ziggurat, four glass and steel towers rising somberly from a plinth almost a city block in area. Access is by means of a wide but very steep series of polished wooden steps. There are no banisters or rails and when the stairs are wet, purchase is difficult. Elderly scholars very often lose their footing and fall badly. If the library is a monument to poor design and clumsy architecture, it is also a link in the unbroken chain of libraries that extends from the ancient world to the twenty-first century. The collection that it contains is matchless, one of the glories of French culture.

But whatever those glories, I had a cold. It was that time of year. Everyone in Paris was sniffling. The *métro* had been chilly and full of hoarse honkers, all of them looking peevish and indignant. The library was at least warm and comfortable, a kind of pastel glow suffusing all the reading rooms and the long echoing corridors. There was no one waiting in the rare books and manuscripts division. The seats at the central table were unoccupied, and the computers arranged in rows like so many squat and waiting penguins were all blank, their open eyes sightless.

The librarian was a tall, elegant woman. She knew and understood the manuscript collection, but like everyone working at the Bibliothèque, she had come to regard visitors as a considerable inconvenience. I had asked permission to see the library's copy of Major-General Sir Henry Creswicke Rawlinson's *The Cuneiform Inscriptions of Western Asia*. Rawlinson was one of the great soldier-scholars of the nineteenth century, a man whose fine intelligence and wide-ranging curiosity had elephant-walked over the entire Near East. I was interested in volume III of his four-volume work—*A Selection from the Miscellaneous Inscriptions of Assyria*. The folio edition is the very key to ancient astrology; it marks the place where every path led somewhere new. The librarian was dubious. Special permission was needed even to look at the thing.

I spread out the stamped letter of authorization that the chief librarian provided me. I placed my *carte de séjour*, my birth certificate, and a recent telephone bill on top of it. The librarian studied each document with great deliberation. Everything was in order. She filled out a yellow special request form and passed it to her assistant, a young man with red eyes and a wet nose. He counter-signed the librarian's form and briskly disappeared into the forbidden stacks, returning after five minutes with Rawlinson's folio underneath his arm. Very carefully, he placed the volume on the counter. I could not touch it. The librarians would open the cover and turn the pages.

I could see the point of their concern. The book was a large folio edition, perhaps three feet tall and one and one-half feet wide. The paper was thick and gray with age. The book contains the first printed edition of documents that are more than twenty-five hundred years old. The stone-cut originals are in fine shape at the British Museum. They may well last another ten thousand years. The book reproducing them is falling apart. The binding is cracked, and pages torn; there are water marks on almost every page, and a shapeless gray stain on the cover. Directly after I looked at the book, I was informed, it would be sent to the department of conservation and preservation for special treatment. It seemed a little late to me.

I asked the librarian to open the book for me. After smoothing her hair behind her ears, she pulled on a pair of pink surgeon's gloves and began slowly turning the pages. I was fascinated and so was she. Each page is divided more or less into quadrants, and the quadrants filled with hand-drawn cuneiform inscriptions, both troubling and incomprehensible. The symbols are wedge-shaped and quite ugly, resembling flags mounted on thin stalks, but they have the power to compel the eye. There is drama in their shapes. The book is introduced by a table of contents spread over four enormous folio pages. The document titles are in English. Plate III contains "Fragments of Inscriptions on Votive Offerings." Plate XLVII is more down to earth. It depicts "ten loan tablets." Life went on in the ancient world, just as it does today. Loans needed to be recorded and debts repaid. But Plate XLIX hints at a great domestic drama: It is a deed of sale. Nabu-Ricktu-Azar and his sons have sold his daughter, Bilat-Khazin, to a woman named Nikhte-Sar, for *her* son and his wife, and this for sixteen shekels of silver.

Plates LI–LXIV are of particular interest to astrologers. These plates, Rawlinson wrote soberly, contain "the great Chaldean work on astrology." Altogether, there are seventy tablets in these sections, collectively known now as the *Enuma Anu Enlil.* It is here that astrology's dark desert flowers first opened to the night air.

I could read nothing of the originals. I had simply wanted to breathe in the air of centuries. Now I had seen enough. Very carefully, the librarian closed the great, moldy book, and then asked me to counter-sign the original forms and initial the places where I had counter-signed them. I think she was sorry to see me go. We had shared a moment of mystery.

Some weeks later, I began to study the English translation of the *Enuma*. I was interested in the astrological omens, warnings, and predictions. One in particular caught my eye:

> If the Star of Dignity, the Vizier of Tispak, approaches the Scorpion, for three years there will be severe cold, cough and phlegm will befall the land.

Everything was clear. There was severe cold, cough, and phlegm throughout Paris. It had been the Star of Dignity and the Vizier of Tispak all along.

♈

IT IS SEVEN CENTURIES before the birth of Christ. The Assyrians are masters of the Fertile Crescent. They control the heaped granaries and the sun-baked, river-washed fields. Waters flow at their command. Alien deities rule the sky. The king, the great Ashurbanipal, moves heavily to his accustomed place at the center of the world. He is the descendent of kings as well as a king himself, the royal line—*his* line—stepping backward through the long years until it touches the magnificence of Sargon II. Ashurbanipal wears a rolled grape-black beard; his eyes are black and often troubled. Chiefly a warrior, he has for years been occupied with savage campaigns of conquest or subordination, often against his brothers, who resent his eminence and fear his power. But he is also a man of sophistication and some learning: a competent mathematician, skillful with all sorts of formulae; an astrologer, the student of famous astrologers in his youth; a linguist, proud of his ability to speak not only Assyrian, but Akkadian, as well. Alone among the great kings in his line, he can read Sumerian, the ancient language of scholarship. Ashurbanipal carries the weight of centuries on his royal back. The Near East was literate. The evidence was everywhere. Every civilization had its scribes. They had scribbled away on wet clay for centuries. The world was bursting with things that had been said and then written. The further back it went, the further the Assyrian tradition divided itself into an ever-finer network of memories. But in spite of all he knows, Ashurbanipal remains a man of great melancholia, the mysteries of existence and the pointlessness of man's fate an ever-present torment. Like Shakespeare's Richard II, he is in the habit of sitting upon the ground and telling sad stories about the fate of kings. "To the King, our Lord, from your servant Balasi," an astrologer had written. "Good health to the King, our Lord!" And then the revealing question: "Is one day not enough for the King to mope and eat nothing?"

At some time in the seventh century B.C., Ashurbanipal conceives the idea of collocating the texts, inscriptions, legal codes, funeral orations, poetry, and celestial ominia of the ancient world. He is determined to create a royal library. The project obsesses him. It is his boast. Scribes, scribblers, and court scholars, accompanied, no doubt, by a retinue of imperial thugs, depart the palace to scour and then loot the Mesopotamian world's private libraries. It is plain that Ashurbanipal has a vision in which the light from various separate centers of literacy is fused so that it becomes, like the king himself, a single, glowing sun. Great wagonloads of clay tablets make their way from the corners of the empire to Nineveh. Dust rises along the roads and ox-trails; broad-backed farmers turning from their wooden plows to stare in stupefaction at the endless plodding wagon trains, their platforms piled high with stone tablets. The oxen snort through their velvet noses.

Years and then decades go by. The library is at last complete, the cool marble of its corridors containing tablets in all the languages of the ancient world, a vibrant record stretching back more than a thousand years to make contact with all the old lost civilizations. The central hall contains a spectacular frieze of a lion hunt. Scholars gather there to read, and since none of them are able to read without reading aloud, the library is filled with a low drone, a kind of gabble. There is another sound: a muddy, wet plop. Scholars using the library needed to keep notes. Each man kept a supply of moist clay in a box. Seized by a thought, he would reach into his box for a wad of clay, plop it onto a flat surface, and then flatten the bolus, committing his thoughts to clay by means of a stylus and then leaving the tablet to dry. Beyond the gabble and plop, there is a sober sense of security throughout, Ashurbanipal's censorious warnings prominently displayed on almost every tablet:

May all these gods curse anyone who breaks, defaces, or removes this tablet with a curse, which cannot be relieved, terrible and merciless as long as he lives, may they let his name, his seed be carried off from the land, and may they put his flesh in a dog's mouth.

Sometime in the fourth or fifth decade of the seventh century, Ashurbanipal simply withers into inexistence, his affliction unknown. "To the King, my Lord, from your servant Urad-Nanna," an astrologer writes. The usual formula follows: "May the gods Nunurta and Gula give happiness and physical well-being to the King, my Lord." And then the astrologer addresses the heart of the matter. "The King, my Lord, keeps on saying to me: 'Why don't you diagnose the nature of this illness of mine and bring about its cure?'" Beyond this, nothing. Court historians and chroniclers are unforthcoming.

But the terrible urgency of Ashurbanipal's desires have frog-marched the centuries to topple, burning and blood red, into our laps.

Υ

THE ROYAL LIBRARY'S treasure is the *Enuma Anu Enlil.* It is one of the great documents of the human race, ageless as a lizard, and like all such documents, troubling in its significance. The *Enuma* comprises seventy stone tablets and covers more than one thousand years of speculation and commentary, the Assyrian codification of numerous astrological traditions that had swirled throughout all the ancient kingdoms of the Near East. Some parts of the *Enuma* suggest an even older astrological tradition, one making contact with the fabled Sumerian empire, the first literate civilization in world history and dead for more than fifteen hundred years at the time Ashurbanipal's physicians were worrying about his melancholia. The *Enuma* is a continuous record of observation and prediction rather than a religious or artistic treatise. The source of its science is the ancient impulse to study the largest patterns of human affairs, matters of general well-being, as they are reflected in the sky at night. Time has, of course, broken the original tablets into fragments. Patient scholarship has been required to fit the shattered pieces back together. A part of the collection may be found in the British Museum, but there are thousands of fragments lying unclaimed in the desert, chewed up by the centuries and scored by the ever-blowing desert wind.

The work that Rawlinson published reproduced the omens of the *Enuma* in the form in which they had been found. Over the next 130 years, scholars managed to crack its code, life emerging from the stones in stages, a word here, another word there, a series of linked thoughts, an inference. The omens have now reacquired a part of the human voice they once had. As one might expect, given the grief that time imposes, the voice is very often spastic. "If an eclipse occurs in Arahsammna and i[ts] redness [is red]...." reads one omen, the dots trailing off into eternity. Another omen considers an eclipse taking place on the first of Kislimu. "The land of Akkad," it begins confidently, but then there is silence, the blistered tablets too chipped to be revealing. Scholars are still uncertain about the meaning of basic words. "If the sun is seen in a black web, people will tell lies, heaviness will disappear from the country." *Heaviness?* In other places, the meaning of the omens is all too clear: "If on the first day of Nisannu the sunrise [looks] sprinkled with blood, grain will vanish from the country, [and] there will be hardship, and human flesh will be eaten."

Where the omens of the *Enuma* do convey a complete message, it is most often expressed as a warning, one whose minatory effects survive transliteration into modern English:

> If Nergal approaches the Scorpion, there will be a breach in the palace of the Prince.

> If in Month I, the Demon with the gaping mouth rises, then for five years in Akkad at the command of Irra, there will be plague, but it will not affect cattle.

> If the True Shepherd of Anu's navel is red, and there is a black spot in its right side, then there will be a revolt.

> If an eclipse occurs during the morning watch, a high-level official will seize the land.

Part of this is, of course, vague. The breach in the palace of the prince might cover anything from civil insurrection to an outbreak of shingles, and a good many omens refer to geometrical features of the sky that we can imagine but cannot specify precisely. *Nergal* denotes Mars, and *the Scorpion,* the constellation

Scorpio; but while Anu is a god, just where is his red navel? It is pointless to expect astronomical precision in these reports. The ancient astrologers were observing the heavens with unassisted eyes. They had no telescopes; they could do nothing about clouds or storms of dust. Records were cut into wet clay, hardly an efficient method for keeping meticulous notes. Things in the sky were massive, or deformed, or spread apart (the Demon with the gaping mouth), cosmic distances measured pretty much by the astrologer's spread fingers. For all that, some details are entirely literal. As high officials so often are, a high official is up to no good. And some parts of the series are remarkably specific. It is plague and not typhoid fever that is in store; it will not affect cattle, a nice distinction among afflictions.

The omen series of the *Enuma* is many things, but in its fundamentals, it expresses an *astrological* perspective, although very little in the omens suggests the modern astrological system. There are no signs. No horoscopes. No birth dates. Various tablets deal with the sun, the moon, and with Mercury, Venus, Mars, Jupiter, and Saturn. The constellations figure as reference points in the night sky, just as they do in modern astrological systems, but there is no fixed zodiac straddling the ecliptic. No ecliptic, in fact. And there are eighteen rather than twelve constellations in all: the twelve in use today, as well as the Pleiades, Orion, Perseus, Auriga, Shinunutu (a mystery still, its name rather suggesting a Shinto deity), the Swallow, which incorporated parts of Pisces and Pegasus; and Anuitu, busy swallowing the tail of Pisces. Nevertheless, the *Enuma* expresses the essential astrological idea very well. The following words come from a diviner's manual of the seventh century B.C., the end of the ancient astrological period. Their powerful emotional effect is best appreciated by seeing their meaning emerge through the filter of an alien language:

Same u ersetim istenis ittati ubbanluni
ahenna ul BAR.MES samu u eretu ituzi
ittu sa ina same lemnetu ina ergetim lemnet
sa ina ersetim lemnetu ina same lemnet.

These incomprehensible words have something of the effect of an insistent chant. Pidgin English allows some meaning to break through:

Sky and earth together produce omens
Each separate, not divided; sky and earth are
interconnected. A sign which is bad in the sky is bad on
earth; a sign which is bad on earth
Is bad in the sky,

until modern English reveals their true sense:

The signs on earth just as those in the sky give us signals;
[the] sky and [the] earth both produce portents, though
appearing separately, they are not separate [because the]
sky and [the] earth are related,

and discloses a surprisingly modern scientific sentiment, the doctrine that the heavens and earth form a unity.

If the omens of the *Enuma* may now be read in modern English, their interpretation is another matter. Scholars are often divided about the meaning of certain words, just as ancient astrologers were often divided about the significance of certain signs. "Whoever wrote to the King, my Lord," an astrologer named Nabu-ahhe-eriba complained, claiming that "Venus is visible," is "a vile man, a dullard, and a cheat." For the rest of us, the omens of the *Enuma* are intriguing because they seem at once familiar and alien. There is in the British Museum an ancient copy of an ancient copy of the earliest of the *Enuma* tablets, the Venus Tablet of King Ammisaduqa. The series of copies steps backward in time to a hypothetical origin at roughly the beginning of the second millennium, 1750 B.C. or so, but despite its great age, the tablet has an oddly familiar tone:

> If in the eighth month, on the eleventh day, Ishtar disap-
> pear[s] in the East and stay[s] away from the sky for two
> months and [?] days, and [becomes] visible again in the
> West in the tenth month on the [?] day, the harvest of the
> land will prosper.

This is nothing more than a weather forecast, and stripped of its archaic language, one similar in its form (and no doubt accuracy) to contemporary meteorological predictions. It is familiar fare. A cause has been specified, an effect foretold. The omens seem to contain the hard seed of a powerful method, one destined to ger-minate in the seventeenth century A.D. Within various scientific disciplines, the antecedent of a conditional statement specifies the cause of some effect, and its conclusion, the effect of some cause. A bottle containing a tincture of mercury reads, *if swal-lowed, then death may result.* Swallowing mercury is the cause, death the effect, and the hypothetical ties the two together. With the addition of a specific fact—some idiot *did* swallow a tincture of mercury—the hypothetical issues in a prediction, in this case death, or, at least, very grave distress. The future has been pene-trated by a logical inference, one based on a causal connection. The omens are likewise, and in some cases likewise *exactly.* One report from the Assyrian State Archives (Volume VIII) begins:

> If the Goat star produces a mishu, the gods will for[give]
> the land, [they will have] mercy on the land.

The very next line reads:

> This night it [the Goat Star] produced a mishu.

The conclusion that the gods will have mercy on the land now follows as a matter of pure logic.

This way of considering the omens of the *Enuma* is gratify-
ing, if only because it suggests so strongly what we wish to see, an
ancient culture endeavoring to become modern and, if not succeeding, then at least trying diligently. Even if the ancient astrologers lived in a world of gods and demons, in the end they,
too, were bound by logic, and when *we* clarify *their* thoughts,
what they reveal is a universe governed by the same formal powers that we ourselves recognize and respect.

If this is so, why then do astrological warnings very often
reach the threshold of prediction only to gutter out inconclusively, the logical inference simply lapsing? For the curious fact is
that ancient astrologers often tempered their counsel, advising
kings on methods they might adopt to avoid their fate or preserve
their kingdom from catastrophe. If signs portended disaster, specific *Namburba* rituals were required. And if not required, then
surely advisable. Threats to a king or his kingdom often man-
dated the month-long substitution of a surrogate for the king
himself. The surrogate would attend the great affairs of state, and
take his ease with a surrogate queen; he would be treated with
deference by the palace courtiers. He did nothing of note and was
allowed to make no decisions. The king himself, as this charade
was taking place, might occupy himself profitably in meditation
and purification. Thereafter, the substitute went to his destiny.
"To the King, my Lord, from your servant, Mar Istar," one astrologer wrote. "Good health to the King, my Lord! May the
gods Nabu and Marduk bless the King, my Lord! May the great
gods bestow long days, well being, and joy upon the King, my
Lord!" These words are purely ceremonial. The awful message
follows: "Damqi, the son of the bishop of Akkade, who had ruled
Assyria, Babylonia, and all the countries, died with his Queen on
the night of the . . . day as a substitute for the King, my Lord, and
for the sake of the life of the Prince, Sama-sumu-ukin. He went
to his destiny for their rescue." The drama proceeds: "We pre-

pared the burial chamber. He and his Queen have been decorated, treated, displayed, buried, and wailed over." The King, my
Lord, the astrologer concludes somberly, "should know this."

These rituals, and the fearful world that they reveal, suggest
quite another interpretation of the *Enuma*. Sharp logical inferences now lapse. Antecedents of various omens do not so much
specify a cause as indicate a sign. Far from constituting a series of
scientific inferences, the *Enuma* comprises a way of coordinating
the language of the gods with the language that men speak. The
astrologer is a man capable of determining what celestial events
mean rather than what effects they cause. Some omens suggest
this interpretation at once. "When I wrote to the King, my
Lord," the astrologer Nabu-ahhe-eriba (the same) writes in a letter of explanation, "saying that 'the gods have opened the ears of
the King, my Lord,' I meant if something happens to the King
and he worries, the gods first send a message from heaven saying:
Let him be on his guard." The messages that the gods send are
written in *their* language, which just happens to make use of celestial objects. *If an eclipse occurs during the morning watch, a
high-level official will seize the land.* The eclipse *means* that a high-
level official will seize the land. It is a sign, but not a cause, the
eclipse standing to the ancient astrologers, bearded and often
baffled, precisely as their original words stand to us. To determine
the meaning of these celestial signs, the astrologers made use of
the *Enuma*; we make use of our translations. We are in the same
position.

Once the omens of the *Enuma* are interpreted in this way,
their form makes perfect sense. There are no logical inferences in
place, and so no place where logic lapses. An identity lies at the
heart of each omen, with the celestial sign in the antecedent, its
meaning in the conclusion. This removes from the omens their
charge of dreadful inexorability. Signs may, after all, be misread
or misinterpreted, or the astrologer's warning may be rendered

irrelevant because the gods and goddesses, like the human beings who observe them, have changed their minds.

"Interpretations of [the] omens are like this," the astrologer Balasi remarked modestly. "One is never similar to another."

♈

FOR THE MOST PART, the omens deal with affairs of state: the fate of kingdoms, the king's health, the supply of food. A number of omens deal with more practical concerns, and as so often happens, these plain matters of fact have the power to leapfrog the centuries with their troubling implications entirely intact. "If Jupiter reaches the middle of the Scorpion," one omen reads, "in the land of Akkad the market price of one *kor* of barley will be reduced to one bushel." On one interpretation—the logical one—the omen is clear enough. A prediction has been made, and an attempt undertaken to penetrate the future. Cause and effect are in force. By reaching the middle of the Scorpion, Jupiter *causes* an adjustment in local market prices. And this, of course, raises a characteristic problem. Just how does a distant planet bring about a local effect without making use of any obvious chain of intermediate causes and their effects? The ancient astrologers had no idea how action at a distance was conveyed.

And neither do we.

Let us pass, then, to a second interpretation—the symbolic one. The omen is again clear enough, even if it remains false. A prediction has been made, and an attempt undertaken to penetrate the future. Symbol and meaning are in force. Reaching the middle of the Scorpion, Jupiter *signifies* an adjustment in local market prices. The position of the planet functions as a sign. It indicates the intentions of the gods, their plans for the future. And this, too, raises a characteristic problem. A sign acquires its significance from the men and women who use it. So, obviously, the celestial signs. So, *necessarily,* the celestial signs. They express the wishes of the gods, or their demands, desires, and commands.

The gods bring the future into being by an exercise of their will. It is some form of personal *force* that lies behind celestial action. The letters from various astrologers to the kings Esarhaddon and Ashurbanipal reflect this view: indeed, it is the common view of religious language at all times and all places.

This way of thinking has by no means disappeared. Metaphors evoke a very long racial memory, as when clouds are *threatening*, hurricanes *ferocious*, or ocean waves *proud, tempestuous*, or *sullen*. Many places still seem haunted by alien presences—magic mountains, odd little grottoes, Greek islands, forbidden caves, full of malignant feeling and deadly. The earth's landscape retains some of its old power to evoke the reverence due an indwelling god.

But however familiar this way of thinking may be, it does suggest a deep and ineradicable problem. The ancient astrologers had no explanation for the fact that the gods had the power to bring the future into existence by an act of their savage will. They had no explanation for the fact that the king could do as much. They had no explanation for the fact that, in their daily life, *they* could do as much.

And neither do we.

⍊

HENRY RAWLINSON published the third volume of his four-volume series in 1870, when he was sixty years old. Portraits made at this age show a man with a high, smooth forehead, and a great mop of still-brown hair fluffing over his ears and neck. He has wide-open, thoughtful, staring eyes; something of a Pinocchio nose; full sensuous lips; and a plump chin turned up like an open tulip. Both sensitive and trusting, it is the face of a man devoted to the oboe. How appearances are misleading! Rawlinson was an adventurer, just recently returned from thirty-five years spent in the Near East and the Orient; he was a military man and a leader of men; and he was a smooth diplomat, polished enough to have slithered adroitly through all the treacherous court in-trigues of nineteenth-century Persia. "The situation being one of very considerable difficulty," Rawlinson's brother recounts in a sober and respectful memoir, "and the relations between the British Envoy and the Persian Court being from time to time greatly strained, and appearing to threaten a rupture, an unusual responsibility devolved in the accomplished linguist, whose com-munications were sure never to be misunderstood, and who never failed to understand the exact bearing and intention of the communications, whether official or semi-official, which reached the British Residence from the Court." A world of intrigue, sus-picion, malignant elegance, and corruption is hidden in these remarks.

Rawlinson was, of course, a great scholar as well as a suave diplomat, a man immersed in and master of almost all the swirling currents of Near Eastern research in the mid-nineteenth century. Together with Jules Oppert and Edward Hincks, men well worth the price of admission to the nineteenth century, he created the modern field of Near Eastern studies. Rawlinson was above all one of those nineteenth-century figures whose intelli-gence indicates how Victorian England came to conquer so much of the world and whose character suggests why they were per-suaded that they had every right to do so. "Lose no opportunity of making yourself useful," he had written to himself. "Grasp at everything and never yield an inch."

Feeling that old age was upon him, hardly the most romantic of reasons, Major General Creswicke Rawlinson, diplomat, sol-dier, and scholar, married in 1862, and after the obligatory tour of various European capitals, returned to London, the British Mu-seum, and his studies. He led a life of high purpose. He dined out often; he knew the great men of his time—Gladstone, Disraeli, Palmerston—and they knew him. He was widely respected. He is there in history, solid, imperturbable, dignified, and assured.

Rawlinson was fond of wild animals and, while serving the Persian government, he kept a pet leopard named Fahad. On his return to England, he presented the animal to the Zoological Gardens at Clifton, near Bristol. He was in the habit of visiting the zoo to conduct amicable conversations with the beast; he often reached his hand into the cage to pat and rub the leopard's head. "Once," his brother recalls, "as Major Rawlinson was petting and rubbing his head, the keeper rushed in, and exclaimed in great alarm, 'Sir, Sir what are you doing? Take your hand out of the cage. The animal's very savage and will bite you!' 'Do you think so?' said the Major. 'No, I don't think he'll bite *me*.'"

Rawlinson the adventurer may be allowed to disappear; so, too, the soldier and diplomat. It is Rawlinson the decipherer whom time has revealed as a man with a taste for dangerous disciplines. It is this Rawlinson who has given astrology back to the astrologers by fixing their art in the flux of time. And knowing what we now know of the omens, we can see what a dangerous business ancient astrology really was—for the ancient astrologers and for us. They were using methods they could not control, and asking questions they could not answer.

Rawlinson's leopard is forever there, just behind the bars of his cage, and we are where Major Rawlinson was and is, petting and rubbing the leopard's head and hoping that he will not bite *us*.

CHAPTER TWO

TAURUS
♉
A GOLDEN TONGUE

About a small lion, whether he will be tamed.

Year of Diocletian 199, Epiphi [1] 4, 1st hour of the day. The sun in Libra 18, moon in Aquarius 10, Saturn in Scorpio 11, Jupiter in Gemini 19, Mars in Libra 6, Venus in Leo 7, Mercury in Cancer 18, Horoscopos in Leo 2, Midheaven in Aries 24, ascending node in Capricorn 23, [preceding] full moon in Capricorn 11. Lot of fortune in Aquarian 29.

The Horoscopos [Leo] indicated the kind of animal, and the dodekatemoria of the Horoscopos, sun and moon and Mars, which fell in four-footed signs, showed that the Katarche was about animals.

Because Venus is in the Horoscopos and Jupiter in the Agathos Daimon, about to receive the contact of the moon, tameness is indicated; and especially the third of the moon and the seventh from Venus showed that the lion would be tamed and brought up with man.

That the moon and the Lot of Fortune happened to be in the setting sign showed that the lion would go abroad on a ship, because the setting sign was watery.

I T IS 483 A.D. An astrologer has cast the horoscope of a small lion. His client is eager to assure himself that the lion will become a disciplined member of a domestic household. The watery signs indicate that before entering into a tranquil routine, the animal must face a voyage on board a ship.

Sometime later, seasick and wobbly, the lion braces his tawny head against a sailor's knee.

♉

BEROSSOS THE CHALDEAN—Berossos the *Astrologer*—was born in Babylonia during the reign of Alexander the Great. Berossos was in his early life devoted to the service of Bel, the Babylonian god, whose accomplishments included the creation of the stars, the sun, the moon, and the five planets. "Berossos" in Akkadian is *Bel-re-usu,* meaning roughly that "Bel is his Shepherd." Berossos very quickly established a reputation in the Greek-speaking world as a gifted astrologer.

While still a young man, Berossos moved to the island of Kos, which is located in the Mediterranean Sea off the coast of Turkey. The island descends toward the ocean in a series of hard chalky cliffs, which like elephant feet fold themselves at their base into the toes of small grottoes; there are sparse stands of trees clinging to the cliffs' lower flanks, giving out to pebbly beaches. Like all of the Greek islands, Kos, although made of stone, is shaped by light, the sun blinding in the whitened sky, the sea a deep, improbable aquamarine.

I have not seen any of this myself, but I have been assured that it is so.

The days passed. Somehow Berossos arranged his meals, found lodging, and acquired slaves or servants. At some time after his arrival on Kos, Berossos opened a school. He attracted disciples and enthusiasts, and he must have earned his living by offering predictions. He became known.

Both an astrologer and a historian, Berossus published three books in which he traced the course of Babylonian history. These histories, like his astrological predictions, exist only in later scraps from Greek and Latin commentators. Consulting records that are now dust, Berossos apparently persuaded himself that the Babylonians were a people more than 490,000 years old, an estimate the modern scholar regards as generous. Whatever the dates he assigned the Babylonians, it is in these lost works that Berossos describes a great flood, an account suggesting the biblical narrative, at least to the extent that it mentions both a devastating inundation and the timely appearance of an ark.

"A most able man," Tatianus remarked of Berossos.

THE DISTINCTION BETWEEN fact and myth eluded Berossos the historian, possibly because it does not exist or cannot be drawn, but a number of the myths that he recounts touch on profound philosophical problems. Berossos found perplexing the fact that, alone among the animals, human beings know a great many things beyond what they need to know in order to survive. A story that he tells explains the acquisition of human knowledge by depicting a gift from the sea. "In Babylonia," Eusebius writes in his recapitulation of the Babylonian histories, a large number of people "lived without discipline and without order, just like animals." The time is the distant past. A frightening monster named Oannes then appeared to the Babylonians after clambering out of the Red Sea. "It had the whole body of a fish, but underneath and attached to the head of the fish, there was another head, human, and joined to the tail of the fish, feet, like those of a man, and it had a human voice." This is a description that unnervingly reconciles the evolutionary and epistemological history of the human race. The monster "spent his days with men, never eating anything, but teaching men the skills necessary for writing, and for doing mathematics, and for all sorts of knowledge." Since that time, Eusebius adds regretfully, "nothing further has been discovered." In the early part of the twenty-first century, the answers that we might offer to the question that Berossos raised, although richer in their detail, are hardly more penetrating in their scope. The origins of civilization are still a mystery.

LIKE MANY ANCIENT and modern writers, Berossos was persuaded that the world was shortly to perish. His analysis reflects all of the moody currents of Babylonian thought. "Berossos," Seneca writes, "attributed [the end of the world] to the movement of the planets." The causal sequence listing inexorably toward disaster begins "whenever all the planets, which have different orbits, converge in Cancer." When later they converge in Capricorn, a second great flood may be expected.

This is the Babylonian strain. Ancient astrologers were interested in the odd and the unexpected. Berossos reasoned from deviation to deviation, just as a physician might pass from boils to blisters in predicting the outcome of a disease, leaving the mystery of ordinary good health unexplained and unacknowledged.

But these inferences may be flipped, revealing on their backside a pattern of regularities. The result is a claim that Berossos did not make and could not see; namely, that the survival of the earth is contingent on the stability of the solar system. Although both sides of the chart are logically equivalent, they are very different in their practical effects. The attempt by Berossos and other astrologers to predict celestial anomalies led nowhere. The attempt made by modern astronomers to predict celestial *regularities* led directly to the idea of a law of nature. The solar system *is* stable, and the planets turning in their orbits will continue to turn serenely, the earth safe, at least until it is enveloped by the swollen sun. It is this that Kolmogorov, Arnold, and Moser established in their great theorem of 1954.

Berossos must have lived his life as ordinary men do, waking, bathing, and trudging off to the academy that he founded, but the domestic details have vanished. With one exception. The historian Pausanias tells the story of a prophetess living among the Hebrews in the occupied territories beyond Palestine. Her name was Sabbe; her father, Pausanias claims, was Berossos. "Some say she was the Babylonian Sibyl; others called her the Egyptian Sibyl." Whether Babylonian or Egyptian, the woman made claims to prophetic powers. Berossos reached his conclusions about the future as he reached his conclusions about the past, by following a rational method. He required neither inspiration nor possession. His daughter required both. It is possible to imagine the man's perplexed astonishment at her choice of career.

♉

BEROSSOS HAD COME TO the island of Kos as a Chaldean; he was a man of the East. Some years before his arrival, the armies of Alexander the Great had left Greece in order to conquer the world. They swept toward Mesopotamia and with insolent ease dismembered the solemn, ritual-bound Persian empire. The Greek world followed the Greek armies.

The Greeks of the fifth and fourth centuries were philosophers of genius, but they were neither competent astronomers nor careful astrologers. Winter weather is often cloudy in Greece, but clear in the Middle East; perhaps the Greeks failed to develop either discipline for the most trivial of reasons: They could not properly see the stars. The Babylonians, peering out at a sky unclouded both in winter and summer, had by the end of the seventh century B.C. developed an astronomical system of remarkable power. Its discovery and re-creation by Otto Neugebauer has been one of the glories of twentieth-century scholarship. Although Babylonian astronomical techniques are now understood, they remain as strange as they are powerful, for the Babylonian scribes approached astronomy from a computational point of view, regarding their very complicated schemes as tools and nothing more. Their ambitions were satisfied when they could figure out the phases of the moon or the time of the next eclipse. They lacked entirely the idea of a law of nature.

The Greeks they must have regarded as primitives. It is delicious to imagine one of the Babylonian scribes, a master of those complicated numerical techniques, asked to comment on Greek astronomy and astronomers, as he comes to understand that while *he* could offer astronomical forecasts with rare precision, his Greek counterparts were consumed by the debate whether the stars were—quite literally—living or not. In the *Apology,* Socrates finds himself answering the charge that he—of all people!—has been advocating the thesis that "the sun is a stone, the moon [made of] earth." What injustice. "These claims," Socrates affirms, "are so absurd." Standing unobserved at the rear of the courtroom, that Babylonian scribe can think of nothing better to do than shake his oiled head.

With Alexander's conquest of Babylonia, the conquered taught their conquerors. The Greeks had come to use the zodiac as early as the sixth century B.C.; the Babylonians now gave them a systematic and rational way of interpreting the sky in terms of the ecliptic, the sun, the moon, and the planets. They acquired the duodecimal and sexagesimal systems of measurement and they gained access to a matchless astronomical record—tables and charts describing the course of the planets over hundreds of years. Vitruvius credits Berossos with the invention of the half-circle sundials that can still be found in a great many Roman villas and Italian palaces.

The Greeks were intrigued, then fascinated. They had long been consumed by the idea that the future is accessible. For centuries they had studied the migratory pattern of birds for signs, or they had looked at fires, sifting the blackened ashes left behind for a suggestive shape, or, squatting on their haunches, they had attended closely to the flow of streams and rivulets, trying to assess the significance of the fact that, coursing through the brown and arid earth, a rivulet had carved a figure resembling the genitals of a goat. Babylonian astral techniques, charged as they were with precisely observed detail, must have struck them as sharply as a slap.

This should come as no surprise. The Greeks have entered history disguised as men who are rational, literate, civilized, and dedicated to lofty thoughts. In every conversation celebrating the arts of civilization, it is the Greeks who, with a discreet cough, never fail to mention that they were there first, if only to give names to concepts that we now take for granted: tragedy, geometry, fate, democracy, philosophy, proof. But in any realistic assessment of Hellenistic emotional life, thermometers go to red. Mystery cults were widespread, men sworn to secrecy trooping off into the mountains to lash themselves into a frenzy or to participate in savage rites. At the end of the fifth century B.C., Euripides had called attention to the growing cult of Dionysus; by the beginning of the third century B.C., the cult had become widespread, its influence felt in Italy as well as Greece. A sense of aimlessness predominated. Religious impulses that the Attic Greeks had kept under control one hundred years earlier now snapped their leads, and, gaining influence as they lost restraint, persuaded some men to conquest and others to withdrawal.

It is in this world that the modern astrological system was created.

♉

BEROSSOS THE CHALDEAN must have cast thousands of horoscopes. None have survived, and any conclusions about how he worked or what he offered his clients can only be speculation. But not entirely fanciful speculation. Several hundred horoscopes have survived intact from the ancient world, the earliest papyrus fragments datable to the period almost immediately after Berossos lived and died, the latest from well after the fall of Rome.

These earliest of the classical horoscopes are found on fragments of Egyptian papyri. They are original documents, the very ones that astrologers in busy offices handed to their anxious clients; we know their dates with some precision because these fragments offer a vivid if compressed description of the heavens at the time they were composed. Given the astronomical details, modern scholars can roll back the sun, the moon, and the planets to their position at the time the charts were cast, dating even documents whose Greek or Roman dates are missing. The friable papyrus and scratched inked signs form a physical connection between the modern student of astrology and the ancient astrologer.

Although fragmentary, these early papyri nonetheless have all the urgency and whispered drama of the human voice. A typical fragment dates to the years between 15 and 22 A.D. There are a series of telegraphic inscriptions, the ellipses indicating where the papyrus fragment was ripped. Some of them are strictly matters of astronomy:

—The moon in Taurus, a female sign...
—Saturn and Jupiter in Sagittarius, a male sign...
—Venus in Scorpio, a male sign...

But the astrologer's voice breaks through as well, alert and attentive:

—Thinking it proper...
—Your descendants, dear Tryphon...
—I shall try to [set forth] for the dates [which you have given us]...

For all his deference, the astrologer is something of a bungler, the editors of the collection observe, since Scorpio is a female and not a male sign.

Some fragments are found as graffiti, their cryptic astrological references a hasty throwaway, the astrologer, or his assistant most probably, using a vacant wall for details that he could not commit to papyrus. The fragments have a deferential tone, one that time has stripped of sycophancy, leaving only a current of human tenderness behind:

—Dearest Lady...

And there is something else as well, a certain cheeriness. One horoscope dating to 283 A.D. is very typical. It begins with a summary of the facts:

—Nativity of Pichime
—Year 1 of Carinus, Phamenoth
—27, 1st hour of the day
—Horoscopus [and] sun in Aries
—Mars in Taurus
—moon [and] Jupiter in Cancer
—Saturn in Capricorn
—Mercury [and] Venus in Pisces

and concludes with a brief, bursting salutation:

—Good luck!

Still other fragments display a melodramatic internal rhythm. One papyrus fragment, dating to 95 A.D., has become famous because it contains the only extant copy of the long-lost funeral oration of Hyperides; the other side contains a Greek horoscope and an astrological treatise in Greek and early Coptic. The fragment was purchased in Egypt in the mid-nineteenth century, under circumstances that suggest one of those curious dramas in which an alert scholar notices by chance some hidden treasure lying in an antiquarian's warehouse or store, merchant and scholar emerging from their endless haggling each well pleased with what he takes to be the other's miscalculation. It is by no means an easy fragment to read or translate, but the predictions have an exuberant quality, a spurt of life. The chart was probably commissioned on the birth of a child. The astrologer dips his hand into the flow of time. He sees "well being and an abundance of pleasure," adding with gusto that "if he is a slave he will be set free, [and] if he is poor he will become rich." If he should happen to be rich, the astrologer adds grandly, "he will become *richer.*" His children "will have inborn in them a fine nature." The predictions continue like a mounting wave: "And he will have excellent associations extending everywhere."

And then all at once the tone changes. "He will suffer from colds or fevers or other illnesses, such are the things that Mars portends." What is more, Venus is in *Apanaphora.* "He will be cold as regards women." And there is worse, the wave so recently cresting now dropping into a black trough. "He will be tried before the magistrate for unspeakable accusations... He will suffer miserably, and will live a miserable life abroad." The first lot, the astrologer explains stolidly, is a separation; likewise the second lot; and likewise the third.

Standing by their darling boy's crib, as the infant cooed and gurgled, just what did those proud parents think when the astrologer, his hand clasping the shawls of his toga, suggested by means of a decorous cough that perhaps they might now wish to regulate their bill?

♉

SOMEWHERE IN THE ancient world, an astrologer has been consulted on a matter of some importance. After listening attentively to his client, he sets down the chief fact about the case in the crabbed hand of the busy professional:

Another inquiry in Smyrna regarding fear about a ship

These words release their weariness like a sigh, the astrologer's "another inquiry" calling to mind the physician's "another patient." But the words that follow—*fear about a ship*—with their ominous intimations of disaster, suggest that the astrologer, scribbling at his charts in a wharf-side office, had just been consulted on a problem of great urgency. Every voyage in the ancient world was an expedition into silence as well as space. Unable to cancel distance, men and women regarded the astrologer as a way of conquering time.

The ship had been expected long before to arrive from Alexandria, and it had not arrived.

The astrologer's report leaves open the circumstances prompting the client's question; and, for all we know, the client may have been a merchant concerned about woven goods, or a husband vexed by his wife's long absence, or a mother determined to know her child's fate. The astrologer's clients were as varied as the men and women of the Greek and Roman world, and the astrologer himself was the ancient amalgam of a number of familiar modern figures: the private eye, shambling down mean streets; the physician, tracing a causal connection through a daisy chain of symptoms; the molecular biologist, seeing in the beaded string of the human genome glistening astral objects.

With the client finally gone after eliciting a promise from the astrologer that he will send word at once—*at once, please, you won't forget*—the astrologer at last gets down to work. He has a number of charts to prepare. In his line of work, business is as steady as the wind, and, lady, just as evil. This astrologer is not forecasting the future: The future has already arrived. The ship is somewhere safe at harbor or somewhere lost at sea, but its fate has been consummated.

Smoothing out a fresh papyrus sheet, and rubbing his palm over the dome of his bronzed scalp, the astrologer settles his astrolabe on the top of his polished desk, and after idly spitting a few pomegranate seeds into the corner of his office, settles down to his calculations.

The routine is always the same. The horoscope is determined by the time and place:

It was the year of Diocletian 195. Epiphi (XI) 20, 3rd hour of the day, Saturday.

Using various sophisticated ephemerides, tables of planetary positions widely available in the Roman world, the astrologer then writes a trenchant description of the heavens as they appeared on that day and that time.

Sun Cancer 19, moon Scorpio 16, Saturn Virgo 16, Mars Virgo 18, Jupiter Aquarius 8, Venus Gemini 6, Mercury Leo 4, retrograde, Horoscopus, Virgo 2, Midheaven Taurus 26, ascending node Aries 11, Lot of Fortune Sagittarius 29.

No ship sails in this hard world without leaving traces of its journey in the heavens. And so the astrologer's account of the facts is also an inquiry into its fate.

The ship had met with a great storm.

This is an alarming moment.

But [it was] saved because Venus in Midheaven and moon were in aspect to Jupiter, and the moon's position on the seventh day was moving away from Jupiter and its dodecatemorion was also moving away from Jupiter.

Relieved, the astrologer exhales.

The ship is secure but damaged; the astrologer now allows his art more completely to penetrate the future:

Having observed that the Horoscopos was in a bicorporeal sign, and that the ruler of the Horoscopos was in retrograde, and the ruler of the midheaven, Venus, was in a bicorporeal sign, and the ruler of the Lot of Fortune was in a bicorporeal sign and the planet which receives the ruler of the Lot of

fortune was in a bicorporeal sign and the house ruler of the
moon was in a bicorporeal sign—I said that they would change
from ship to ship. Virgo was a winged sign and also Sagittarius.
I said they were bringing some feathered things with them.
And because the moon was in the house of Mars and terms of
Mercury, I said they were probably bringing books and papyrus
with them and some bronze objects because of Scorpio. Having
noticed that Asclepius was rising with the moon, I said they
were bringing medical instruments with them.

There remains a final prediction to be made.

As to when it [the ship] ought to come, I said the moon would
be in Aquarius on the seventh day.

Pausing to blot his copy with sand, the astrologer allows himself
a moment's quiet satisfaction, and then, as the oil lamp sputters
and the wind over the harbor moans, begins to record the details
of another case. "In his 48th year," he writes, "the client witnessed a great sorrow, the death of a beloved child."

♉

THE LIFE OF VETTIUS VALENS, conceived on the thirteenth of
May, 119 A.D., and born on the eighth of February, 120 A.D.,
reads like a horoscope. He came to his adult work with the enthusiasm of a man recovering from a misspent youth. At the age
of thirty-four, he found himself living abroad, where he kept
company with great men and loose women, then as now an unstable combination. A year later, he is on the high seas, in danger from pirates and from a storm. Egypt is next. He is searching
for esoteric wisdom, and although "he suffered much, [and] endured much," he also "spent money that seemed inexhaustible,"
an interesting reference to financial techniques that sadly Valens
does not explain. And thereafter Vettius Valens consecrated himself to astrology. "The truth [of astrology]," he writes, "keeps the

mind free and out of bondage." If astrological stoicism offers the adept some conveniences, it is a comfort purchased at some cost: Valens refers to himself as "an intelligent slave of a harsh master," his liberation from bondage less a matter of freedom than compliance.

The papyrus fragments are interrupted stories; what they gain in immediacy, they lose in coherence. Complete horoscopes, on the other hand, have been preserved in various literary sources, the most famous of which is Valens' *Anthologiae*. Although the book is a trot for professionals, the horoscopes contained in the *Anthologiae* are literary artifacts, almost all of them composed long after the events that they record. Valens was looking on the past from the perspective of his present. It was a perspective that included the future, as it was seen in the past. Valens had made himself time's master. His horoscopes explain what happened to men and women and slaves and animals long dead. It is a polished performance, involving the multiple displacement of the past, the present, and the future.

The horoscopes are cut to a common two-part pattern. In the first, the astrologer offers a description of the heavens, an astronomical flash freeze of the position of the sun, moon, and planets against the background of the fixed stars. The language, although accurate when read by a professional, is also deliberately contrived to be obscure to the layman. In this it very much resembles legal or medical language. In the second, the astrologer offers an interpretation of the astronomical facts. His art is now invoked. The chart spread before him, the astrologer searches for patterns, or remembers an odd comment made in the professional literature or offered in passing by another astrologer on his way to the baths, or simply waits for the moment when his memory gathers and discharges itself.

The astrologers did not, in general, limit their practices to specialties. Their opinions and judgments ranged widely, every question met with an astrological answer, the astrologer's art coextensive with the demands of life. Many clients were understandably concerned to know the length of their lives and the means of their deaths, and since these deliberations involved specific dates, numerological methods were often employed. One astrologer offers this account:

—The minimum period of the moon—twenty-five years;
—The rising time of Cancer in the clima—thirty-two years;
—The house ruler of the moon, Jupiter—twelve years.

These numbers sum to sixty-nine, the astrologer concluding that his client would die in his sixty-ninth year.

As, in fact, he did.

There is, in these various calculations about length of life and the means of death, a certain morbid strain. In a chapter entitled "On Violent Deaths, with Examples," Valens trundles down a list that is as horrible as it is bizarre. Mars was in Cancer, one horoscope reveals, a wet sign. Very wet evidently. The person choked to death in water.

—This person was beheaded;
—This person hanged himself;
—This person burned to death in a bath;
—This person was banished and committed suicide;
—This person had in the fated places injury and tender feet and most of all he was lunatic;
—This person was killed by wild beasts;
—This person was drowned in bilge water.

Afflictions short of death are frequently mentioned, Valens recalling those fated by the stars to be hunchbacked, lame, halt, short-armed, lunatic, or disabled in their penis owing to the dominance of Saturn.

The horoscopes are by turns lurid and measured, either addressed sharply to specific questions or concerned generally with

the patterns of a man's life, its shape. One horoscope begins in
102 A.D. The horoscope's subject began as a deputy governor—
Valens does not say where—"but falling into the governor's dis-
favor in his thirty-fourth year, was condemned to the quarry."
Valens attributes his misfortunes to the joint influence of Mars
and the sun. Two years later, he obtained his freedom "as disabled" and "owing to the aid of greater persons." If his benefac-
tors were able to provide assistance, this in turn was caused by or
reflected in the stars, for "the beneficent [stars] then were strong."
Three years later still, the former deputy governor's fortunes
again fell; he was condemned to an oasis, a form of exile less
harsh but no less lonely than hard labor. The stars are now
malefic. In his fortieth year, Valens recounts, the deputy governor
"lived precariously and fell ill." The stars, however, have become
ambiguous in their configurations, and as it happens "his wife
[accompanied] him and affectionately comforted him, and shared
her possessions with him."

It is easy to treat this horoscope with some skepticism. Valens
is, after all, recording events that have taken place. The pattern is
already plain. But the horoscopes suggest more than they reveal.
The movement of the sun, the moon, and the planets is continuous, without pause or break; a horoscope succeeds only in freez-
ing action at a particular time and place. The astrologers had for
the first time in human history confronted the great question of
modern science. The heavens are in continuous motion; so, too,
a human life. *We* have only words or pictures to play with. How
might we fashion from the second an instrument adequate to the
description of the first? If the astrologers did not succeed in answering this question, their practice indicated that they knew its
nature and were perplexed by the problem that it posed.

☿

IF ALL THINGS COME to an end, classical astrologers believed, they
also return to their beginnings. On sun-washed, sun-whitened

Kos, Berossos is still calmly attending to his clients, listening attentively to their questions, nodding, and then patiently recording the movement of the sun, the moon, and the planets against the ever-changing sky. Not a word of his remains, but his reputation is such that one can be sure that, after depositing their drachma in his collection bowl, mounted discreetly on an iron tripod (a few drachma placed ostentatiously on its blacked bottom to prompt payment), his clients must have left his chambers persuaded that they had been given what they had come to seek, a picture of their past or future.

"In knowledge of various things," Pliny the Elder remarked, "various men stand out. It is . . . proper for me to pick out the best. In astrology, it was Berossos."

And then the extraordinary detail. "In honor of his divine predictions," Pliny adds, "the Athenians set up in the gymnasium a statue of him with a gold tongue."

♉

DURING THE EARLY 1970S, archeologists discovered the remains of a Roman villa somewhere on the coast of Africa. Sand had covered its walls but protected its interior. The villa had obviously been the home of a provincial official, a local consul, in fact, for it was spacious, one suite of rooms facing an interior garden. When the archeologists finished carefully brushing the terracotta walls, they could just trace the faint outlines of a series of delicate frescoes in the Roman style. In the bottom of the villa, they discovered the family crypt, the hawk-nosed consul and his fleshy wife having made preparations for their interment long before their deaths. Two regal sarcophagi were mounted on a marble pedestal, with bas-relief portraits of both husband and wife. The couple was evidently childless, but there is a third sarcophagus nonetheless, mounted at right angles to the consul's feet.

Above an inscription that time has defaced, there is a bas-relief portrait of a small lion.

CHAPTER THREE

GEMINI

♊

THE GREAT LIBRARY

A T SOME TIME between 180 and 145 B.C., the Jewish scholar Aristeas recounts, seventy-two learned Alexandrian rabbis were asked to translate the five books of Moses into Greek. The work was conducted at the Royal Library. Those seventy-two rabbis are gathered around a long table in the private reading room. Sunlight streams in from the high windows, and entering the room from the city beyond the library, there are all the soft sounds and spicy smells of a Mediterranean port. Bearded and dressed in caftans, their feet in sandals, the rabbis sit there, pulling at their ear locks, fidgeting, allowing their knees to jiggle, or eyeing furtively the elaborate buffet mounted along the room's far wall, each man wondering whether by the time his scholarly colleagues got through stuffing themselves, the delicious date rolls sure to be gone in a flash, *he* would find enough to eat.

The chief rabbi raps the table with his knuckles.

The work commences.

♊

THE BABYLONIAN ASTRONOMERS were masters of exceptionally clever mathematical techniques, but in all the long years stretching from the fall of the Sumerians in roughly 1900 B.C. to the creation of the Roman Empire, astrologers worked without a massive and complete astronomical theory, a structure powerful enough to encompass their intuitions and rich enough to sustain their efforts. We think very naturally in terms of a particular backward-looking view, one in which Tycho Brahe, Nicolas Copernicus, and Johannes Kepler liberated human beings from the wearisome superstition according to which the earth is at the center of the universe. If nothing else, modern science has endowed modern scientists with a remarkable capacity for self-congratulation. That superstition was, in fact, a powerful scientific theory, one with walls so massive that, like the Coliseum, it endured for more than fifteen hundred years, not because it represented a superstition, but because in every respect it seemed to meet the facts and explain their nature.

The Greek Egyptian astrologer Claudius Ptolemy was born in 100 A.D. and died seventy-eight years later. Very little is known of his life. Some popular accounts place him in the Egyptian city of Alexandria; others in Canopus, fifteen miles to the east. The greater part of his research he conducted at the library in Alexandria, and the library serves retrospectively to endow the man with a familiar aspect. Surrounded by exotic gardens, and flanked by elaborate terraces, the library was considerable in its luxury. A zoo was included on the grounds; inside, there was a reading room covered by a dome, classrooms and observatories, a spacious dining hall, washstands of marble, gold chalices filled with oil, the perfume of a thousand flowers drifting through the rooms, study halls, and private reading alcoves. It is satisfying to imagine Ptolemy trudging up the library steps and, after settling into the domed reading room, parchments stacked in front of him (the library's patron, Ptolemy III, having banned papyrus), releasing one of those soulful sighs that only scholars know. Gossips assigned Ptolemy the same lack of interest in personal hygiene that they assigned philosophers in general, and if Ptolemy drew the attention of his colleagues because he had neglected to bathe or clip his yellowed toenails, his endearing piggishness must have softened a personality that judging by his work must otherwise have been as austere as cold water passing over ice.

Ptolemy wrote widely and on a number of subjects: astrology, of course, but astronomy, history, geometry, music, and geography as well. He addressed himself to various disciplines as a mathematician, and his temperament was tough, demanding, rigorous, and skeptical. When the occasion demanded, he wrote popular accounts of his scientific results, as in his two-volume treatise entitled *Planetary Hypotheses,* a work occasioned, I am persuaded, by certain unspecified financial embarrassments. Among astronomers, Ptolemy is best known for the *Almagest,* Arabic commentators later adding the Arabic *al* (the) to the Greek *megiste* (greatest) to signify the book's stature. Quite right. The book *is* a marvel. It is in the *Almagest* that Ptolemy outlines and defends a geocentric view of the cosmos. Astrologers quite naturally regard the *Almagest* as the unavoidable prologue to the *Tetrabiblos* (Four Books), Ptolemy's comprehensive astrological treatise. Then as now, the *Almagest* is a work that professional astrologers either propose to read or remember having read. The *Almagest* is organized as a geometrical tract, and while the mathematics is never difficult, it is always dry. The book's drama lies with its subject, which is the structure of the universe; its execution appeals to those with a taste for desert landscapes. The *Tetrabiblos,* on the other hand, is quite accessible, and although theoretical, it is a book of some human warmth. In any case, Ptolemy regarded astronomy and astrology as two aspects of one discipline. In astronomy, he writes, we apprehend "the movements of the sun, moon and stars in relation to each other and to the earth, as they occur from [one] time to [another] time." The astronomer's business is the prediction (or retrodiction) of the movements of the sun, moon, planets, and stars. The astrologer, by way of contrast, is concerned "to determine the changes that [the heavens] bring about in that which they surround." The heavens surround the earth; the changes they bring about are changes in human fortune.

II

THE CELESTIAL PANORAMA commences. The sun rises and sets; so, too, the moon, the planets, and the stars. The sky is filled with light, or withdrawn in darkness. The moon that was but a sliver turns into a glowing sphere. The fixed stars wheel in the heavens. The seasons change, the sun moving northward by degrees, stopping, and then turning to the south.

Raising himself from his library seat, and, of course, knocking over the table's inkwell, Ptolemy asks that these appearances be brought under some form of intellectual control. "The first order of business," he remarks, "is to grasp the relationship of the earth taken as a whole to the heavens taken as a whole." It is the last order of business as well, I might add, for once that relationship *is* grasped, the details of the Ptolemaic system follow logically. Whether the first *or* the last order of business, the project that Ptolemy is proposing has a dangerous grandeur, if only because it suggests that the human mind is capable of grasping the heavens as a *whole,* a thesis as uncertain today as it was two thousand years ago.

Whatever our astronomical allegiances, some readers persuaded against all reason that the sun is at the center of the solar system, the heavens, as they are *observed,* form a canopy covering the earth. The canopy's height, judged by the relative brightness of the celestial objects, never changes, no matter our own change in position along the surface of the earth. By the same token, celestial objects, as they are *observed,* are in continuous and periodic motion, the sun, moon, planets, and stars smoothly returning to the places in the sky from which they started. There is only one two-dimensional shape that completely captures the idea of an eternal return and that is a rotating circle, and there is only one three-dimensional shape that encompasses an indefinite number of rotating circles, and that is a rotating sphere. Ptolemy very sensibly concluded that the moon, the planets, *and* the fixed stars are rotating around the earth once every twenty-four hours. The direction of rotation is from east to west. This hypothesis brilliantly simplifies the night sky. Instead of many celestial objects in motion, there is only one.

"Absolutely all phenomena are in contradiction," Ptolemy writes, "to [any of] the alternate notions that have been propounded."

THE ROTATION OF THE celestial sphere explains the largest features of space and time, and it is again spherical rotation that explains the peculiar motions of the sun. In the northern hemisphere, the sun seems to move northward in the spring and southward in the fall; in the southern hemisphere, it is the other way around. As the sun moves, it sheds heat as well as light, and as it withdraws, it leaves the earth in cold as well as darkness. These facts must be explained geometrically. If the sun's path is observed over the course of a year, it describes a line curving around the interior of the celestial sphere. Twice each year, this line, if projected downward, intersects the earth's equator, and thereafter reaches a maximum distance from the equator of twenty-three and one-half degrees. This curved line—the sun's apparent path—astronomers designate the *ecliptic.*

The ecliptic, Ptolemy argued, is the equator of a *second* sphere. Although nested within the celestial sphere—Ptolemy does not say *how*—this sphere lies at an angle to the celestial sphere, its north pole south of the celestial north pole, and its south pole north of the celestial south pole. Like the celestial sphere, the solar sphere is perpetually in rotation, but while the celestial

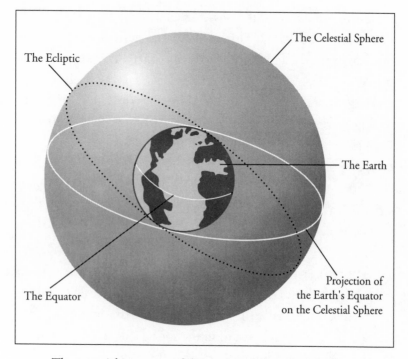

The essential geometry of the earth and the celestial sphere.

sphere carries celestial objects from east to west, the solar sphere carries the sun from west to east. The celestial sphere completes a revolution during the course of a day; the solar sphere, during the course of a year, and as the sun dips north and then south and then north again like a great glowing pendulum, it warms whatever it covers and cools whatever it leaves.

It is in this way that the Ptolemaic system expresses geometrically the three great facts of observed astronomical experience.

The days turn.

The seasons change.

The years pass.

II

PTOLEMY BEGINS the *Tetrabiblos* with a theoretical defense of astrology. Then as now, a defense was expected of astrologers, and then as now, a defense served chiefly to assure the astrologer of

A fifteenth-century copy of Ptolemy's *Almagest,* based on the thirteenth-century manuscript by Nasr al-Din Tusi. Ptolemy's great work disappeared from the West for more than eleven centuries, preserved against the worm of time by its translation into Arabic.

the legitimacy of his calling and the irrelevance of his critics. Ptolemy does not appear to have been a practicing astrologer. His brief is impersonal. That the heavens have some effect on human life, he observes, is evident. The sun and the moon affect the earth directly, the sun by its warmth, the moon by means of the tides. It is reasonable to suppose that what holds for the sun and the moon holds for heavenly bodies in general. This is inarguable, the burden of proof falling on the scope of the word *reasonable*. Whatever its scope, the word that best describes the way in which heavenly objects produce their effects is *influence*, a term that does not appear, and so is not needed, in the *Almagest*. It is not completely a magical concept, since its effect is contingent on very specific features of the night sky, but like the concept of *force* in mathematical physics, which it anticipates, influence will never be mistaken for a precisely defined idea.

Influence is, most obviously, very difficult to measure, and this because it is conveyed not only by individual objects in the sky, but by their ever-changing configuration as well. The very richness of the data introduces an unavoidable risk of error into all astrological calculations. "It is clear," Ptolemy admits, "that even though one approaches astrology in the most inquiring and legitimate spirit possible, he may frequently err, not for any of the reasons stated, but because of the very nature of the thing and his own weakness in comparison with the magnitude of his profession."

Limited by standards of observational accuracy, astrology is nonetheless the source of knowledge that is both accessible and important. In a section of the *Tetrabiblos* devoted to the birth of monsters, Ptolemy considers the prospects for children born under what he calls "four footed signs" (that is, the animal signs), and this at a time when the two maleficent planets, Mars and Saturn, are centered. Such children, he reports soberly, "will not even belong to the human race."

There remain the details necessary for the astrologer's art. The ecliptic has been etched onto the interior of the celestial sphere. Astrologers divide the ecliptic into twelve equal units of thirty degrees. The ecliptic's origin is determined by the sun's rotation around the earth, zero degrees fixed by the moment that the sun intersects the earth's equator in spring. The ecliptic has by means of two simple intellectual snips become a one-dimensional celestial coordinate system, a measuring ribbon and so a measuring rod. Although stars fill the night sky in every quadrant, the sun, moon, and planets appear to follow a circular orbit around the earth that stays within eight or nine degrees of the ecliptic; these are the instruments of astrological influence. To accommodate them, the ecliptic is extended to either side by roughly eight degrees, so that what was a circle becomes a curvilinear band. The origin of this system remains the same, but its units are now two-dimensional regions on the interior of the celestial sphere and not intervals along a curved line. Each region is fifteen degrees in width and thirty degrees in extent. Twelve units in all, as before, the whole traditionally designated as the zodiac. Carried as it is by the celestial sphere, the zodiac rotates around the earth on a daily basis, a new part of the zodiac passing over a fixed point on the earth once every two hours.

By tradition, the units of the celestial coordinate system were named individually after the twelve constellations or signs, beginning with Aries and ending with Pisces. The signs of the zodiac represent either Greek or Babylonian constellations or star clusters, and the names assigned the constellations are an exercise in simile. The various constellations apparently looked to ancient astronomers like a bull or a lion or even a fish. It is a point of similarity that even now escapes many observers. It has certainly escaped *me*.

Now a secret must be imparted. The signs of the zodiac have nothing to do with the physical constellations. There are, in the first place, thirteen rather than twelve constellations visible in the zodiac; and there is, in the second place, no regular principle of coordination from year to year between Aries, considered as a star cluster, and Aries, considered as the first two-dimensional section of the zodiac. The signs of the zodiac designate a certain two-dimensional region of space on the interior of the celestial sphere. They do nothing more.

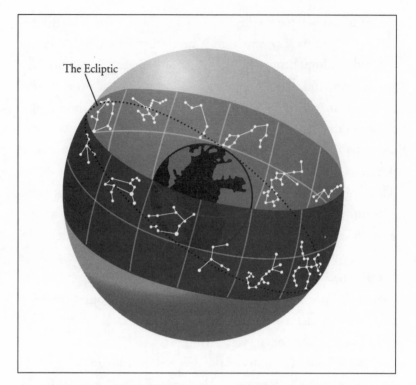

The signs of the zodiac designate a certain two-dimensional
region of space on the interior of the celestial sphere. Carried as
it is by the celestial sphere, the zodiac rotates around the earth
on a daily basis, a new part of the zodiac passing over a fixed
point on the earth once every two hours.

The zodiac functions as a rotating celestial diorama sweeping around the earth in regular periods, the show both unwavering and familiar. It is the sun's annual movement that takes it
through the signs of the zodiac. On March twenty-first, it enters
Aries and as time moves forward, crosses Aries on a diagonal
axis. This is the basis for sun sign astrology, an undertaking of
little interest but wide appeal. Shuffling forward in the sky, the
sun moves through the zodiac over the course of the year, stay-
ing in each sign for a month. (There is a curious contrast in as-

trology between two impressions: the sun bursting anew upon the world, and then scuttling quickly across the sky; and the sun shuffling along the ecliptic, slow to reach the vernal equinox and slow to climb into the summer sky.) If the sun is in double rotation around the earth, so are the other planets; bound as they are to the celestial wheel, they revolve around the earth once every twenty-four hours. But like the sun, the planets revolve around the earth at different speeds, some fast, others slow, all of them moving doggedly. It follows that, in addition to the sun, the planets *also* make their way through the zodiac, and like the sun, they are eager to be represented in a chart, if only to have a record of their influence. At different times—of the day, year, hour, minute—various heavenly objects may be found within different signs—found *physically.*

♊

IF THE LIBRARY in Alexandria was famous, its librarians were famous as well. Callimachus of Cyrene, the great elegiac poet of Hellenistic Greece, managed the library's collection during the later portion of the third century B.C.; he created an index of the library's holdings that itself contained 120 thousand scrolls. He was followed into the stacks by Erastosthenes of Cyrene, famous for his measurement of the earth's circumference, who, in time taken away from the study of geography, put together "a scheme of the great bookshelves." Aristarchus of Samothrace was the last of the librarians. Having taken up his position in 180 B.C., he was relieved of his duties shortly thereafter, the victim of an unhappy struggle between two Ptolemies, each eager to extend his patronage to an institution they were both willing to destroy. The library's books reduced the world's three-dimensional wonder to two dimensions; the librarians then reduced the library's books to an index. The mental maneuver that they undertook was the one that Ptolemy was himself undertaking.

If the earth is a point from the perspective of the cosmos, Ptolemy observes, it is locally a sphere, human beings aware of and often haunted by its size. Access to the heavens is always partial and frequently denied (by clouds or darkness, for example). Under the best of circumstances, observers can see only a part of the whole, the entire panorama of the rotating zodiac blocked simply because they cannot see through the earth to encompass a 360-degree perspective.

Astrology as a discipline represents a sophisticated attempt to reconcile the facts of human life, which are local and time-bound, and the global panorama of the heavens, which is forever in motion and indifferent to time. The astrologer must establish some sense of the grand pattern of the universe by tools that can directly reveal only its parts. The technique developed to this end is the chart, and together with the coordinate system of the zodiac, it represents the second—and last—purely astrological concept developed by ancient astrologers, or anyone else, for that matter.

A CHILD ENTERS the world at a particular time and at a particular place, his cry separating the flow of time into two halves. Birth is an important astrological event. Conception marks the initial stage in the development of a human being, Ptolemy acknowledges, but "the child at birth and his bodily form take on many additional attributes which he did not have before, when he was in the womb, those very ones indeed which belong to human nature alone." The astrologer attending his birth, or consulted sometime later by his parents, requires some system linking time and place to the rotating zodiac.

The simplest of such devices is a list; although charts may be found throughout the ancient world, busy astrologers, with no time to waste, often used a list as a kind of shorthand:

Year of Diocletian, Epihi [1], 4, 1st hour of the day. The sun in Libra 18, moon in Aquarius 10, Saturn in Scorpio 11, Jupiter in Gemini 19, Mars in Libra 6, Venus in Leo 7, Mercury in Cancer 18, Horoscopus in Leo 2, Midheaven in Aries 24, ascending node in Capricorn 23, preceding full moon in Capricorn 11. Lot of Fortune in Aquarian 29.

Everything is evident, and yet, as in so many forms of shorthand, everything is hidden; the list is too cryptic to be of use, the astrologer recording these details frequently missing their significance. The list that I have displayed does not specify the relationship between and among the planets.

It is here, with an astrological list in evidence, that the Ptolemaic insight becomes insistent. Nothing short of a picture will do what a picture does. A star map is precisely such a picture; it does what maps do, and that is to represent a complicated three-dimensional object in two dimensions. The earliest star maps were found in the caves at Lascaux, drawn more than seventeen thousand years ago. The following star map shows the sky over Alexandria in early January of 140 A.D.; it is the view that Ptolemy might have seen if, after working late at the library, he strolled into the gardens, the gentle plop of the waves breaking on the near shore of the esplanade a curiously tender sound, eased his hands onto his hips, and with his toga drawn against the chill, looked up at the sky.

A star map is a beautiful device, one reason, no doubt, that it figures so prominently in pre-historic cosmology; but from the astrologer's point of view, a star map is like a woman's face seen in profile: it offers a part of the whole. What Ptolemy could see at night, and what he might have recorded on a map, was hardly the whole of the heavens, and on the other side of the globe, the turning celestial sphere would present a quite different face to an

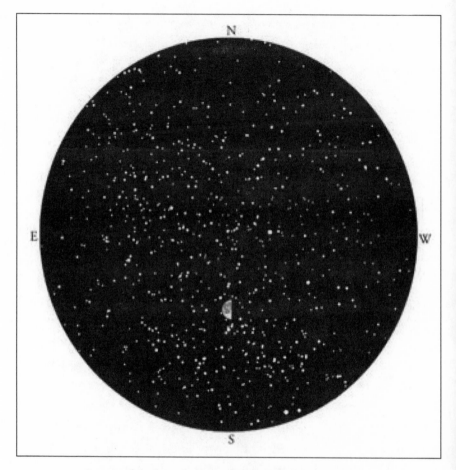

A map of the heavens as Ptolemy might have seen them;
and, like any map, a representation in two dimensions of a world
existing in three dimensions.

astrologer improbably studying the sky from the Fiji islands.
Planets are in opposition to one another across a distance of
180 degrees. Heavenly bodies form complicated triangular and
quadrilateral relationships. The sun scuttles across portions of the
zodiac, invisible at times and hidden. And all of this is important,
the heavens exerting their influence, whether malefic or benefi-
cial, across the *whole* of space. The earth's bulk is no impediment
to astrological transmission.

Now it often happens that the future of an art hinges on the discovery of a symbolic form. Musicians sang, clapped, chanted, and played instruments before the eleventh century; but the discovery of musical notation by Guido d'Arezzo opened wide the doors of art. So, too, Laban notation, phrase structures, or Feynmann diagrams. Art and science are both struggles to reduce the world's dimensional complexity downward, the same struggle, apparently, that life undertakes in reverse as a living creature reads its genetic code in order to construct itself.

The astrologer's chart now enters into the community of symbolic forms as a summary of the night sky. It reveals *everything* the astrologer needs: the zodiac, the planets, the observer's horizon, the planets' position with respect to the horizon, the planets' position with respect to one another; and beyond this, the bare record of the astronomical facts. The astrologer's chart allows the astrologer to add that layer of detail that is distinctively astrological, the congregation of relationships among signs and planets. It is this that the astrologer captures in a chart, employing an instrument that by means of discrete symbols can somehow accommodate the complexity of heavenly bodies in continuous motion.

The displayed chart follows the sky map in depicting the heavens on January 30, 140 A.D., and like the heavens themselves, the chart must be read.

The earth is at the center of the chart, the celestial sphere in rotation around it. The chart reveals what the earth conceals, those parts of the celestial sphere that lie below an observer's line of sight. The straight line bisecting the chart represents the horizon, moving as the eye moves from east to west. The pie-shaped sections of the chart are its houses. They serve to designate corresponding regions of the sky.

With the horizon fixed, other details fall into place. Passing over the earth like bright clean pennants, the signs of the zodiac

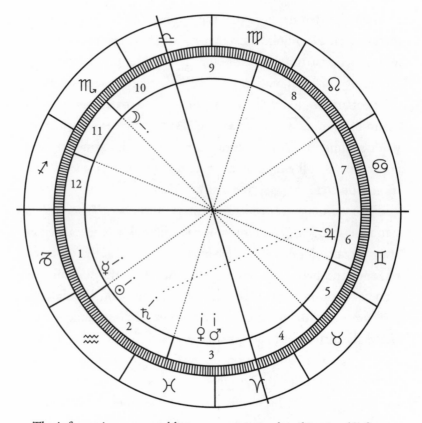

The information expressed by a star map reproduced in circular form, with an amazing improvement in lucidity and compression.

are for a moment stopped. The chart's outer ring designates the signs of the zodiac, regions of space, bits of fire. The planets are positioned against these signs.

A few places on the chart have particular importance. The ascendant is the star, or constellation, just breaking over the eastern horizon. If the sun is just above the ascendant, it is daybreak; if, on the other hand, it is approaching the western margins of the chart, it is sunset. In this way, the chart has effectively been made a clock, a sundial, in fact, if time is measured by its shadow. Temporal and spatial intervals have been coordinated. No bigger than the astrologer's palm, a chart is nonetheless capable of capturing in the alembic of its symbols the universe frozen in its forward flow.

♊

A LIBRARY IS MORE than a collection of books, the library at Alexandria more than a collection of scrolls. Callimachus, in his *Pinakes,* or tables listing the library's holdings, divided the library's subjects into mathematics, medicine, astronomy, geometry, and philology. This division was presumably reflected on the library's shelves as well. Ptolemy, when vexed by a problem, could stretch his legs, and, after trying in vain to track down an errant thought, amble through the cool corridors containing, say, scrolls dealing with the library's holdings on medicine. Interested in the causes of violent death—a section of the *Tetrabiblos*—he could begin with any particular reference in the *Pinakes* and then, by a process in which carelessness and serendipity both play their role, scout the adjacent sections where other scrolls were kept, finding, if he were lucky, not only the single text for which he was looking, but a whole series of texts organized around the mournful theme of violent death. Thus satisfied, he could in good conscience walk to the dining room, refresh himself with Egyptian delicacies, and return later to his desk, his sense of the patterns inherent in violent death invigorated by the library's stacks. He knew what every scholar knows. It is far easier to move around a library than to move around the world.

A chart is a map of the heavens; it contains the twelve houses, twelve signs, sun, moon, and six planets. This is, of course, theoretically interesting, but the astrologer concerned to counsel his clients or to advise an anxious politician has taken up casting charts to make a living, and before the information recorded in a chart can be used, he must figure out what it means. This is more difficult than it might seem. There are as many charts as there are times. Prediction, Ptolemy observes, cannot be based on a study of "the combination of all or most of the stars, because it is manifold and well-nigh infinite." The heavens are complex; charts are complicated; and time, like life, is short. A pattern is needed, what modern science would call a *law*.

The *Tetrabiblos* contains a rich account of what various charts might mean, and no doubt these accounts provoked the same reaction when Ptolemy displayed them at the library that they might today provoke. A pattern? And up there? And one with the power to inform human life? Tell me more. It is a question to which Ptolemy is responsive. His account reaches its rhetorical climax in a section of the book entitled "On the Quality of the Soul." Some configurations of the heavens (those involving Mercury) produce souls "fitted for dealing with people, fond of turbulence and political activity, glory-seeking, moreover, and attentive to the gods, noble, mobile, inquisitive, inventive, good at conjecture, and fitted for astrology and divination." Other configurations are not quite so happy. They "make souls complex, changeable, hard to apprehend, light, unstable, fickle, amorous, versatile, fond of music, lazy, easily acquisitive, prone to change their minds." The asseverations become more and more gorgeous. If "Saturn alone is ruler of the soul . . . he makes his subjects lovers of the body, strong minded, deep thinkers." If Saturn's position is opposite and without dignity (an astrological, not a social, term), "he makes them sordid, petty, mean-spirited, indifferent, meanminded, malignant, cowardly, diffident, evil-speakers, solitary, tearful, shameless, superstitious, fond of toil, unfeeling, devisers of plots against their friends, gloomy, taking no care of the body." Or under other circumstances, "uncultured, mad, easily frightened, superstitious, frequenters of shrines, public confessors of ailments, suspicious, hating their own children, friendless, hiding within doors, without judgment, faithless, knavishly foolish, venomous, hypocritical, ineffective, unambitious, prone to change their minds, stern, hard to speak with or to approach, cautious, but nevertheless foolish and submissive to abuse."

The attributes that emerge from Ptolemy's torrent of adjectives are quite palpably *characters,* men, in fact, with coherent personalities; but the law of nature connecting the heavens to human affairs—that Ptolemy never specifies.

II

DURING THE CENTURIES in which it stood as a symbol of literacy, the Library at Alexandria was often destroyed and almost as often rebuilt. In the course of his campaign in Egypt, Julius Caesar is said to have lit fire to wharves whose warehouses contained forty thousand books. No doubt fuming with indignation on discovering that the sad, torched volumes included innumerable remaindered copies of his own *Gallic Wars,* Caesar went on to do what Caesars always did. He stomped away in a fine fury. The patient Alexandrians, having put out his fires, rebuilt the wharves, restocked the library's shelves, and simply carried on. It is in this library that those seventy-two rabbis are gathered. The buffet luncheon has been consumed, and just as each scholar feared, the date rolls were quickly devoured. No man has had his fill, but each man has had enough to eat.

But there came a time when no reconstruction was undertaken. The library was destroyed in the sixth century A.D., and it was not rebuilt. The scrolls in its magnificent collection were lost, or burnt, or sold, some careless merchant, baffled by the languages of literacy, doubtless employing a priceless Aristotelian treatise to keep accounts or even to wipe his nose.

If the library was destroyed in fact, it has remained imperishable in thought, like the lighthouse outside the harbor at Alexandria, one of the wonders of the ancient world, still lit long after its lamps have gone out.

CHAPTER FOUR

CANCER
♋
LATIN LESSONS

Fata volentem docunt, nolentem trahunt.
(Fate leads the willing, drags the unwilling.)
—SENECA

UGUSTUS WAS THE FIRST of the Roman emperors. Before he assumed power, savage civil wars had already brought the Roman republic to its knees; Augustus brought it to its end. Almost five hundred years would follow before the last of his imperial successors would totter off into oblivion.

Augustus' path to power was enabled by an astrological forecast, one pegged to the date of his birth in 63 B.C. The Roman writer Suetonius recounts the story in his light-hearted but blood-flecked *Lives of the Twelve Caesars.*

> At Appolonia, Augustus and Agrippa [his closest friend and confidant] together visited the house of Theogenes, the astrologer; they had both wished to consult him about their future careers. Agrippa went first and was prophesied such incredibly good fortune that Augustus expected a far less encouraging response, and felt ashamed to disclose the time of his birth. Yet when at last after a great deal of hesitation,

he grudgingly supplied the information for which both were pressing him, Theogenes rose and flung himself at his feet, and thus gave Augustus so implicit a faith in his destiny that he even ventured to publish his horoscope, and struck a silver coin stamped with Capricorn, the sign under which he had been born.

Now Theogenes was certainly not the first astrologer to comment on Roman politics. In one of his immensely tiresome speeches, delivered to a Senate long accustomed to seeing the man rise and then unwind, Cicero observed with some asperity that astrologers had often offered various politicians soon to perish by assassination assurances of a long life and a tranquil old age. Cicero took the inaccuracy of their judgments as an indictment of their craft.

But whatever the predictions of other astrologers, Theogenes was in this case correct. Augustus came to power as he had anticipated and ruled for more than fifty years.

The emperor's faith in his fate, however, had its limits. As Augustus grew older he became vexed and then alarmed that astrologers were occupying themselves in predicting the length of his life. Such calculations were an affront to his majesty. They were malicious in their effect. Who knew what foolishness might be prompted in men persuaded that the emperor's time in power was growing short? Having treated the astrologers with great respect when they and he and fate were on a first-name basis, he now determined that whatever fate had had in store for him, the astrologers would be well advised to shut up. In 11 A.D., he issued an imperial edict. Calculations concerning the length of the emperor's life were forbidden. Calculations concerning the length of *anyone's* life were discouraged, even if such calculations were undertaken in private. It might be well for the astrologers to give up entirely the morbid practice, whether the subject was the emperor or an ordinary Roman citizen. The astrologers were pleased to have the emperor confirm the potency of their art, and if they refrained from making their predictions on such matters public, this served only to enhance the mystique of such predictions when they were made in private, behind garden walls or in the quiet refuge of the baths.

♋

THE ROMANS WERE not an immensely curious people. They took their philosophical and scientific culture from the Greeks, and they were content to borrow their gods from people prepared carelessly to lend them. Their genius was expressed in military discipline, law, commerce, statecraft, and hydrodynamics.

In the world beyond the imperial court, ordinary men and women carried on, whether as slaves or masters; they married, attended to their children's education, formed business enterprises and exchanged contracts; they entered into complicated litigation, sold goods, repaired shoes, made clothing, practiced law or medicine; they managed households. The Romans were optimists of the ordinary. Nevertheless, a dark, superstitious strain ran throughout the history of the empire, a general sense, noted even when the empire had seemed indestructible as the sea itself, that both its glory and its power would one day be squandered.

Rome never lacked for priests, vestal virgins, soothsayers, magicians, mystery cultists, esoteric teachers, sect leaders, phrenologists, palmists, fortune-tellers, or men capable of reading entrails; omens were widely noted and assiduously interpreted. And astrologers were everywhere. Forced as they were to make a living in trade, they opened offices and accepted consultations; they solicited business; they looked to advertising; and when the heavens were economically unrewarding, they dabbled a bit in medicine, offering their patients the benefits of a double diagnosis, one based both on their symptoms and on the stars.

Dorotheos of Sidon, writing in the second half of the first century, has left an account of the astrologer's art that could well have been in the Augustan air or carried through the Roman streets by the astrologers' anxious voices sixty years before. Although writing in Greek verse, Dorotheos seems to have drawn his astrological inspiration from Egyptian culture. He refers to himself as the king of Egypt. His text, the *Carmen Astrologicum* (Song of Astrology), although concerned with horoscopes and birth dates, is concerned as well to supply techniques by which specific questions might be answered, and answered at the time that they are asked.

The book that Dorotheos left is gloomy. There is a burst of bright, brittle cheer, and then the bad news follows. Is a client considering marriage? "Look at Venus," Dorotheos advises, "and consider the first, second and third lords of its triplicity." The burst of cheer now follows. There is a good indication in certain configurations. And about that good indication, Dorotheos does not say another word. Those certain configurations now vanish, replaced by others more grim. "Those who are born under *these* circumstances," he writes, "will be those who never marry, or whose marriage is with slave girls or whores or old women who are disgraced, or those young in years, or he [will be] a leaser of whores." Taking one thing with the other, things indicate "disaster and disgrace because of women, and anxiety and grief because of them."

When it comes to children, Dorotheos is more specific and still more pessimistic. "If Saturn is in quartile to Mercury in the tenth sign from Mercury, it will bring many misfortunes to those nativities and will make the native base, listless in work, a cheater—he will love the fault that is not his own and with this he will be afflicted, a lisper, or a mute, or a deaf man." Given another equally likely astrological configuration, he will suffer "a flaw in his manner of walking and a chronic illness in his body will come upon him, and he will not be courageous for any of his work, and he will spoil his mother's properties, and there might be among them some who hate their fathers."

If the *Carmen Astrologicum* is gloomy, at the same time it is never short on awful detail. Cicero had argued that astrological predictions are too vague to be tested, a thesis that we in the twenty-first century find persuasive. The prediction, from a popular column, that those born in Aries might expect a change in fortune in the first week of May can hardly be faulted, even if it cannot possibly be challenged. This is not true of the *Carmen Astrologicum*. Its claims are as exposed as a tree in winter.

"If Mars is in left quartile of the Sun," Dorotheos writes, "then it will be harmful in the matter of his father and of himself, and he will abound in calamity, misfortune in his property will reach him until everything he possesses disappears, and he will be frightened, perplexed, obsessed with delusions, and his vision will grow dark and his sight will be in error; in a diurnal native, the misfortunate will be worse except sometime he will die from this and perish."

In the bright Roman sunshine, a good many senators and politicians claimed to regard the astrologer's art as an absurd superstition. But in the gloomy night, when fog slithered through the streets, the astrologer's complicated charts seemed rather less ridiculous than they had by day, and buoyantly confident men made suddenly insecure would send for their personal astrologers to hear firsthand what the stars might have in mind.

♋

DESPITE HIS POWER, Augustus had the gift of evoking his subjects' assent without seeming to offer them his commands. His character was constant: He was modest, tactful, generous, and fair. When necessary, he could be unforgiving. He regarded promiscuity in others with none of the indulgence that he allowed himself, and when he discovered the extent of his daughter Julia's adultery, long after her indecorous affairs had been flaunted before the imperial court, he had her exiled to some inhospitable island. For all that, Augustus' own vices were no more flagrant when death forced him to relinquish power than when ambition prompted him to seize it.

In 15 A.D., Tiberius ascended the imperial throne with a show of marvelously insincere reluctance. He had waited patiently for more than twenty-five years to assume his stepfather's power, and he had grown lean and sullen in its service. Now it was his. He commanded an immense empire. Sophisticated stone-paved roads carried his commands to the ragged edges of the world, and after circulating around the circumference of the empire and sweeping up military reports, taxes, news, architectural plans, and all the gossip of the state, returned to evacuate themselves joyously at Rome. In the west, Britain had since the time of Julius Caesar been a half-conquered Roman province, Roman legions tramping over the muddy fields, the blue mist drifting as they set up camps, the legions dismaying their enemies by means of a dreadfully efficient military machine. What is now France was divided into three parts and it remained Gaul under Augustus, with southern Gaul, or Aquitania, famous in Roman times as a very pleasant place to live and work. Roman legions occupied Lusitania, the Spanish coast, and they occupied Tarraconensis as well, the interior of modern Spain. In the East, the empire surged to the very ends of the Mediterranean, incorporating Bithynia, Galatia, Cilicia, and Syria, absorbing and then transforming all of the dissolute, weak, old kingdoms. The Roman standard flew over much of northern Africa and included the greater part of ancient Egypt; the Carthaginian empire, which had in the second century B.C. challenged Roman power, lay in ruins, the very ground seeded with salt. Roman legions occupied the Rhine basin and straddled the lawless German frontier. If Rome was the center of the empire, the imperial court was Rome's center, the single quivering point where every line of force began. Lurid and irresistible, it was the scene of endless intrigue. Men in power schemed to stay in power, and men close to power schemed to get closer. Blood flowed like a dark shifting current through the cool marble of its corridors.

Tiberius was a large, demanding, and forceful personality. He commanded respect, but did not evoke affection. Almost one hundred years after his death, his life and the nature of his rule came to occupy Cornelius Tacitus, if not the greatest then the most realistic of the Latin historians. The portrait that Tacitus offers in the *Annals of Imperial Rome* is not naïve. Tacitus was a man of the world. He had few illusions. Tiberius had come to power under dark circumstances. Men had died conveniently to ease his path. Tacitus knew that no one acquires power without corruption, a fact that he regarded as unacceptable and accepted as unavoidable.

The man who emerges from the *Annals* is intelligent, perceptive, sour, secretive, disciplined, unrevealing, and cruel. He had a remarkable capacity for concealing his emotions, hardly an unwelcome gift in a politician, but Tiberius' skill in this regard was so considerable that in the end he seems to have concealed himself from himself and, like Stalin, who was seen doodling wolves over and over again before his death, Tiberius spent his last days lost in a sinister fog of indiscriminate suspicion. A cold oil had seeped into his soul.

DURING THE LATTER PART of Augustus' long reign, Tiberius found himself in difficult personal circumstances. He was a man of ambition. And he had made painful personal sacrifices in order to place himself in the line of imperial succession. His marriage to the emperor's daughter Julia, brought about only when he divorced his beloved wife Vespina, represented a concession to reality that he could neither avoid nor abide.

With Augustus still in possession of his faculties, and so of his power, Tiberius retired to the island of Rhodes, a bright artistic and cultural center. He read widely; he thought solemnly; and he waited. Far away in Rome, the emperor, who was the author of his misfortune, continued to rule, advancing into his own old age while giving no indication—a helpful catarrh, an outbreak of kidney stones, a decent sign of wasting—that he was at any time soon helpfully prepared to shuffle off. A bust made of Tiberius expresses these vagrant and conflicting aspects of his personality. It depicts a man of perhaps thirty-five who stares out from the cut and polished stone. His hair is worn in a Caesar-cut, shaped in delicate bangs over his forehead. There is a certain boyish plumpness to the face, with even the faintest hint of a double chin, an effect that must have cost the sculptor something by way of anxiety. And there is more: a kind of petulance to the way the face is set, the eyes far away in their lost look.

Waiting—that is what he did, the days and weeks and months of Augustus' long life plashing like a mocking water clock in Rhodes as well as Rome. It was while waiting that he made the acquaintance of a Greek astrologer named Thrasyllus. By profession a grammarian, Thrasyllus was a member of the imperial court's outer circle. His advice was widely sought; it was frequently valued. He seemed to have kept a hand in a number of divinatory arts. Stories circulated about his shrewdness. Details of his life are locked between myth and fact.

Tiberius' claim on the imperial succession was never considered a closed case. Roman power was like a river, and rivers could be dammed, re-channeled, or blocked with silt. If power was within his reach it was not yet within his grasp. And there he was, in Rhodes of all places, the intrigues that make men master of their fate taking place far beyond the island's beaches. Tiberius wished to know whether—and when—he would acquire supreme power; the questions consumed him. He had spent years in the service of Augustus and he had the sense that in some unvoiced way, Augustus regarded him with regret. In this he was correct. Augustus appreciated his intelligence and valued his military abilities, but he simply did not like the man.

Having invited Thrasyllus to Rhodes, Tiberius now subjected the astrologer to an interrogation, one that Tacitus places on the terrace of Tiberius' villa. The sea is far below—*very* far below—the sky blue, the terrace flower-mad but insect-still. Chattering nervously, Thrasyllus spread out his charts, Tiberius grunting in assent or clearing his throat before lapsing into his notoriously unforthcoming silence. Tiberius could read and speak Greek fluently, and he was devoted to Greek literature, but beyond rhetoric, poetry, and military affairs, he was hardly an educated man. He had no grasp of any scientific technique. The charts fluttering on his tabletop reflected an astronomical tradition that he certainly did not understand.

Pulling on his earlobes, I imagine, and then offering his nose a nervous pinch-and-tug, the kind that begins at the bridge and sweeps off from the nostrils, Thrasyllus undertook various calculations. General insights about his life or personality would have insulted Tiberius, the very idea an affront. Thrasyllus' chart addressed a specific question, with the position of the sun, the moon, and the planets all dated from the moment the question was asked. Thrasyllus covered his parchment with scratches and astrological symbols. He measured angles and drew arrows. He may well have doodled in a few esoteric formulae. His most accurate instruments must have been a water clock and the elaborate planetary tables available in the Roman world for hundreds of years. Thus occupied, he must have spotted his own fate be-

ginning suddenly to creep around his sandaled ankles like a vigorous jungle vine.

Never mind the imperial succession, and never mind the sun,
the stars, and the sparkling sea. *He* was in peril. The man glower-
ing at his side, his unrevealing face set in its heavy, habitual scowl,
might well regard another man's death as an especially tidy way of
resolving his own emotional problems.

Thrasyllus glanced over the fluted white wall that separated
the terrace from the sea far below. Tiberius' personal guard stood
at attention on the walkway leading from the terrace to the villa.
These brutes would be pleased to pitch him from the terrace and
then, without pause, resume standing at attention, the hot sun
beating down on their bronze helmets. The voice of common
sense sounded with a simple message: Tell Tiberius what plainly
he wished to hear.

And then flee.

But just what did Tiberius wish to hear? Bad news might
prompt Tiberius to disappointed fury. Good news might persuade
Tiberius that he was being flattered. Too many men were prepared
to flatter Tiberius to his face; he hardly needed an astrologer to
flatter him through the stars. The psychological complexities of
this encounter are considerable. And then all at once, Thrasyllus
must have seen his way clear through his own enveloping fog.
Tiberius would ascend to the throne, he announced.

The stars had spoken, and if not spoken, then signed themselves in their habitual language of curved gestures. Tiberius received his astrologer's prophecy in silence, his dark, familiar bile
neither diminished nor displaced. Thrasyllus stood nervously in
the shedding sunlight; from time to time, he regarded Tiberius
with an assessing glance. Tiberius for his part had heard what he
had hoped to hear, of course, but he had not discovered what he
had wished to know.

What, Tiberius now asked, did Thrasyllus' *own* chart for the coming year suggest?

> Thrasyllus, after measuring the position and the distances of the stars, hesitated, then showed alarm. The more he looked, the greater his astonishment and fright. Then he cried that a critical and perhaps fatal emergency was upon him. Tiberius clasped him, commending his divination of peril, and promising that he would escape it. Thrasyllus was admitted among his closest friends, his pronouncements considered as oracular.

An interesting story, and one that if properly read reveals the infinitely receding landscape of mirrors that is the human heart.

THE EXCHANGE BETWEEN Tiberius and Thrasyllus marks a new place in history, one of those odd little dimples in the flow of time. The men were not at all equal, of course, and power flowed in one direction, from Tiberius, its gushing source, to Thrasyllus, its hapless sink. Tiberius could certainly have had Thrasyllus flung from the terrace to his death on the shore-side rocks far below. This is something that Tiberius, Thrasyllus, and Tacitus all knew.

But the story has another aspect, one that restores an odd degree of symmetry to its protagonists. If allowances are made for Tiberius' brutality, allowances also should be made for his vulnerability. He stands there on that sun-freckled terrace, forever frozen by the description that Tacitus offers, a large man, plainly uncomfortable in his skin, waiting glumly for a clever Greek astrologer to undertake the calculations that would reveal his fate. The concept of fate has played its role in the life of every civilization, but for the most part, the scribes of the *Enuma Anu Enlil* thought a man's fate was the expression of some system of personal forces. Those forces were quite beyond a man's control, but they were well within his comprehension. A man's fate was determined by the action of the gods, and if it was written in the stars, that was largely because the gods had chosen stray bits of the cosmos on which to record their thoughts.

Thrasyllus was confronting Tiberius with the powers of a very different system. The stars were revealing, just as they might have been to astrologers advising a king one thousand years before; but these stars were different. No gods animated the sun's forward sweep, and no gods drove the moon in revolutions around the earth. The gods or goddesses might still figure in Greek and Roman cosmology, but they could no longer be appealed to or appeased, and for all *practical* purposes, they had vacated the astrological system. Now there was something new: a chilling and precise impersonal concordance between an astronomical system and a man's life.

No wonder Tiberius hesitated. And in the concord and exchange between the two men, a new relationship was forged, the wizards and magicians of old vanishing in a twinkle, replaced by men who made claims to a new kind of knowledge, objective but inaccessible, its elucidation a matter of training, education, discipline, expertise, and perhaps a certain innate gift.

∞

SUETONIUS TELLS another story about another emperor, Domitian, the last and least of the Flavian line, and another astrologer, Ascletario.

Tiberius was a man of great personal force, compelling to his contemporaries even in his sourness. But the Julian-Claudian line had come to an end with the lamentable Nero's death; thereafter the emperors Galba, Otho, and Vitellius occupied the imperial throne while managing to leave it vacant. Domitian was heir to the Flavian dynasty, a successor to Vespasian and Titus, his father and his brother. He served to consolidate the vices of his predecessors while doing little to enhance their virtues.

Domitian was born on Pomegranate Street, Suetonius recounts, in Rome's sixth district, his childhood both "poverty stricken and rather degraded." Roman gossips claimed that, as a child, Domitian was sexually abused by his successor, the Emperor Nerva, although Suetonius does not say why, in an empire in which children were sometimes executed, their sexual abuse should have prompted indignation. It is more difficult to satisfy the claim that his upbringing was poor. Suetonius says only that his otherwise aristocratic family lacked silver to place on the table, a circumstance that, if it excludes wealth, hardly indicates indigence. Whether poor or not, Domitian slithered toward power by means of cunning unrelieved by courage. He was one of history's inveterate schemers. When the Emperor Titus fell ill—his brother, after all—Domitian left instructions that his attendants should presume that he was dead.

And soon he was.

Thereafter Domitian ascended the imperial throne, amusing himself largely during his early time in office by catching flies and stabbing them with a needle-sharp pen. "For a while," Suetonius writes, "he governed in an uneven fashion: that is to say, his vices were at first balanced by his virtues." This was, of course, true of almost all the Roman emperors. "Later," Suetonius adds, Domitian managed to "transform his virtues into vices," thus ending the division in his personality that had tempered his early rule. "Lack of funds made him greedy, and fear of assassination made him cruel." Domitian was not under the best of circumstances a man of intellectual curiosity, and so Rome was ruled by a man who was stupid as well as avaricious and cruel. On a Roman relief, now in the Vatican, Vespasian is seen in profile facing the young Domitian (his son). Vespasian is depicted as a bald, large-nosed man with tight, thin lips, and, curiously enough, an insecure look in his stone eyes. His hand is raised. It is remarkably difficult to determine whether the sculptor intended to de-

pict Vespasian pushing his successor back or about to pat him
on the shoulder.

ASTROLOGICAL PREDICTIONS, Suetonius writes, had long foretold
the year, the day, the hour, and the manner of Domitian's death.
He would perish by means of an assassin's knife. As he grew older,
Domitian grew more dissolute, and as he grew more dissolute,
he became more fearful; his horoscope, which had for so long
seemed a dark but distant threat, came ever more to oppress him
as the years tapered into the familiar funnel of middle age. Lightning terrified him, he saw omens in the most ordinary of events,
and his dreams disturbed him profoundly, the more so since they
were dreadful. The goddess Minerva, who had been charged with
his protection, appeared one night gravely to inform him that she
had been disarmed by Jupiter and that he, the emperor, now
stood defenseless before the world.

"What disturbed him *most*," Suetonius observes, "was a prediction by the astrologer Ascletario." The sunny Tiberian terrace
is gone. Suetonius sets the scene somewhere in the imperial
palace, and it is left to the reader to imagine the deep resonating
gloom of the place, especially at night, Ascletario facing the emperor and offering the man the unwelcome news that he was
mortal and that he would soon die. Having offered the homici-
dal Domitian his counsel, Ascletario could not have been in any
doubt about his own fate. He would be punished either for
telling or denying the truth, and since in logical fact he was obli-
gated to do one or the other, he would be punished. In Domitian's circle, as in Stalin's court, there was only one punishment.

But if Ascletario knew his fate, Domitian did not; he was in
an agony of uncertainty, the astrologer standing there in the imperial chamber regarding him with a cool, insolent regard. There
is no record in the classical literature of anyone remarking that
Domitian was psychologically shrewd. Yet curiously enough he

found the means to settle his doubts, hitting on just the psychological strategy that Tiberius used in confronting Thrasyllus.

Domitian demanded to know whether Ascletario could "prophesy the manner of his *own* end." Ascletario at once replied that he was very soon to be torn to pieces by dogs, an answer similar in spirit, although not in detail, to the one that Thrasyllus had offered Tiberius.

Torn to pieces by dogs? It seems an odd response. There were no dogs in the imperial palace, and even if there had been, the emperor's dogs would be more likely to beg for food than risk biting their dinner from the living flesh of one of his guests.

Calling in his palace guard, Domitian had Ascletario executed on the spot. He then gave orders that the man's "funeral rites be conducted with the greatest of care, *as a further proof that astrology was a fake.*"

The story now unfolds with all the chilling logic of the Monkey's Paw. While the funeral was in progress, Suetonius writes, "a sudden gale scattered the pyre and dogs mangled the half-burned corpse."

Thereafter the scene that Suetonius sets is dreadful. His power unavailing, the emperor faces a prospect he is unprepared to accept and unable to reject. Suetonius writes:

> On the day before his assassination, someone brought [the emperor] a present of apples. "Serve them tomorrow," he told the servants, adding:—"if only I am spared to eat them." Then turning to his companions he remarked: "There will be blood on the moon as she enters Aquarius, and a deed will be done for everyone to talk about throughout the entire world."

Time now slows. It is nearly midnight in the imperial palace. Domitian's death, Ascletario had predicted, would occur at five in the morning.

With the approach of midnight Domitian became so terrified that he jumped out of bed; and at dawn, condemned to
death a soothsayer from Germany who was charged with
having said that lightning portended a change in government. Domitian then scratched a festering wart on his forehead, muttering: "I hope this is all the blood required."

Domitian asked his servants for the time.

As had been prearranged, his freedman answered untruth-
fully: "The sixth hour," because he knew that it was the fifth
he feared. Convinced that the danger had passed, Domitian
went off quickly and happily to take a bath, whereupon his
head valet, Parthenius, changed his intention by delivering
the news that a man had called on very urgent and important business, and would not be put off. So Domitian dismissed his attendants and hurried to his bedroom—where
he was killed.

Nullo fata loco possis excludere, as Martial wrote. Nowhere can you
shut out fate.

⊙

AT THE END OF the second century A.D., the Roman Empire was
not yet in decline, but like a spear thrown into the air, it had
reached its apogee, and sensitive observers could see that having
risen, it must in the end descend. The empire, although prosperous, had begun to fray at its margins, even as Rome was itself undergoing a deep and ineradicable coarsening of its taste and
temperament. Mystery religions, which had represented a subversive current of sentiment in the republic and the early empire,
now emerged from the shadows. In Egypt, there was the cult of
Isis; farther east, men and women worshipped the Great Mother;
and in Persia, the Unconquerable Sun, the Mithraic religion
spreading westward by seeping through the Roman army. In Italy
and throughout north Africa, the Christians were a powerful

presence, their rites acquiring great appeal in virtue of the specific historical story that they told.

By the end of the third century A.D., its currency wracked by inflation and its authority gravely compromised by tribal insubordination along its borders, the Roman state had taken on many of the aspects of those oriental despotisms that free Roman citizens had long held in contempt. During the early part of his reign, which began in 284 A.D., the emperor Diocletian, a man of coarse sensibilities but considerable cunning, indulgently tolerated the Christian sect. When he later realized that it had formed a state within the Roman state, his fitful attempts at suppression served only to call attention to the remarkable capacity of the Christian church to bear suffering without losing influence.

Diocletian resigned the throne in 306 A.D., and after a number of mediocrities seized and then squandered imperial power, he was succeeded by Constantine the Great. The emperor, his biographer Eusebius recounts, had seen a cross flaming in the sky before the battle of the Milvian bridge. The Christians had promised that their Christ would come bringing not peace, but a sword. Here was proof. Constantine had been previously persuaded of the virtues of the Unconquerable Sun. He now underwent a conspicuous conversion and commanded the empire to follow. However sincere his change of heart, Constantine took care to have his coins inscribed *both* with the Christian cross *and* the sign of the Unconquerable Sun, interesting evidence that while he was affirming his faith he was also hedging his bets. If Christianity had survived persecution, it now enjoyed power.

Church leaders of the fourth century were men of uncommon intelligence and ability, and they moved quickly to secure their ideological control of philosophy, science, and literature. Astrology had been a part of the very fabric of Roman society for more than five hundred years, and if Ptolemy had not quite succeeded in making it a science, he had certainly succeeded in suggesting it was a system. But Roman astrology and Christian doctrine, Church authorities suspected, were in conflict. Astrologers were looked on first with suspicion and then with intolerance.

In 365 A.D., the Council of Laodicea officially prohibited clergy from practicing either astrology *or* magic, the Church fathers drawing little distinction between the two. The Council of Toledo, held thirty-five years later, offered an anathema to anyone considering astrology "worthy of belief."

It was left in this, as in so many other matters of doctrine, for Augustine of Hippo—Saint Augustine—to offer a theological justification for Church strictures. Writing in north Africa in the fifth century A.D., Augustine was, of course, forming his thoughts against the background of a great civic catastrophe, the eclipse of the Roman Empire in the west; there is throughout the *City of God* an anguished appreciation of the grandeur of a culture in dissolution. The argument that Augustine advances against astrology has some of the drama of a man renouncing his own heritage.

If the stars hold the power to control human affairs, Augustine writes, then that power is either independent of or dependent on God's will. So much is clear as a matter of logic, and it is logic again that now drives the argument forward. If they are independent of divine will, the stars, it would seem, are for this reason beyond divine control. This Augustine rejects as a form of atheism. "For what does this opinion really amount to but this," he asks, "that no god whatever is to be worshipped or prayed to?" The question is unanswerable, whether in the fifth century A.D. or in the present. It troubles the imagination. But if the stars are *dependent* on divine will, then they must be nothing more than a cause transmitting another cause. But if the stars *are* causes reflecting a divine cause, what then is left of free will? If nothing, as Augustine suspects, then the great Christian drama of contrition, forgiveness, and redemption stands emptied of its meaning.

There is a pause in the argument. Augustine is not, let us acknowledge, a superb dialectician. His style tends toward overflow and afterthought. The inevitable afterthought now comes overflowing. Why assign causal powers to the stars at all? What "if the stars are said rather to *signify* these things than to effect them, so that the position of the stars is, as it were, a kind of speech, predicting, not causing future things"? This interpretation of astrology Augustine attributes to the mathematicians, but it runs backward, of course, to its true source in the omens of the *Enuma*.

There is an additional odd note, one that runs through the entire story of astrology. Whatever his philosophical conclusions, Augustine admits, astrologers are often correct in the predictions that they make.

And thereafter Augustine's argument trails off inconclusively. Early Church fathers quite knew that they were opposed to astrology. They were not entirely sure why. Augustine had taken their animadversions to the cusp of an argument, but no further. An unfocused sentiment and an incomplete argument nevertheless reinforced one another. An art which had been considered no more shady than any other Roman art, such as extispicy (the examination of animal organs) or fortune-telling, found itself proscribed, the astrologers themselves, if unwilling to renounce their beliefs, forced instead to renounce their practice.

A long decline commenced.

CHAPTER FIVE

LEO

♌

AN ARABIAN NIGHT

Sometime in the latter part of the eighth century, the English deacon and astrologer Alcuin made a voyage from his home in York to the continent. He was already well known as a scholar able to read and write classical Latin, and as the master of the church school at the Archbishopric of York, known as well as a superb, even an inspiring, pedagogue. Church affairs had taken him to Rome. The trip must have been arduous. Europe was still largely covered by forests of beech, oak, and spruce; there were wolves in all the woods, even in France, and the few roads that connected one demesne to another, or that straggled through derelict villages, were impassable in autumn and again in spring.

On meeting Charlemagne in March of 781, Alcuin found himself captivated by the man's boisterous confidence, even as Charlemagne, who could barely sign his name, found himself deeply impressed by Alcuin's gentle cultivation. Alcuin became the master of the Palace School at Aachen. And more. He became Charlemagne's confidant, teacher, advisor, and astrologer, and although he probably bathed no more than a dozen times in his life and regarded a change of underwear as a considerable luxury, as, indeed, it is, as master of the Palace School he was nonetheless in a position to convey the burden of the classical and patristic heritage from the scattered monasteries in which it had been entombed to the raw new centers of European culture.

Suppose now, in one of those magical undertakings that prose makes possible, that Alcuin were suddenly sent on a journey down from Aachen and the imperial court, through the boot and heel of Italy, and across the Mediterranean Sea, closed in the eighth century to European scholars as well as sailors, the baffled cleric, clasping his cloak tight, sailing past Palestine, through all the old Roman provinces in Syria and across the vaulted sky until at last he came into view of the spires and minarets of the city of Baghdad.

This is what Alcuin would have seen, as seen somewhat later by Yaqut ibn Abdallah ur Rumi, an Arab geographer and slave:

The numerous suburbs, covered with parks, gardens, villas, and beautiful promenades, and plentifully supplied with rich bazaars and finely built mosques.

And:

The palace of the Caliph in the midst of a vast park which beside a menagerie and aviary comprised an enclosure for wild animals.

And:

The palace grounds laid out with gardens, and adorned with exquisite taste with plants, flowers and trees, reservoirs and fountains, surrounded by sculpted figures.

And:

The palaces of the great nobles, not made of stucco and mortar, but of marble, the palaces and mansions lavishly gilded and decorated and hung with beautiful tapestry and hangings of brocade or silk, the rooms lightly and tastefully furnished with luxurious divans, costly tables, unique Chinese vases and gold and silver ornaments.

And:

Kiosks, gardens and parks of the grandees and nobles on both sides of the river Tigris, marble steps leading down to the water's edge, and the scene on the river animated by thousands of gondolas, decked with little flags, dancing like sunbeams on the water, and carrying the pleasure-seeking Baghdad citizens from one part of the city to the other.

I mention all this to convey a sense of that compelling contrast between ninth-century Europe—slops running through streets that had once been served by sophisticated sewers, a haze everywhere, the mice scampering over the cobblestones—and the Moslem world when Abbasaid power was at its height, and Caliph Harun-al-Rashid, his bearded chin held high, could be seen in the streets of Baghdad, surveying in calm contentment the city of his glory.

Ω

ABU MASHAR Al-Balkhi Jafar ibn Muhammad was the most famous astrologer of the ninth-century Moslem world. He was a citizen of Baghdad, whose very streets had been laid out by astrologers a century before, and he was a man of great sophistication, accustomed to marble and silk and the swish of flag-capped lantern-lit gondolas as they made their way from one Baghdad waterfront palace to another. His long name tells the reader that he was born in Balkh (*Al-Balkhi:* from Balkhi), which is located in the province of Khurasan near the Afghan border, and that he was the father (*abu*) of Mashar and the son (*ibn*) of Muhammad, but it says nothing of the long reach of his racial memory, which by means of all the contrivances of art—lyric poetry, exquisite painted miniatures, letters, the Persian script itself, and much besides—carried the man back to the sensuous and corrupt Sassanian Empire, which Ahnaf ibn Qays had conquered 150 years before.

With his hand discretely cupping the coarse cloth at Alcuin's unresisting elbow, Abu Mashar could conjure up for this earnest primitive the sights *he* took for granted: Jews in beaded prayer shawls; Nestorians, against whom Alcuin had argued in combating the Adoptionist heresy; Manicheans, forever dividing the world like two halves of a walnut; Buddhists; coal-black Hindus from the south of India; gabbling religious scholars from every corner of the globe; merchants in caftans; street-corner astrologers, dust boards on their knees; scribes who for a small fee would compose love letters, wills, or business documents; jewelers working in gold and ivory and precious metals; and food stalls selling lemon chicken, or lamb cooked over a spit with cardamom, or small rolls dipped in honey, or flat slabs of pita bread smeared with fat.

In the gentle Baghdad evening, the muezzin calling the faithful to prayer in the distance, Alcuin and Abu Mashar might have talked shopped about astrology. I doubt very much that Alcuin could properly cast a horoscope. He might have read Maternus. Ptolemy remained untranslated into Latin and Alcuin had no Greek. His astrological system, whatever it was, must have been nothing more than the stump of ancient systems. The luscious doctrines and details available to Abu Mashar, by way of contrast, pile up like wine-soaked raisins in a Sicilian wedding cake. Dorotheos of Sidon, and Vettius Valens, *yes, of course,* but Buzurjmihr, Andarzghar, Zaradusht, and the *Zij al-Shah,* as well, the rich quickening currents of the Pahlavi Greco-Indo-Iranian tradition in astrology *and* astronomy, Varahamira, Kanaka, the *Sinhind,* the *Zij al-Arkand,* and Aryabhta, the great figures and the classics of the Sanskrit-Greco-Indian tradition.

It was a world beyond the world that Alcuin knew, and a world beyond the world we know.

ABU MASHAR began his professional life as a master of *hadith,* a discipline rather like Talmud study, in which the adept commits

to memory the sayings of the Prophet in order to use them for ex-
egetical or pedagogical purposes. He suffered a psychological crisis in his forty-seventh year. His biographers do not say why. And
sometime later he came under the influence of Abu Yusuf Yaqub
ibn Ishaq al-Kindi, the greatest of early Moslem philosophers,
and one of the synoptic intellects of the Middle Ages. Al-Kindi
acquired a disciple, and Abu Mashar a master, and for the first
time since Ptolemy, astrology fell under the analytic scrutiny of a
profound intelligence.

Al-Kindi was interested in divination and in magic. It was
this large and general interest that served to focus the wandering
gaze of his intelligence onto astrology. The root of magic has always been with certain incantations, forms of words with the
power to affect material objects. Legends allude to words so terrible in their power that writing them, whether in sand or on
paper, causes sudden death. The man who foolishly utters them
out loud dies at once, and so, too, the animals who might have
overheard him. It is for this reason that these words are conveyed
from magician to magician by being written on water, their letters disappearing as soon as they are formed.

Could one, I wonder, possess these terrible words without
knowing that one knew them? What if they were silently
mouthed? Or uttered inadvertently, or in a fit of pique, and what
if they were uttered as a part of a longer, entirely innocuous word,
the way "cat" is uttered as the first part of "catatonic"? And suppose two magicians were simultaneously to pronounce anathe-
mas on one another using the same minatory words? Would each
be responsible for the other's death? Or would the coroner return
a verdict of a double suicide, explaining soberly that, appearances
notwithstanding, each man quite literally talked himself to death,
as when professors perish in committee rooms?

These fascinating questions have a misleading effect, if only
because they suggest that it is magical acts that are inherently

mysterious. Not so. The mystery goes beyond magic. It is action in general that requires an explanation. This is the topic that al-Kindi addresses in a treatise entitled *On Stellar Rays*, a book with a significant influence on the history of astrology, and still the subject of Internet citations today. Its Arabic source having been lost or otherwise misplaced (and occasionally denied), those stellar rays have made their way into the world in medieval Latin.

The phenomenon that provokes al-Kindi's puzzlement directly is action at a distance, the fact that objects separated in space may have a causal influence on one another. The obvious examples of action at a distance lie close at hand. Words have the power to reach the past or the future, or to bring a vanished city or romance to life. They achieve their effects at a distance. "Discourses...and entreaties," al-Kindi writes, "are performed by men for the purpose of making events happen by means of devoted minds and intense desire." It sometimes happens that one man's will comes to dominate another man's behavior. This is again a form of action at a distance. The stars, in achieving *their* effect, act across the cold and emptiness of space. Action at a distance once again. Our most natural explanation of action is by means of contact, one object influencing another directly. But when action at a distance takes place, contact is obviously lost. What, then, serves to bridge the gap between a cause and its effect?

In dealing with these difficult issues, *On Stellar Rays* proceeds by assertion, and it achieves its control over disputed matters by repetition. It is neither a work of physics nor metaphysics. It does something else. It *suggests* how action at a distance might be accommodated within a physical theory, one that did not exist at the time al-Kindi was writing his treatise, but one that he could nonetheless have imagined.

In his reflections, al-Kindi retained the ancient Aristotelian idea that change in all its forms is, in the end, reducible to change in place, and that change in place is brought about only when objects are in contact. One thing bangs, hits, jams, rams, knocks, crumples, touches, pushes, or shoves another. *Contact.* And thereafter the thing banged, hit, jammed, rammed, knocked, crumpled, touched, pushed, or shoved *changes* in some way. How then to accommodate the influence of the stars, or the power of words, or the mystery of prayer, within this scheme? How, for that matter, to accommodate the evil eye, or the sorcerer's hypnotic influence, or even the teacher's control of his pupil's development?

Al-Kindi attributes his theory, and so his answer, to various "ancient fathers."

> For looking up they saw certain conditions of the many stars; and they especially sought to investigate and to know which of the seven planets' properties were more well disposed than the others, for they had proved by long experience that they were the special stewards of the world. They acquired undoubted faith, through sense, that the arrangement of the stars ordered the world of the elements and all things in it which are composed of them, comprehended in every time and place and that therefore no substance subsists here which is not figured in heaven in its own manner and that this happens by the rays of the same stewards sent down into the world is not to be doubted

The idea that the planets play an especially important role in regulating human affairs is a straightforward account of astrological doctrines already old in the eighth century A.D., but the last twenty-one words express Al-Kindi's own theory, for it is there that he introduces the idea that one set of celestial objects transmit their influence by means of another set of objects—the stellar rays. One can see the quickening of a current of thought that will in the West lead to the creation of the electromagnetic field or various theories of sociobiology. Having been introduced into astrology and astronomy by executive decision, al-Kindi's stellar rays have precisely the properties that are required to settle the questions that al-Kindi finds troubling. The rays arise in the planets; they convey their force to the earth at the center of the universe; and they are as varied as the stars themselves, "since the whole operation of the stars proceeds through the rays which are themselves varied in every varying aspect."

It is not only the stars that possess rays. On the surface of the earth, men, minerals, and mountains are the source of their *own* rays: obviously so, since "fire transmits the rays of heat to an adjacent place, and earth the rays of cold." Once rays are acknowledged, their usefulness is multiplied, al-Kindi failing to ask only how stellar rays succeed in transmitting *their* influence, a question that modern mathematical physics still is hardly in a position to answer.

Whatever the details of his theory, al-Kindi's purposes in *On Stellar Rays* are not at all in line with orthodox Islamic doctrine. Action at a distance is the hallmark, the very sign, of magical practices in general and astrology in particular; but action at a distance is also the mark of prayer, and a philosopher concerned to provide a physical explanation for the power of prayer is very much in danger of cutting the heart out of a sacred doctrine. *On Stellar Rays* is a dangerous book—one reason, perhaps, that in 1277, Bishop Tempier of Paris condemned as heretical ideas similar to those it espouses.

The details of the personal drama between al-Kindi and Abu Mashar have been lost. It is clear only that Abu Mashar fell under al-Kindi's spell, striking evidence that when these men wrote of the powers of the mind to control the distance between personalities, they were appealing to circumstances they knew well. Abu Mashar took counsel from al-Kindi; for a time he became a disciple, the two men studying mathematics and the philosophers of antiquity together. He enlarged the margins of his understanding. He became learned and somehow promoted himself into an astrologer of some note, and then into an astrologer of great influence. Did he take the doctrine of stellar rays intact from al-Kindi? I do not know. But he seems to have taken something more important, a methodological principle: *no action without explanation.* The principle carried more weight than its four words might suggest. By an *explanation,* the al-Kindi of those stellar rays meant a physical explanation, and by a physical explanation, he meant a scheme in which *no* force or influence is transmitted at a distance, the universe filling with intermediaries simply to keep on going. In this way lay heresy.

Abu Mashar, having taken so much from al-Kindi, took this as well: He ended his days as an atheist.

♌

ABU MASHAR'S services did not come cheap. Serving as the court astrologer to al-Mutazz he received one hundred dinars in land revenues, thirty dinars in real estate, and one thousand dinars as an emolument. These stipends made him a wealthy man and so a figure with real influence in society.

In the early decades of the ninth century, Abu Mashar may be observed casting the horoscope of an Indian prince. Together with another astrologer, Abu Mashar accompanied al-Mutamid on a military campaign against the Zang. On another occasion, al-Mutamid asked his astrologers to cast a chart that would reveal the specific thought he had had the day before. It appears that he devoted himself to thoughts of a pregnant cow. Abu Mashar and his companion were able successfully to describe its calf. It is impossible to determine whether the story is false, or fabulous, or whether al-Mutamid did think of a pregnant cow, or even whether imagined pregnant cows could give birth to astrologically visible calves.

Sometime later Abu Mashar is offering astrological advice to a number of men dissatisfied with the caliph's rule. Astrological duties with the Prince al-Muwaffaq follow. He is accompanying the man on some long forgotten military campaign in Basra. In time taken from his professional duties, he composes a series of influential astrological texts: *The Book of Nativities, The Book of Conjunctions, The Book of Subtleties, The Book of Elections, The Book of Thousands, The Book of the Conjunction of the Two Malefics in Cancer,* and *The Book of Rains and Winds and of Changes in the Weather,* whose second part deals with the astrology of prices. And there is the odd claim that Abu Mashar *plagiarized* several of his most notable works from one Sanad ibn-Ali. The thought of Abu Mashar, alone in his marble-floored, Chinese-vased library, suavely lifting words, sentences, passages, or even chapters from some long forgotten tract by Sanad ibn-Ali, and then covering his traces by means of a few verbal alterations and a light cosmetic dusting of misdirection, is one that it is not possible to contemplate without satisfaction.

He had clients, I imagine. In the stillness of the early afternoon after prayers, he would greet a palace official or prosperous merchant with a knowing smile, order tea, and have the servant bring out baklava on silver dishes. Then he would ask delicately of his guest when the ceremonies had ended whether *he doubted his wife, the companion of his heart?*

Or perhaps, somewhere in the palace, the caliph's vizier would propel him by the elbow down a long marble corridor, and then, slipping into the obscure demotic of palace politicians, ask by means of a thousand artful allusions whether the moon had fallen under the sun's gaze, traditionally the time of intrigue, and when the stars might favor a certain—and with a deft movement of his hand, the fingers curving into a fan, the vizier would signify an assassination.

How else could he have lived?

ALTHOUGH ABU MASHAR's thoughts were intended to encompass the universe, they could be inscribed on a single piece of paper.

He took from Aristotle the division between the earth and the celestial sphere, the one corrupt and ever-changing, the other pure and eternal, and since some part of this ancient doctrine had survived in Europe, conveyed, of course, in texts that were themselves corrupt, Abu Mashar's metaphysical scheme would not have surprised Alcuin at all. Like al-Kindi, Abu Mashar took as well from Aristotle the idea that all forms of change are in the end reducible to change in place. This thesis is simple enough to serve both as the premise of a philosophical system and as a slogan capable of explaining the essentials of astrology to a caliph notably lacking in a taste for metaphysical niceties.

Abu Mashar's major work, *The Book of the Establishment of Astrology*, was famous throughout the Moslem world. Having, I am sure, predicted its own disappearance, the book is now lost forever. But if the work has been lost, there is also Abu Mashar's *Great Introduction*, a work composed during the fifth decade of the ninth century and twice translated from the Arabic into medieval Latin in the twelfth century, once by John of Seville, and again by Hermann of Carinthia. It is by means of the *Great Introduction* that Abu Mashar's voice was heard throughout the Christian West, astrologers as far afield as England coming to frame their predictions on the basis of the book.

The *Great Introduction* is largely a standard introduction to astrological descriptions. Abu Mashar begins with the basics: the zodiac, the twelve signs of the zodiac, and the planets. And thereafter he discusses what it means for the planets to be *in* various houses. This is the essential astrological idea, and Abu Mashar's treatment breaks no new ground. If Mars is *in* Aries, its "nature is hot, dry, fiery, yellow bile, its taste is bitter, and it is masculine . . . cut in its limbs, prone to anger, possessing two colors and two forms, libidinous, having few children, and sometimes it indicates twins, royal, possessing four feet of the sort that are cloven, half-voiced." There are, in addition, medical associations:

Mars in Aries controls the head and the face. And geographical associations as well. When in Aries, Mars dominates Babylonia, Persia, Azerbaijan, and Palestine.

There are times in the course of his discussion when Abu Mashar indulges in an almost giddy logical incoherence. When he describes Saturn as *malefic,* we astrologers quite know what he means. A malefic planet is one that indicates bad news in prospect. Had Abu Mashar left matters at that, no one would scruple. But in his hands, Saturn becomes a kaleidoscopic symbol, rather like a multi-limbed Indian deity. In addition to conveying bad news generally, Saturn *indicates* "moisture, waters, rivers; it *signifies* wealth; it *governs* misers; it is *associated* with long journeys, hatred, cunning, perfidy, and every activity of evil." This seems straightforward enough. Saturn is altogether a bad influence. But as it happens, Saturn *also* "designates trustworthiness in speech, old age, slowness, deliberateness, intelligence, experimentation, obstinacy, sadness, fear, griefs, misfortune, the dead, grandfathers, fathers, older brothers, eunuchs, slaves and the rabble."

How one symbol could signify so many things, Abu Mashar does not say; nor, for that matter, does he explain how Saturn might signify "every activity of evil" *and* at the same time "trustworthiness in speech." These are mysteries of the astrologer's art; they require analysis. But no further analysis could possibly explain what Abu Mashar meant by affirming that Saturn is "dark," "ill-smelling," and "gluttonous." If Saturn is a symbol, then Abu Mashar seems to have confused the symbol with what it signifies, a vice that logicians consider akin to original sin.

It is in his book (or books) of the mysteries (*Libri mysteriorum*) that Abu Mashar goes beyond his own inheritance from Ptolemy or Firmicus Maternus or any of the scattered astrological texts to which, as a man of the Arab east, he had easy access. Ce-

lestial objects, he believed, spell out a message; they are quite literally elements of a symbolic system, but unlike a human language,
the system that Abu Mashar entertains is a system of similes:

> When Venus is with Mars it is similar to a woman who
> searches for pleasure and who joins a man that is perverse
> and is a whore-monger; she fears him, flatters him, and she
> has a loving attitude towards him and shows affection to
> him; and however these things are pretence, she does them
> for fear.

> When Venus is with Saturn, it is similar to a young woman
> with a good figure who keeps company with an old impo-
> tent man.

> When it is with Jupiter, it is similar to a woman who is in
> the prime of life, and who joins up with an honest man and
> there is affection between them.

There are in these claims a disturbing degree of specificity. The
idea that Venus—the *planet* itself—is like a woman is old in
human mythology. The Sumerians imagined that Venus embod-
ied *Inanna,* the goddess of love and battle; much later the Greeks
and the Romans followed suit, confounding the planet and the
goddess. Venus has continued to seem dreamy and romantic to
poets and lovers alike, although of the poets, few could actually
pick Venus out from the jumble of stars in the sky at night. By
the same token, Mars has always seemed rather war-like, the
planet's aspect embedded in its adjective—*martial*—and even a
few nouns such as *marzipan*—the bread of war. Mars often appears red and so, by means of an imaginative hip-hop, bloody as
well. But Abu Mashar goes quite beyond any kind of loosely-
leashed linguistic connections. Venus is like a woman—*yes,* this
we have heard before—but bent on pleasure? This is new. Mars

is martial—an old message—but a whoremonger and a *perverse* whoremonger at that? New again. And what are we to make of Abu Mashar's claim that the concourse between Venus and Mars is *like* the relationship between a woman with a carnal urge and a man who quite literally scares her pants off?

The confident details dazzle, but they also confound.

In other parts of his text, Abu Mashar reposes his faith in what is almost a doctrine of algebraic opposition. The signs, he argues, are naturally opposed to one another. Taurus and Capricorn are opposite to Virgo; Leo is opposite to Aries; and Sagittarius opposite to Leo. The pairings continue until they exhaust the signs of the zodiac. Abu Mashar was a sensitive astronomer as well as an astrologer, and he certainly knew what Ptolemy had known eight centuries before: The signs of the zodiac bear only the loosest relationship to the constellations themselves. What, then, do the oppositions actually signify? If the signs designate varying regions of the sky so that Leo is the name of whatever star cluster happens to be peeping from behind the scrimshaw of the zodiac, then why should Leo be in opposition to Aries? Those regions in space are not constant, and Aries considered during one year is not Aries considered the next. This suggests that Abu Mashar, like many other astrologers, was tapping his way blindly down a certain algebraic corridor, the opposition that he recorded with such zest sparking between various symbols and not whatever they might designate or represent.

Whatever the methods by which Abu Mashar constructed his astrological interpretations, he succeeded in persuading both his contemporaries and the future that his gifts were extraordinary and that he had the power to give the veil of time a good sharp yank. Skilled at answering interrogations, he once was presented with the debris left over from another astrologer's chart. The ascendant was in the tenth degree of Scorpio; the moon was in the fifteenth degree, Jupiter in the sixteenth, and the Lot of Fortune in the twenty-ninth degree. Saturn was in the second house; Venus, which is lord of the seventh house, was in twenty-six degrees of the eleventh house and in conjunction with Mars.

Looking over this chart with a practiced eye, Abu Mashar observed that the Lot of Fortune was in the ascending sign; and that the lord of the seventh house and the lord of the ascendant were in conjunction in the eleventh house. These were *not* matters of interpretation; they reflected nothing more than the application of traditional astrological descriptions to the astronomical facts. Abu Mashar nonetheless concluded that the questioner calling the chart to his attention was asking questions about his *own* situation, the interrogation having a direct and immediate urgency.

It is by no means clear how Abu Mashar reached this conclusion: He did not say, although possibly nothing more than a guess was involved. What followed, however, was altogether remarkable. The questioner, Abu Mashar asserted, wished to marry; the original interrogation posed a question about the questioner's bride. The woman, Abu Mashar went on to claim, was far from chaste, and this because of the conjunction between Venus and Mars. Abu Mashar's mysterious system of similes now shed rather a more penetrating light on the scene. "When Venus is with Mars it is similar to a woman who searches for pleasure." And vice versa apparently. Abu Mashar affirmed the couple would nonetheless marry, and the man prosper, but the woman would "be in peril because her husband would devour her property." The explanation that he offered enlarged on that fateful conjunction between Venus and Mars:

He [Abu Mashar] said the reason why the man would prosper through the woman was Venus as lord of the seventh, with the Ascendant in sextile aspect, while the woman would be injured and deprived of her property because of Mars, lord of the Ascendant, being in quartile aspect with the eighth house, which was the place of a woman's money, just as the second house is that of a man's money.

These bitter domestic predictions, one gathers, were confirmed by events.

And thereafter, let us allow Abu Mashar's elegant Persian-accented Arabic voice to trail off as with a discreet whisper he takes his leave.

♌

ALTHOUGH THE TWO MEN were very different, al-Kindi and Abu Mashar form a single figure in the history of astrology, the suave and polished astrologer forever enveloped by his erudite master. They were both men of great ebullience. There was about them a permanent froth. No one running an index finger over the ninth century could possibly pass al-Kindi in the lists without wishing to rescue him from his perpetual captivity in the cage of his own lost words. The subjects that he is known to have discussed suggest a culture about to burst its boundaries and then overflow.

Just imagine. There are any number of standard tracts on philosophy, astronomy, and mathematics: a work entitled *On Psychology,* another entitled *On Rhetoric;* there is a treatise on medicine and another on *tested* medicines; there are works discussing spherical geometry, optics, arithmetic, Indian numerals, and the principles of first philosophy. There is a book in which al-Kindi proves that the universe and everything it contains must be spherical in shape, a demonstration on roughly the same intellectual order as those current in cosmology today. There are tracts with tantalizing titles: *On the Explanation that the Body of the World cannot Possibly be Infinite.* And practical trots: *On Surveying Rivers, On the Geometrical Construction of a Marble Sun*

Dial, On Mirrors that Burn. There are books about leprosy, rabies, and delirium; a work entitled *On Fits Resulting from Phlegm and the Causes of Sudden Death;* another on gout, still another on the spleen. Lisping requires a treatise. And there are, of course, a dozen separate tracts dealing with divination: *On the Foreknowledge of Events,* then a first, a second, and a third treatise on astrology, a work describing the signs of the unlucky stars; and a curious work entitled *On the Duration of the Rule of the Arabs,* in which al-Kindi, using astrological techniques, estimates—correctly—the anticipated reign of the Arabs dating from the *Hijrah* of the Prophet. There are numerous polemical works, al-Kindi prevailing over his opponents by exhausting them. And a work in philosophical psychology, *On the Unanimous Agreement among Philosophers regarding the Erotic Signs.*

This last title is irresistible. Unanimous agreement? Concerning erotic signs? Among *philosophers?*

Alcuin is there, of course, an observer from another world. Nothing in his experience could have prepared him for an estuarial intelligence that quite literally seemed to encompass a thousand brooks, streams, rivulets, rivers, waterways, tributaries, and canals, even the slow-moving sluggish waters of some dun-colored irrigation channel sending up a thousand colored sparkles into the warm Arabian air.

But having shifted poor Alcuin through time and space in order that he might see these Arabian nights confabulations, it is now necessary to reimpose a real world on one that is imaginary. He is in Rheims, or in Aachen, or even in York; he is what he is and limited as always by what has always limited him. The Arabian nights vanish to a twinkling and disappear just as, almost six hundred years or so later, they were destined to disappear in fact as well as fiction. Do not be misled by ebullience. There is a dark stain in early Moslem thought. Men who had begun their adult lives persuaded of the miracle of the Koran ended their days admitting to themselves that they no longer believed in God. In action at a distance, al-Kindi had diagnosed the disease infecting astronomy *and* astrology. The remarkable Arab intellectuals who followed him would accept his diagnosis while rejecting his remedy. The distance between causes and their effects cannot be crossed. There is only faith. And there is neither astronomy nor astrology.

Alcuin may be allowed a moment of satisfaction. The future lies in Europe and not Arabia, and the future is his.

CHAPTER SIX

VIRGO
♍
THE SWORD
OF SKEPTICISM

WHATEVER THE theoretical demands of his craft, the astrologer, poor schnook, needed to make a living. Serious astrologers attended an institute or served as apprentices with a master. The great observatory of Uleg Beg in Samarqand and the observatory at Istanbul had both astronomers and astrologers in residence. The course of study was as demanding as instruction in medicine. Astrologers with established reputations very often served political masters. Some Persian kings were persuaded that horoscopes were best cast for the moment of conception, and not the moment of birth. They stationed astrologers outside their bed chamber and signaled the magical moment of climax with the exuberant tinkle of a royal bell. And astrologers were frequently called to the sickbeds of princes. Having fallen ill, Caliph al-Watiq requested his astrologers; after considering his horoscope, they assured him that he would live another fifty years. He died ten days later.

The astrologer with a clamorous family and little time for higher things, on the other hand, needed to master just the essentials—the astrolabe, that certainly, and the various ephemerides, the tables of planetary positions. And he needed to have a limited but arcane vocabulary at his disposal. A serious look suggesting alert sobriety was no doubt important. A dust board was necessary, if only to convey to clients the many calculations involved in computing a horoscope. Some men could make a living with only a smattering of real knowledge. Setting up shop in the streets, dust boards held between their knobby knees, they offered advice and analysis on the fly. The Baghdad police often rousted them from their habitual quarters, so that like a flock of pigeons, they were forced to flutter and then regroup. Their modest competence did nothing to impede the reach of their art. The astrologers, the historian George Saliba remarked, "claimed they could answer any question that could occur to the human mind." Old-fashioned omens of the sort familiar from Babylonian astrology and the *Enuma*? Baghdad street-corner astrologers were willing to try. Studying the conjunction of the planets, or shooting stars, or comets, they would offer a judgment concerning the fate of various kingdoms, or even, if the price were right, the entire world.

Interrogations and elections, on the other hand, were the street-corner astrologer's stock in trade. Lost objects might be recovered by these techniques, or missing husbands. One astrologer, a woman, oddly enough, was asked to survey a caliph's army, pointing out soldiers destined to survive in battle. It is hard to imagine that her counsel improved the troop's morale.

The police were often charged with making quite certain that the astrological riff-raff kept to the streets and did not practice their trade within the shops. There follows an odd erotic aside. Most Moslem women were either illiterate or capable only of reading classical Arabic. This is still true today in parts of the Moslem world. Professional letter writers held court in many of the shops, where they offered their services to women unable to write their own letters. When astrologers were allowed to practice by their side, shiftless young men would scan their horoscopes, using the various intimate details to later approach the women.

♍

ABU HAMID MUHAMMAD AL-GHAZZALLI was born in Baghdad in 1058. He was obsessed in childhood with the appearances of the divine, his study of the Koran and *hadith* blossoming before his own adolescence into an encyclopedic grasp of dogma and doctrine. He was trained in law as well as theology, disciplines so far apart on the curved manifold of scholarship that they might well appear to touch back to back, but they gave to his intelligence a double distinction in dialectics so that in argument, he was matchless. As a young man, al-Ghazzalli achieved fame in Baghdad. A commanding public personality, he was accustomed to deference even on those infrequent occasions when he did not demand it.

At some time toward the end of the eleventh century, he suffered a terrifying spiritual crisis. Skepticism overwhelmed him. He could find in the various sciences at his command—astronomy, astrology, mathematics, geography, and law—no reason for belief. The burning fringe of his certainty contracted until he came to distrust his very senses. The stars seem small when seen, he wrote in his autobiography, "no larger than a *dinar*," but astronomy indicated that the stars were larger than the planets. An object cannot at once be small and large. Al-Ghazzalli found it impossible to reconcile what he had seen with what he knew. He then began to mistrust his reason and the truths of logic. This is an affliction that, like Alzheimer's, often allows its victims impotently to witness the deterioration of their faculties, unreason fastening on them like a vulture. Unable to combat doubt and unwilling to accept it, al-Ghazzalli stood naked in his torment. God "put a lock" on his tongue. He fell mute. His physician, a smooth Baghdad professional, wisely remarked that there would be no way to treat his affliction unless "his heart [were] eased of its anxiety."

Although God restored his reason, al-Ghazzalli's spiritual torment was not permanently abated. He left his family and vacated Baghdad, making toward the end of his life the discovery that such men often make, that his soul could find refuge only in a doctrine of annihilation. His book of spiritual exercises, the *Iyah alum al–Din* (Revival of Religious Science), describes for the faithful a routine intended as much to calm the intellect as to evoke the divine. An unvarying ritual is prescribed, thought discouraged. The book is revered in the Moslem world.

EVERY MAN WHO suffers—and all men do—suffers alone, but no man's suffering is unique. Al-Ghazzalli was of his time, and connected in a thousand ways to the often fractious currents of medieval Islamic thought. Caliph Harun al-Rashid, the fifth and the most notable of the Abbasid caliphs, ruled over an empire that by the end of the eighth century stretched from the eastern coast of the Mediterranean to the frontiers of India, and when in 809 A.D. the great caliph died, his power fell to his sons, al-Amin and al-Mamum. They then squandered their inheritance by disputing its division. The short, violent conflict that followed was won by al-Mamum, and thereafter Baghdad transcended itself to become the cynosure of every wandering eye in the Orient and the Near East. Like his father, al-Mamum was devoted to learning, but where the great caliph was content to leave learning to the learned, al-Mamum was determined to see that it flourished. It was al-Mamum who found the financial resources to establish the greatest of all medieval academies, the Bayt al-Hikmah, the House of Wisdom, and to attract to his academy scholars from the entire Mediterranean world. "The scholar's ink," the Prophet was overheard to remark, "is holier than the martyr's blood."

Men speaking a dozen different languages floated through the House of Wisdom's marble corridors. The Moslems had been made heir to the weight of classical learning. The ancient texts were everywhere and, unlike European scholars, who had carelessly lost or otherwise misplaced the keys to their culture, Moslem scholars could read Greek. They were, after all, within hailing distance of Byzantium.

The unknown classics of the ancient world entered the House of Wisdom murmuring in Latin or Greek and left speaking brisk and excellent Arabic. Thereafter they made their way to academies in Toledo or Cordoba in Spain, or on the wild inhospitable Afghan border, or far ports in the Arabic archipelago. Mathematicians were in residence in the House of Wisdom, men such as al-Jawhari, the geometer, who proposed a fallacious proof of Euclid's fifth postulate; al-Kindi, Abu Mashar's contemporary and mentor, much occupied with a thousand delirious intellectual projects; and al-Khwarzmi, the master of medieval algebra, the algorithm as an idea fluttering from his symbols.

During the four centuries that followed its founding, the House of Wisdom fell on evil times, scholars forming political intrigues against one another, and as often recovered, its luster reacquired, the disputes forgiven or forgotten. Its writ ran wherever the Arabic language was read or spoken. By the eleventh century it had, like the library at Alexandria, become an institution beyond space and time.

The philosopher ibn Sina was, for example, born in Karmaithen, which is a province of what is now Uzbekistan. Baghdad is impossibly far away. It is the latter part of the tenth century. Ibn Sina was, at the age of sixteen, treating patients as a physician, and he was known as a young man with a healing touch. Having cured the Samanaid ruler, Nur ibn Mansur, of an unspecified illness, whether by herbs, diet, massage, or magic, he was offered the use of the Samanaid Royal Library, and had his patrons been able to maintain their power, he might have passed his days peacefully as a scholar. Instead, he spent the next thirty-five years more or less on the run, an uncommonly sturdy leaf bobbling in the savage currents of Near Eastern history. He served as a jurist under the rule of the Turkish Qarakhanids, and then, in the words of one historian, "as a jurist in Gurganji, a teacher in Gurgan, and an administrator in Rayy." These are also places far from Baghdad. As he was nimbly assisting various political masters while assiduously avoiding their enemies, an enterprise that traditionally demands all of a man's strength, ibn Sina managed to carve out a career in scholarship, bringing to completion his masterpiece, the *Kitab al-Shifa* (Book of Healing). The *Kitab al-Shifa* is an encyclopedic treatise on all of the sciences, infinitely more advanced than anything that would be produced in Europe until the seventeenth century, a tour of Euclidean geometry, astronomy, arithmetic, and even music, the tour taking divagations to touch on mapmaking, statics, hydrostatics, and optics. It is in the *Kitab* that ibn Sina deduced—God only knows how—that the velocity of light is finite. Theology, of course, attracted his attention and then his pen. God is a form of intelligence, ibn Sina argued, the human mind partaking of the divine by grasping at his intelligibility. Like branches on a spreading pear tree, his voice seemed to bend slowly in the Arabian winds.

The most notable physical scientist of the eleventh century, Abu Arrayhan Muhammad ibn Ahmad al-Biruni—altogether a character with a harder edge than ibn Sina—was born in Uzbekistan, again far from Baghdad's dimpled pleasure palaces and bathing pools. Al-Biruni wrote widely and he kept in touch, his collected works running to more than thirteen thousand folio pages. With the generous curiosity that the House of Wisdom made possible, he wrote on subjects that exuberantly burst free of any obvious scholarly categories. A book entitled *Shadows* is an account of the rich Arabic system for describing various shadows and the shade they offer. What a superb idea! There are long shadows and short shadows, shadows that mark an oblique angle with the ground and shadows that do not; there are shadows that may be found in darkened corridors and shadows running the length of sun-lit piazzas; there are strange phenomena associated with shadows, and odd colors, and it is shadows in the courtyard that determine the five-fold time of prayer for the faithful; and while some shadows are blue, and others blue-black, still other shadows retain in their somber heart a rouged touch of the sun's red-eyed fury.

AT THE CENTER OF the Moslem renaissance, time now flows like the Arabian sands. Astronomers and astrologers who were famous, or were destined to become famous, gathered in Baghdad, the clear night sky an open invitation. In the latter part of the ninth century, Abu Mashar was joined in the House of Wisdom by astronomers such as Habash al-Hasib and al-Farghani, the author of *The Elements of Astronomy*. The long golden moment prolonged itself into the tenth century, when the astronomer Al-Nairizi wrote an elaborate commentary on the *Almagest*. His colleague Thabit ibn Qurrah in turn defended the theory that the equinoxes had their origins in spherical oscillations—essentially Ptolemy's view; and *his* colleague Abd al-Rahman al-Sufi created in his text, *The Figures of the Stars*, something like a map of the fixed stars, rare in its accuracy, remarkable in its beauty, a forerunner, in fact, to G. O. Abell's *Catalog of Bright Cluster Galaxies*. Astronomers and astrologers drew no distinction between astronomy *and* astrology. Both were a part of the sciences and both reflected the world's causal scheme. Al-Biruni explicitly made the assumption that all Moslem scientists made, that influence in the world proceeds *from* the heavens *to* the earth. If this was so— who could doubt it?—then astrology had precisely the same authoritative credentials as astronomy itself, and the star map that al-Biruni set out in his own *Canon of al-Masudi* was one that Abu Mashar might have used, the same complicated geometrical scheme animating the astronomer's heaven at work as well in the astrologer's heaven, the two heavens when seen rightly coinciding calmly in one firmament.

Astrology and astronomy were at their zenith. These were the long years in which Moslem science seemed ready to conquer the world.

♍

IN ARISTOTELIAN LOGIC, Greek culture had given Moslem intellectuals a superb sharp tool, a systematic way of stating and then assessing arguments. The "miracle of the Koran" had given them an instrument of revelation. Tendencies, as everyone quite understood, were in opposition. And beyond the astrologer's drawing room, or the hushed tranquility of the House of Wisdom, they were *profoundly* in opposition. They had, in fact, been in opposition from the very beginning, when Baghdad was yet a new city ruled by tough Arab administrators with little time for speculation.

The fissures in medieval Arabic culture opened as early as the period of Umayyad rule in the seventh century, and thereafter widened alarmingly and often without warning, enlarging suddenly in a roar and then consuming thousands. Prophets and preachers and mad theologians were everywhere. The Imam Hasan al-Basri had, in the early eighth century, urged his followers to conduct themselves with piety, austerity, and discipline. Frugal, he encouraged others to frugality. Regarding the Koran as a great refreshing fountain, he urged a life spent in its contemplation. Had al-Basri said no more, he would have broken no new ground. But al-Basri argued as well that God had endowed men and women with freedom of the will and so quite unknowingly crossed the ominously pulsing red line separating philosophical dispute from dangerous theological doctrine.

Like Augustine of Hippo, the mullahs of the early Moslem world were quite able to follow an argument to its most distant conclusions. If men are free, they reasoned, there are things that God does not know and that he cannot control. If this is so, is not God diminished? And if diminished, is not God not God?

Almost at once, sects arose in opposition. The so-called *Jabria*—three sects in one, actually, the Jahmia, Najjaria, and the Ziraria—argued in favor of a strict, unrelenting doctrine of fatalism. The plan of the world is fixed. It has been fixed from the moment that time began. It is unalterable. It cannot be changed without compromising the authority of God. And the authority of God cannot be compromised. The Koran, above all, demands submission to *his* will, all other wills proving illusory in their nature, impotent in their effect. Just how the Koran could *demand* submission to God's will, if men have no free choice, the Jabria did not say.

During the period of Umayyad rule, the Qadarites, who had argued in favor of freedom of the will, lost the support of the political establishment, free will proving a subversive doctrine to politicians alarmed, then as now, at the prospect that someone might decide to act according to his conscience. Their leader, Mabad al-Juhani, was beheaded, interesting evidence of the extent to which free will stops at the sword's edge. If the movement was oppressed and its leader killed, the Qadarites' spirit nonetheless proved irresistible in the face of oppression. With its pleasure palaces, broad boulevards, and delicate delightful gondolas, what use for fatalism did eighth-century Baghdad have?

The fierce, idiotic conflict between those in favor of free will and those prepared to deny it gave rise to the Mutazilia movement, which, like the Enlightenment destined to take place in

Europe one thousand years later, represented a moment of complex intellectual compromise. At the root of the word "Mutazilia" there is dissent. Led by Wasa ibn Ata, who regarded Hasan al-Basri as his master if not his mentor, the dissenters dissented both from the fierce fatalism of Jabria sects and the liberalism of the Qadarites. They were concerned to reconcile faith and reason, a project that four centuries later would occupy the great Christian philosophers of the high Middle Ages, and a project that is just beginning to occupy the modern scientific culture of the West. The Mutazilia gained the support of Caliph al-Mamum; in truth, they gained the support of men everywhere who were eager to make theology unrewarding by assuring that it remained inoffensive, and what had been a sect became a creed. Their leaders took refuge in abstractions. The God of the Koran, who to generations of Moslem believers had seemed as real as stone and as palpable as rain, "is no body, nor object, nor volume, nor form, nor flesh, nor blood, nor person, nor substance." He cannot be pictured; and so he cannot personally be addressed. He is, in truth, rather vague and almost dim. And in this respect, he is also safe. The men of the Mutazilia movement also compromised the absolute nature of the Koran, arguing that, although dictated by God, it remained a book like any other, a literary artifact forever in need of interpretation. The Koran's authority, Mutazilia clerics argued, was bounded by its readers. So many great Moslem scholars had seen things differently, arguing with considerable passion that the Koran's readers were bounded by its authority.

These sensible-seeming rational doctrines, with their eerie resemblance to doctrines often preached in Christian churches and reform synagogues in the twentieth century, offered hardly any rational grounds for rebuttal, and so quickly became a matter of orthodoxy among members of the educated Baghdad elite, its physicians, lawyers, traders, philosophers, academics, courtiers, and eunuchs. More than anything else, it was Mutazilia dogma, and the climate of opinion that it enforced, that made possible the growth of Islamic science, its efflorescence in astronomy, mathematics, geography, measurement, and astrology itself. Progress in the sciences is often made possible by bromides in religious thought.

♍

A GREAT SPIRITUAL reversal is coming, a cleansing or a scourge. And let us be honest with one another. It will come as no surprise. The soul longing for the divine has little patience with the chatter of rationalism, and Islam is nothing if not the congregation of such souls. There is the pause between the beating of a heart, and then the streets of Baghdad overflow. Men with furious, strident, harsh, and uncompromising voices are everywhere. Abu al-Hasan al-Ashari was a rationalist who had in a spasm of fierce self-disgust come to see the light. The vague, impalpable, impossibly distant God of Mutazilia dogma he rejected out of hand. His God was a full, forceful, three-dimensional presence, ominous and demanding. "We confess that God is firmly seated on his throne...We confess that God has two hands, without asking how...We confess that God has two eyes, without asking how. We confess that God has a face." It is roughly 880 A.D., the last decades of the ninth century. Men of the most sensitive intelligence and rational disposition are gathered in the House of Wisdom. The Arabic language and the high culture that it represents shelter the civilized world. Gentle Arabic scholars, men who would not hurt a fly, may be found sipping tea in small cafes from southern Spain to Afghanistan. But on the streets of Baghdad, the Imam Ahmed ibn Hanbal is haranguing a great crowd, the froth of a fiery denunciation on his roughened lips. His eyes are rimmed in red. At his death, 150 thousand people thronged the streets of Baghdad to accompany his hearse.

When the Sunni Caliph al-Mutawakkil seized power in the late eleventh century, the Mutazilia movement came to an end.

A "cruel drunken sot," in the words of an observer apparently prepared to withhold his admiration, the caliph settled various philosophical issues in the most direct way possible: He had the Mutazilia theologians and philosophers hounded from office, thrown in prison, subject to torture, broken in pain, and then executed.

"The sword is more telling than the book," the Moslem poet Abu Tammam wrote in words that are still current in the Moslem world.

♍

ABU HAMID AL-GHAZZALLI wrote extensively about his mystical experiences, and he wrote extensively again about the need to reconcile the Koran with various forms of Sufi mysticism, but the work that broke the spirit of Moslem rationalism and that put an end to Moslem science was the *Tahafut al-falasifa* (Incoherence of the Philosophers), and this book, curiously enough, Abu Hamid al-Ghazzalli composed *before* his spiritual crises, when he commanded without skepticism all of his remarkable powers as a man of learning, a lawyer, and logician.

The *Tahafut* succeeds in summarizing and then rejecting an entire philosophical tradition. A way of life is held down (and crushed) under its hump. It is one of the rare works in the history of philosophy that succeeds in canceling the future.

The *Tahafut* is very much a denunciation, and its organization reflects its origins in fury. Although writing *as* a philosopher, it is the philosophers, taken as a class, that evoke al-Ghazzalli's contempt. Part One of the *Tahafut* is devoted to refuting the doctrine of the world's *pre*-eternity. A pre-eternal universe is one that is now infinitely old (and so infinitely old at any given time). Various unnamed philosophers are interrogated and then dismissed. The discussion is in many ways astonishingly up-to-date. Have the philosophers maintained that the world is the necessary effect of some divine and necessary cause? Apparently, they have. A *nec-*

essary cause? Does God then act as he must or as he would? If God acts as he must, then he is not God, and if God acts as he would, then such causes are not necessary. This simple powerful argument drives a wedge between revealed religion and modern science well before the emergence of modern science.

Although the cosmological fireworks are considerable, the book's black beating heart is elsewhere—in the second section, in fact, of Part Two, its seventeenth discussion. It is there that al-Ghazzalli, in the course of a wide-ranging examination of the natural sciences, concerns himself with causality and with miracles, and by means of one magnificent argument urges a form of skepticism so radical that it threatens to burn through the page on which it is printed. The argument anticipates by almost seven centuries David Hume's discussion in *An Inquiry Concerning Human Understanding,* but we are playing here for higher stakes than Hume.

The room is dark. The voices of the muezzins are calling the faithful to prayer. Al-Ghazzalli is pacing with nervous energy, pulling at his beard, screwing up his eyes, speaking without notes in his educated, literary Arabic. Is there another language so divinely suited to denunciation? No wonder these people so often get carried away.

And then he proceeds. Allah has divided the manifold of experience three ways, the faithful and those sunk in unbelief (*kufr*) alike moving *from* the past *into* the present and *on to* the future. Astronomy, medicine, biology, *and* astrology all have as their goal the mastery of time, control over its currents, the subordination of its mystery.

The art of prediction, al-Ghazzalli observes, rests on certain broad claims. A world in perpetual chaos cannot be rationally understood. In the world as it is, there is *order* and *clarity,* the future *like* the past, the *same* proceeding from the *same,* so that *causes* that have evoked their *effects* in the past can be *expected* to evoke the same effects in the future, this *pattern* of causes preceding their effect something that can be *grasped* through the *senses.*

To which al-Ghazzalli replies in words that will be repeated in every madrasa and Moslem academy: "The connection between what is habitually believed to be a cause and what is habitually believed to be an effect is *not necessary,* according to us."

Not necessary?

The argument proceeds by an accretion of cases, as in the law. There is *no* necessary connection, al-Ghazzalli writes, between "the quenching of thirst and drinking, satiety and eating, burning and contact with fire, light and the appearance of the sun, death and decapitation, healing and the drinking of medicine, the purging of the bowels and the using of a purgative, and so on to all that is observable among connected things in medicine, astronomy, arts and crafts." And if there is no necessary connection between these ordinary causes and their effects, there is no necessary connection *anywhere* beyond pure logic itself.

What we see, and so what we can describe, is the *conjunction* of events, one event following another. This is all that we can see and all that we can describe. The *connection* between events "is due to God's prior decree, who creates them side by side, not to its being necessary in itself, incapable of separation. On the contrary, it is within divine power to create satiety without eating, to create death without decapitation, to continue life after decapitation, and on to all connected things."

It follows that the philosophers who argue that it is *fire* that burns or blackens or scorches are quite mistaken. Consider a ball of cotton that has been ignited. Is the cause the match, and the effect the charred cotton?

> This we deny, saying: the agent of the burning is God, through His creating the black in the cotton and the disconnection of its parts, and it is God who made the cotton

burn and made it ashes. For fire is a dead body which has
no action, and what is the proof that it is the agent? Indeed,
the philosophers have no other proof than the observation
of the occurrence of the burning, when there is contact with
fire, but observation proves only a simultaneity, not a cau-
sation, and in reality, there is no cause but God.

And the proof that this is so—the argument has reached its climax—is just that it *is* possible to imagine the universe in which
all so-called causes gutter out inconclusively, and all so-called
effects come dribbling into existence without their causes, the
continuity in things broken, lost, shattered. If it is possible to
imagine this, then causes in nature cannot be necessary. For what,
after all, does the denial of necessity come to if not the declaration that it is possible to imagine certain connections in the
world severed at their source?

Moments before his death, the philosopher Hassan ibn
Muhammad, who had in his life been a man of reason, said:
"God the Most High is right. Ibn Sina has lied."

THE HISTORY OF ideas is the record of conversations that are overheard, or caught in whispers, or muttered in fragments. Al-
Ghazzalli's skepticism is corrosive: It scours everything it touches.
It is at odds with common sense. It dissolves any form of rationality. It makes astrology impossible, of course, if astrology is considered a science, one that traces the course of influence from the
stars to human action. But like an uncontrollable sand-heavy
desert wind, it sweeps beyond astrology to encompass the other
sciences as well, leaving in ruins the rational structure of the world
patiently explored by men of the Moslem renaissance. Some two
hundred years before al-Ghazzalli found his tongue locked by
doubt, the exuberant al-Kindi had written joyfully of stellar rays.
A man with great sensitivity to the currents of scientific thought,

al-Kindi had seen the problem of action at a distance for what it was—a problem. And he had offered a solution—things or rays or fields between what acts and what is acted upon. Al-Ghazzalli heard the meaning behind his words, even if he might not have read the text in which they were expressed. Stellar rays?

I think not. Al-Ghazzalli's skepticism ran deep. It ended the Moslem conversation about natural science. And in a certain respect, we can see that, given the conversation that *he* could overhear, al-Ghazzalli's skeptical conclusions ran truer than al-Kindi's fanciful elaborations. Al-Ghazzalli had seen the connection between skepticism and the old, aching, ineradicable hair shirt of action at a distance. He had seen the connection and refused to compromise with what he had seen. If we live in a universe with diverse material objects, then *all* action, whether astronomical *or* astrological, is action at a distance. And if all action is action at a distance, there is no action at all.

There remains in the face of this devastating skepticism the obvious questions: How then do things hang together? If material objects do not get material objects to act, *what does?*

Al-Ghazzalli's answer is in keeping with his theological commitments, and it is dictated by logic itself. It is some form of personal *force* (or agency) that brings about change in the world, and without such force, there could be *no* change. The force that is required to keep the world aloft is the force expressed by the divine personality. It is "God," al-Ghazzalli affirms, "who destroys and then re-creates the world after every instant of time," and were it not for his actions in sustaining his universe, it would at once collapse into nothingness. The divine force has its obvious analogue in ordinary life. It is the force *we* employ when *we* act on the world in order to bring *our* future into being. We see, we hear, we notice, we register, our senses quivering and alive, and then straight off we act. The things we do change the face of the world, realigning its structure and bringing material objects, which are simply the handmaidens of our thoughts, into new, unsuspected, and unusual configurations. There can be no science of such forces, whether human or divine, because force in nature does not arise from any material cause. And it does not arise from any material cause because there are *no* material causes. The connection between force and action is unmediated. It cannot be further analyzed. It is what it is. "The meaning of the world," the great twentieth-century logician Kurt Gödel once remarked, "is the separation of wish"—what is *wanted* and so the subject of force—"and fact"—what *is* in the world of things.

With this argument, one ancient astrological stream dries up at once. The stars are not the causes of human action. Nothing is. There remains only the possibility that they might be signs. But celestial signs, by their very nature, cannot be the subject of any science. Arising as the expression of the divine personality, they arise at his whim, and whims, like miracles, cannot be studied. One hundred years later, Thomas Aquinas would argue that the stars cannot be signs if they are in any way causes, and caught between these powerful arguments, now as then, the astrologers have found it uncommonly difficult to breathe.

Abu Hamid Muhammad al-Ghazzalli, the Gazelle, died in 1111. The scourge of skepticism that al-Ghazzalli suffered he succeeded in conveying to others. It is yet there, a raw red wound in the history of thought.

♍

THE MOSLEM renaissance came to an end in the thirteenth century. Mongol armies sweeping in from the east sacked Baghdad in 1243, killing tens of thousands and leaving the city lit luridly in flames. The House of Wisdom was destroyed, and forty thousand irreplaceable books thrown into the Tigris by men prepared to place their own interpretation on the concept of force. Unaware of the catastrophe to come, the astrologers carried on. One woman achieved very considerable renown as an astrologer. She was Bawran, the wife of al-Mamum. One day, after playing with an astrolabe, she noticed that a crisis was about to befall the caliph and she predicted it would be conveyed by means of a wooden instrument. She sent her father, al-Hasan, to the court. A great many precautions were taken. After the evening meal had been served, the caliph sent for his comb and his toothpicks. A servant was ordered to use them first and promptly fell down dead.

The most endearing astrologers, of course, were those who practiced on the streets and lived hand-to-mouth. Like psychic readers, the successful street-corner astrologers must have had a gift for listening seriously to their clients and picking up subtle facial clues. They are still there in history, those astrologers, squatting in alleyways during all the high sunny days of the great Moslem renaissance, their somewhat soiled gowns held over their spread knees, unmindful of the deep gathering crises enveloping the Arabic-speaking world that would bring their art to its appointed end.

Carrying a fish, perhaps one of the fat carp still found in the Tigris, a potential client approached a street-corner astrologer. The astrologer grandly opened negotiations by asking for one thousand *dirhams* to cast a chart.

His client regarded him with some skepticism.

One thousand *dirhams?*

Possibly less, the astrologer replied.

A great deal of haggling ensued, the client becoming ever more dubious, and the astrologer ever more desperate. The price was lowered and then lowered again. The merits of the chart were discussed, and then disputed. The price was again lowered.

Finally, the astrologer settled for the fish.

CHAPTER SEVEN

LIBRA

DELIBERATION
OF THE MASTERS

OMETIME IN THE YEAR 1184 A.D., the English chronicler
Roger of Hoveden observed, "all of the world's prognosticators" came to the same conclusion. The year 1186 would see
a planetary conjunction. Dreadful events were expected. The
Spanish astrologer Corumphiza offered a few pertinent details in
his circular Toledo letter. There is first of all the nature of the conjunction: The higher and the lower planets will come together in
Libra. There is then the date: September of 1186. There is next
the doleful consequences: "A strong and very powerful wind will
arise in the western regions, blackening the air and corrupting it
with a poisonous stench." The Arabs will as a result be utterly destroyed. And there is the precisely worded hedge: "That shall
happen *if* God wills it." And finally the hedge is itself unhedged:
"Or rather *since* he wills it, will will it, had willed it, and will not
stop having willed it."

Although Roger of Hoveden mentions *all* of the world's
prognosticators, this, it turns out, is too large a claim. A letter
written by the Saracen astrologer Pharamella, the son of Abdul-
lah of Cordoba as he styled himself, to John, the bishop of

Toledo, contains a superbly contemptuous dismissal of Corum-phiza's astrological predictions. Planetary conjunctions? What nonsense! Conjunctions happen quite frequently, and generally without ill effect. Quoting apparently from Hermann of Carinthia's translation of Abu Mashar's *Introduction to Astrology*, the letter goes on to cite various astrological terms with some authority. And what is more, Pharamella adds with comical assurance, Mars and Venus will *not* be in Libra in September of 1186. As it happened, September of 1186 *did* mark a planetary conjunction.

"This is something that the writer would have known," the twenty-first-century historian Nicolas Whyte sniffs, "if he had been a real astrologer."

Perhaps so. The various astrologers' reports did in any case produce a considerable sense of unease. As the conjunction of 1186 approached, Anselm of Winchester recounted, a lay brother at his monastery, after sadly babbling a number of Latin verses, fell into a trance and died.

♎

THE GENERAL VIEW of the European Dark Ages is that they were dark, an insight that retains its value despite its vulgarity. Early medieval Europe, although Christian, was also superstitious. Beneath the elaborate rituals of the Christian liturgy, designed as much to discipline as to delight, there remained a dark, clouded remnant of pagan belief. Astrology never disappeared in the west, but until the rediscovery of Ptolemy's *Almagest* and the *Tetrabiblos,* it had been gravely diminished. The ninth-century philosopher Alcuin, his voyages to the Middle East now abrogated, was an astrological adept, and it is widely claimed that he taught Charlemagne the principles of classical astrology. Whatever the concourse between the two men, it could not have involved any very sophisticated astrological discussion. The ninth century had lost the ability to tell the time precisely, and even its bishops judged the arrival of Easter or the advent of Lent by scanning the sky, looking at the foliage, and guessing wildly. But during the second half of the twelfth century, the lost treasures of the classical world—Plato and Aristotle, the Greek and Latin poets, the classical scientists and mathematicians—all made their way into medieval Europe, preserved against the worm of time by Arabic scholars and translators. Now there was a spectacular efflorescence as scholars translated into medieval Latin the Arabic versions of long-lost Greek and classical Latin masterpieces. Ptolemy's *Tetrabiblos*, which had disappeared completely from the West for more than six centuries, was translated into medieval Latin in 1160; the Almagest in 1175. Astrologers once again became men of parts. They re-entered popular consciousness, gravely whispering, as they so often did, into the ears of kings.

In the last quarter of the twelfth century, a suppurating wound opened in medieval Europe. The details are obscure. What we do know is that by the time Innocent III ascended to the papacy in 1198, heresy had become widespread throughout the south of France. An obscure Italian abbot, Joachim of Flora, had in a series of incendiary tracts denounced the pope as the anti-Christ. Thereafter, a form of Manichaeism began to flourish near the French trading city of Albi. The world, its leaders argued, was divided between the forces of good and evil, light and dark, spirit and matter. Leaders of the heresy, the Count of Toulouse among them, styled themselves the elect. They commanded respect for their purity, especially when measured by standards of clerical asceticism then current in the south of France, hardly a region of the world conducive to self-denial. Their followers, rumor insisted, threw every moral caution to the winds and occupied themselves in gross sexual indulgence. The less that was known precisely of their rites, the more lurid the tales that circulated. The Christian faith was in danger. Pope Innocent III acted at once, instituting the Inquisition, with all its fearsome apparatus of torture and intimidation, in order to challenge and then crush defiance of the faith.

If force was one remedy for heresy, reason was another. A Spanish preacher—now Saint Dominic—had in the early years of the thirteenth century achieved some success combating the Albigensian heretics in the region of Languedoc. He had discovered that the Church's arguments seemed more attractive than they might otherwise have been when they were delivered by men exhibiting, as well as urging, self-denial. Mindful of Dominic's success, Innocent III created the Dominican order in 1216.

The Dominicans were from the beginning consecrated to a high, intellectual defense of the Catholic faith. Men were accepted into its ranks on the basis of their intelligence, and promoted to positions of authority on the basis of their ability. The order presumed a religious sensibility in its disciples, but its aim was to provide an intellectual structure large enough to accommodate both Aristotelian science and the truths of Christian revelation.

A great intellectual movement was set in motion.

"A MENSTRUATING WOMAN," Albertus Magnus affirmed, "upon looking into a new mirror, sends a cloud of blood to that mirror." Like the other Dominicans of his age, Albertus took his world view from Aristotle. And Aristotle *had* argued that "if a woman looks into a highly polished mirror during the menstrual period, the surface of the mirror becomes clouded with a blood-red color." With lunatic assurance, Aristotle had added that if "the mirror is a new one, the stain is not easy to remove."

These views are so at odds with common sense that it is worthwhile standing them on their heads in order to see better the physical issues that they conceal. Let it be granted counterfactually that women do turn new mirrors red during menstruation. The question that occupied Albertus Magnus, given the anchor of his views in myth, is whether women exercise this power by means of action at a distance. Clearly not, he thought. Under ordinary circumstances, the human eye releases "warm vapors" and "subtle spirits" into the air. During menstruation, blood escapes from all the veins of a woman's body and mingles with those warm vapors. Carried as a fog might be carried, the vapors cover the distant mirror, and everything else, presumably, in the woman's vicinity. Women act locally, a perfectly ordinary series of causes and their effects passing from their eyes, reddened by blood, to a reflecting mirror. There is no action at a distance. A preposterous example has served to ratify a physical principle.

The most notable of the early Dominicans, Albertus Magnus, was born in 1206 in Larvingen, which is on the Danube, and he was educated in Padua. The name "Magnus" is not a tribute to his stature but a Latin corruption of his family name—de Groot—so that Albertus Magnus has entered history *as* great by virtue of being called great, a nicely ironical circumstance with its own power to disturb the imagination. During his youth, legends collected around him. He was said to possess magical powers; his detractors were persuaded that he held amiable conversations with the devil, and some went so far as to insist that he had in secret constructed an automaton, one that could speak. With embroidery now entering into the fabric of myth, still other contemporaries affirmed that they had witnessed Thomas Aquinas destroy the infernal device in a fit of deep indignation. When other contemporaries attributed the discovery of the philosopher's stone to Albertus, his reputation as a wizard was still further enhanced, so that in his youth he seemed to be a dangerous man.

But shortly thereafter, Albertus Magnus had a religious vision in which the Virgin appeared to him, bringing his association with magic and the dark arts to an end. He entered the new Dominican order in 1222 and over the next fifty-eight years devoted himself to natural philosophy. Like al-Kindi, whom he in many ways resembled, Albertus Magnus established himself as an encyclopedic scholar, with interests ranging across philosophy, botany, zoology, physics, and mathematics. He was a fine, if limited, logician. And he was a man of admirable curiosity.

Alone among the scholastics, Albertus Magnus was obsessed with action at a distance; alone again, he seems to have had a troubling, ineradicable sense of its importance. The impossibility of action at a distance appeared to him as a great regulative principle. Action requires explanation. And therefore, *action requires contact*. This principle implies that the Christian God must be everywhere at once, coextensive in his body with the universe itself. Otherwise he could not *act* and without his perpetual intervention, the universe would sag into inexistence. *Dues est ubique conservans mundum,* as theologians said. God is everywhere conserving the world. The body of Christ is ubiquitous. A surge of sympathy may now be observed passing between Moslem and Christian thought.

But having reached one conclusion about action at a distance, Albertus often found himself troubled by examples that undercut his sense of certainty. His thoughts are unstable. He cannot bring them under control. Some men, he observed, have the power of fascination: "The soul of one man acts with his sight or some other sense to the benefit or detriment of another person." A forward glance, a fixed stare, the eyes narrowed and icy, allows such men to invade other men's souls. When the invasion is malignant, many cultures speak of the *evil eye*. Such reports go back to the beginning of time. They are hardly unknown in the twentieth century. If it was the sound of his voice that swayed ordinary Germans, it was Adolf Hitler's stare that dominated his close political associates. The evil eye seems to be a genuine case of action at a distance, an annihilation of space and time. "A certain power to alter things indwells in the human soul," Albertus wrote. And surely he was right: It is foolish to deny this.

Whatever the nature of the evil eye, the problem of action at a distance reappears within the very bowels of theology. Christian doctrine most certainly guaranteed the existence of angels (as well as demons). But angels, since they are distinct, must inevitably find themselves separated in space, some of them residing in one part of the firmament, others in another part. How, then, do they communicate? (*Quo sermone loquantur Angeli?*) In a wonderfully suggestive image, Albertus compared two angels attempting to talk to two widely separated cosmic lighthouses, asking under what conditions the light sent from these sources might meet in a kind of luminous collision. His answer is a marvel of common sense. There must be no absorbing walls or deflecting mirrors between lighthouses; they must be facing one another, otherwise their signals, losing themselves in space, would never meet; and there must be some proportionality between the strength with which each lighthouse emits a signal and their mutual distance. As Albertus remarks, "a light in England does not meet a light in Italy." All of this is in accord with common sense. Lighthouses must use light to communicate and light is a physical signal. When sufficiently far apart, lighthouses cannot communicate at all.

The analogy between angels and light sources now begins to wobble alarmingly, for it suggests that angels separated in space must *talk* to one another, and so must have organs of speech and hearing. It is here that Albertus demurs, his strong grasp of difficult physical principles in conflict with various points of Christian doctrine. If knowledge flows like light from one angel to another, it must be propagated, and however much Albertus considers the matter of angelic propagation, he realized that only a physical system can propagate a physical signal. But angels are *incorporeal,* the Church taught; various doctrines are in conflict.

Albertus resolved his perplexities by means of philosophical strategy that is suggestive without being clear. All angels, he argued, are potentially in a position to know every truth about the world of nature. They do not, however, exercise this power at all times. If one angel wishes to communicate a thought to a distant angel, he does so by admitting the thought into his *own* angelic consciousness, whereupon it immediately becomes available to the angelic consciousness of the second angel. In quantum mechanics, this process is known as quantum entanglement. It is no clearer in theoretical physics than in theology.

The angels may be dismissed. They have done their work. Albertus has allowed the camel's nose of action at a distance to enter the tent. The camel is bound to follow.

As it did some six hundred years later when Isaac Newton published his *Principia Mathematica*.

☍

THE LIVES OF THE great Dominicans were secured by their order. They could afford to consider astrology as a theoretical problem. Working astrologers, with neither the time nor the taste for metaphysics, were obliged to earn a living. The life of Michael Scot is in some respects typical and in other respects exemplary. Born somewhere in Scotland in 1196, Scot commanded the attention of European intellectuals as an astrologer, a magician, and a translator. Very little is known of his early life, except that it was restless, Scot leaving Scotland for the continent sometime in the early part of the thirteenth century. After crossing the English Channel, he made his way on foot to Paris. He required an education. No doubt, he received a surprise.

The universities of Europe had their origins in a kind of twelfth-century riot, where students gathered in the open air to hear lecturers shout their theses from the top of overturned hogsheads. The most popular lecturers survived to charge fees;

others slunk off after a few grim semesters, returning to provincial villages or taking refuge in the smaller monastic centers. In the early years of the twelfth century, Abelard was a great favorite with students, who, when they were not listening to his lectures on logic, were very often banging tankards on table tops and lustily singing his love songs in all the low taverns.

The chronicler Jacques de Vitry offers this fine summary of student life: "Almost all the students at Paris, foreigners and natives, did absolutely nothing." Their time was spent largely in "wrangling and disputation," when it was not, of course, spent in wenching and drinking.

De Vitry's account improves with detail:

[Students] affirmed that the English were drunkards and had tails; the sons of France proud, effeminate, and carefully adorned like women. They said that the Germans were furious and obscene at their feasts; the Normans vain and boastful; the Poitevins, traitors and always adventurers. The Burgundians they considered vulgar and stupid. The Bretons were reputed to be fickle and changeable... The Lombards were called avaricious, vicious and cowardly, the Romans seditious, turbulent and slanderous; the Sicilians, slanderous and cruel; the inhabitants of Brabant, men of blood, incendiaries, brigands and ravishers; the Flemish, fickle, prodigal and gluttonous.

After the exchange of such insults, de Vitry adds with some understatement, "students often came to blows." The faculty hardly represented an improvement. "I will not speak of the logicians," de Vitry remarks, just before speaking of the logicians, "before whose eyes flitted constantly 'the lice of Egypt'—that is to say, all the sophistical subtleties, so that no one could comprehend their eloquent discourse, in which, as says Isaiah, there is no wisdom.

As to the doctors of theology, seated in Moses' seat, they were swollen with learning, but their charity was not edifying.... They not only hated one another, but by their flatteries, they enticed away the students of others; each one seeking his own glory."

Pope Honorius III described Michael Scot as "burning from boyhood with love of science." It is not impossible that Scot's student days, if spent in Paris, should have contributed to his ardor, but given de Vitry's description, neither is it very likely. Without funds or obvious means of support, Scot made a living of sorts by playing the lyre. "Nor is there an instrument," he remarked, "that can better guide [the life of a poor scholar] everywhere, whoever plays it, than the lyre, as it is clear from the experience of anyone who goes from door to door playing it."

The uncertainties of Scot's life resolved themselves in 1217. And there he is—in Toledo, the crossroads of Arabic, Christian, and Jewish cultures, a sun-struck, spice-perfumed, gardened port of call for traders, Jewish scholars, magicians, philosophers, rogue imams, silk merchants, prelates, priests, church officials, love-sick poets writing in Hebrew and Arabic, freebooters, physicians, literary scholars, astrologers, necromancers, and translators from the entire Mediterranean world.

Scot acquired medieval Arabic; he was already in command of medieval Latin. He became a translator, one of the gatekeepers controlling the flood of Arabic texts and commentaries washing over Europe. And although the point is not established in the scholarly literature, Scot must have also read Abu Mashar's astrological works, if only because he was passionately interested in astrology and Abu Mashar's reputation was then at its height.

Roughly five years later Michael Scot is in Sicily, in the employ of the emperor Frederick II. Scot served Frederick officially as a court astrologer, but he seemed to have been an adroit conversationalist, and the two lonely men amused one another by conducting a number of trifling scientific experiments by day and talking into the late hours of the endless night.

It was during his services at the emperor's court that Scot composed the *Liber Introductorius,* his introduction to the arts of astrology, and a book intended, Scot affirms, "for those not over-burdened with intelligence." Scot's book is by no means a complete account of medieval astrological practices. How could it be? It is a personal view, a testament from the trenches. In Scot's hands, astrology is a subject divided into three parts. There is the strictly theoretical business of astronomy itself, and this Scot is content to take intact from Ptolemy; there is the astrological interpretation of Ptolemaic astronomy, matters pertaining to the zodiac, the signs, and the houses; and there is finally the concordance between the position and arrangement of the stars and matters of human interest.

If the idea of a concordance elicits a flicker of contemporary interest, the details that Scot provides evoke skepticism while doing nothing to elicit understanding. Where we would wish to know *how* Scot reaches his judgments, he often says nothing, and where he says something, it is almost invariably expressed in terms that are both general and vague.

There is the moon. When it is in a fire or air sign of the zodiac, Scot is persuaded, "scholars learn better, doctors teach more truly, and artists work more efficiently." Why this should be so, Scot does not say. Nor does he demonstrate that it *is* so. Aries is the sign of the Ram, and rams have both wool and horns. It follows, Scot argues, that those born under the sign of Aries will have wealth and pride. "Also," he adds, "Aries commonly expects death from bloodshed or iron," evidently on the grounds that sheep ultimately make their way to butchers. It is not entirely clear why Scot failed to argue that those born under the sign of Aries are apt to have four legs.

The barely coherent details accumulate. Saturn, when found

in a certain position, signifies "prisons, lamentations, labors, plaints, and sorrows." Leo may indicate maddening slowness, but then again it might indicate firmness and stability. Should a man have an heir by his wife or mistress? "Examine the Ascendant and its lord as to the interrogator [i.e the husband]," and do as well "for the seventh house and its lord as to the other party [i.e. the wife or mistress]." What then? "If both lords...are in conjunction with the lord of that house that signifies sons and daughters...then this is a sign that he will beget and she conceive." What house it might be that signifies sons and daughters, Scot does not say.

There is a great deal more in this style, the book obviously the work of a busy man, and here and there, Scot does offer an interesting aside in which he explains in some detail the nature of his services for the emperor. The subject is again astrological interrogations, the art of answering specific questions. A prince has been confronted by a city in frank rebellion. It is the prince who poses the obvious question—*shall I prevail in battle?*—and thus the prince who is assigned the occupancy of the first house. His opponent is assigned to the seventh house, which is, of course, directly opposite the first.

> I began, as the custom is, to seek the lord of the ascendant for the emperor inquiring and the lord of the seventh house for the hostile party, so that I might know from their positions in the signs...what would be the outcome between the interrogator and his enemies.

As it happened, Scot determined that Mars was the lord of the ascendant, and Venus the mistress of the seventh house. Since Mars is potent, strong, and masculine, and Venus, by way of contrast, is weak, timid, and incompetent, there is no doubt as to the outcome. The prince will prevail.

It would be a mistake to dismiss Scot's astrological interpretations simply because the principles that he cites or the ideas he entertains seem either trivial or inadequate. Frederick II was no fool, and if he attended to Scot's counsel, and the evidence suggests that he did, it is doubtful that he did so because he was invariably disappointed. The medieval astrologer was rather in the position of a medieval English lawyer in that their cases were more interesting than their principles. There is a pressing matter, something that must be resolved. The tenements of Lucy Mills, one plea from the manor of the Abbey of Bec reveals, "are to be seized into the lord's hands because of the adultery which she has committed and the bailiff is to answer for them." What to do? Maud, the widow of Reginald of Challow, is owed certain sheep. How shall they be obtained? John Dun requires mercy for having carried off corn. What is his punishment to be? Geoffrey Coterel is accused of battery. How shall his victim be made whole? Decisions are required and judgments made, and like the astrologer, the harried jurist, forever pressed for time, can expect little from explicit principles of law or the ideas they embody. "Even in Bracton's day" (i.e. the late thirteenth century), Maitland and Pollock remark with some asperity, "the number of legal ideas is very small and public law had hardly an idea of its own." The lawyer, like the astrologer, deals in prior precedents, the accumulated weight of his profession, the contingent record, and the debris of history. The attorney for Lucy Mills considers not only her adultery—a matter of fact, it would seem—but the long compelling record of marital infidelity already recorded in the body of English law, sifting through those complicated cases to find an exculpating pattern, a place where the hammer of justice failed to fall or fell with less than ordinary severity.

There are *no* principles at work here, *no* ideas of note, the lawyer profiting from an immersion into the facts and trusting in some instinct, some sense of pattern, to make his way back from history and into the world his client inhabits.

So, too, the astrologer.

⌒

ASTROLOGY, LET US SUPPOSE, is in the dock. Responsible Church officials are concerned to determine whether divination broadly conceived is something to be condemned. They know very well, and this is something that they feel in their bones, that astrology is somehow a suspicious business; and they are mindful, too, that divination and Catholic teaching are at odds. Their instinct to judgment is tempered by the fact that divination is *also* at the heart of the powerful astronomical scheme that they have inherited from Aristotle and Ptolemy. It is the very foundation of their science.

Albertus Magnus has appeared as an expert witness; he has found in astrology nothing amiss; and his tract, the *Speculum Astrologiae,* has, in fact, explicitly endorsed a great many traditional astrological claims. With the book in evidence on the courtroom table, Albertus argues that, although many occult processes such as menstruation rest on real physical connections between causes and their effect, there remain a troubling residue of cases, such as the evil eye, in which action *is* transmitted at a distance. Shrugging somewhat sadly, he admits that he does not know how. Angelic locution falls somehow between the cases that he understands and those that he does not. It is all very difficult. And thereafter, old and peaceful, Albertus shuffles off, leaving a burbling vortex of confusion in his wake.

THE ISSUE OF ACTION at a distance was not resolved by any of the great Dominicans. And no Dominican followed al-Ghazzalli in arguing that action at a distance is impossible because action is an illusion. The Catholic Church was not about to purchase consistency by embracing lunacy. It is a policy of such obvious modesty that one wonders why it is not more widely employed today. If the stars are the cause of human action, as astrologers maintained, they act as ordinary causes act.

There remains the question whether the stars might be signs. It is a question that engaged Thomas Aquinas, the great master of the medieval manner. Born in 1225 in Rocca Secca, then a part of the independent kingdom of Naples, Aquinas died just fifty years later at a Cistercian monastery in Fossa Nuova in what is now northern Italy. His parents were both members of the Italian nobility, Landulph, his father, the Count of Aquino, and Theodora, his mother, the Countess of Teano. There is something unmistakably aristocratic in Aquinas, a regality of bearing and an emotional discipline that cannot not be acquired, although it may well be imitated.

Aquinas was from an early age marked as an intellectual prodigy, someone capable of absorbing and organizing vast amounts of information in an orderly, entirely disciplined fashion; and he was marked again by an apparently spontaneous religious sensibility. His career was never in doubt. Sometime in 1240, he joined the Dominican order. He was very much the protégé of Albertus Magnus. His first act of friendship was apparently to get rid of the automaton clanking dolefully around the older man's chambers. The two men were warmly devoted to one another, and when Aquinas died in early middle age, Albertus suffered a loss cruel enough to provoke him to tears at its memory many years later.

Portraits of Thomas Aquinas reveal a man who plainly ate too much, the bones of his stern, powerful face outlined in flesh; but the man's body, if round, was also powerful, so that the added weight became less something that he carried and more something he projected.

Aquinas' early life was spent in disciplined study and equally disciplined self-mortification. His biographers report that as a young man he was visited by a "temptress," a woman evidently sent by his family, eager to persuade their son to abjure his monastic vows. The woman entered Aquinas' chamber dressed in scarlet; she offered herself provocatively to Aquinas, who promptly seized a branding iron from the fire and chased her from his quarters. The story may be true, at least in so far as it suggests a synchronous conflagration, the one taking place in the fireplace, the other in Aquinas, but the story's aftermath is very touching. Praying for a release from temptation, Aquinas fell into a pleasant sleep, and was vouchsafed a dream in which two angels promised that he would enjoy the blessing of perpetual virginity. He was thereafter freed from the torment of desire.

Aquinas worked without interruption and he worked with an unhurried aspect. His pace outstripped his writing hand, and in early middle age, he turned to dictation as a technique by which he might encompass his thoughts. And there he may be found: He is sitting stiffly on a stool in an unheated chamber somewhere in Paris, four secretaries seated around him in a semi-circle, quill pens poised over ink pots and parchment as Aquinas began to address objections that he had entertained but not answered the day before.

THE *SUMMA THEOLOGICA* is the great synthetic work of the thirteenth century; it is now also the official philosophical doctrine of the Catholic Church. The project Aquinas had set himself in this work was nothing less than an explication and defense of the Catholic faith on the basis of Aristotelian thought. In this he came remarkably close to success. The *Summa* addresses all the issues of the faith, and it revisits and often corrects Aristotle on many matters of science and philosophy, Aquinas' profound love and respect for Aristotle's intelligence often at odds with his pained recognition that Aristotle, having been born three centuries before the birth of Christ, could not have known the comforts of Christian brotherhood and would, as a result, no doubt spend eternity without the consolations of its religion. The dense, superbly argued *Summa Theologica* contains thirty-eight separate treatises, deals with 612 separate questions, subdivided again into 3,120 separate articles, and raises and answers more than 10,000 questions. It is a cathedral in thought. And like a great many cathedrals, the *Summa Theologica* is a structure that invites admiration while discouraging affection.

It is in the *Summa* that one ancient astrological idea is exposed and decisively emptied of its content. Whatever their role as causes, the stars are not signs.

Aquinas settles himself into steadiness. Intelligence rises from him like heat from a hot stove. Those secretaries are at the ready. Young men, they have all passed through the demanding program of a Dominican education. They are tough-minded, able, and perceptive; and they are aware that the man facing them is addressing eternity. His attitude is somber. And so is theirs. The question, Aquinas affirms, is, "Whether divination by the stars is unlawful?" By "divination," Aquinas explains, he means "foreknowledge of future events acquired by observing the stars." Aquinas is talking about astrology. As Aquinas talks, the scratching sound of the secretaries' quill pens fills the room, that and a delicate *chink* as they dip their nibs into various sooty-looking ink pots.

"There have been various opinions," Aquinas begins. "Some [philosophers] have stated that the stars signify rather than cause the things foretold by means of their observation."

It is this view that Aquinas rejects. An idea is about to undergo dissolution. For the moment, let the stars be placed in abeyance. The idea that signs are physical artifacts signifying, but not causing, the future, was in medieval life as much a matter of common sense as it is today. Every guild in Paris had its sign or glyph:

butcher stalls, the ram's head; surgeons' shops, the beaker and cupping bowl; bakers had their signs, and so did tavern owners, brothel keepers, morticians, doctors, barbers, and chimney sweeps. And in the crucified Christ, the Church itself had its own sign, part mystical symbol and part magical connection to the dread event itself, a series of crosses having multiplied itself throughout space and time to form a universal symbolic form. Signs are physical objects, of course, so much ink or paint on parchment or on wood. As such, they have a physical nature. They are part of a causal stream. The appearance of the butcher's sign has its causes in the sign-maker's lusty strokes, and it has its effects in the way that the sign deflects light or collects dust. Signs share a double nature. They are at once physical *and* symbolic, the first because everything grasped by the human senses is in part physical, the second because signs go beyond themselves to designate or denote. Two streams are at work, the one proceeding from causes to their effects, and the other from symbols to what they signify. And these streams are distinct. The ram's head deflects light, but it designates meat. The point may be resolved into a principle: *signs designate neither their causes nor their effects.*

The argument now gathers force as a cold wind, one that divides itself over two examples. There is, in the first place, smoke and fire. And plainly, Aquinas admits, smoke does *signify* fire. In this it functions as a sign. This is the first example. There is, as well, the common rainbow. And like smoke, a rainbow functions as a sign, one signifying good weather to come. This is the second example.

But if smoke is a sign of fire, Aquinas argues, it cannot penetrate the future. The future, after all, cannot influence the present or the past. Where there is smoke there *was* fire. It follows that to the extent that smoke is a sign, it is a sign that designates something that has already happened.

And plainly this is true as well of the stars. "It cannot be said," Aquinas asserts, "that the dispositions and movements of the heavenly bodies are the effect of future events."

If the celestial signs are rather like smoke, what they designate lies in the past. But at issue, Aquinas now reminds the secretaries, *and he reminds us,* is whether it is possible to have "foreknowledge of *future* events." The example of smoke is of scant help. It points in the wrong direction.

A rainbow is, of course, different, its arc of curved and colored light suggestively moving from the present into the future. The storm has passed. Good weather is coming. Although a rainbow shares its cause with the cause prompting good weather, it does *not* designate its cause as smoke does. Its arrow of information is inclined toward the future. The question rather is whether it penetrates the future as a sign. But a rainbow, Aquinas now argues stolidly, his secretaries scribbling, is a part of an ordinary causal sequence, one that runs from the past (a rumbling storm), to the present (that rainbow), to the future (good weather). In this, it is like any other physical event or process. The storm is the cause of *both* the rainbow *and* the good weather to come, but just as a single blow may lead to a sequence of delayed effects, it is a cause whose effects are staggered. The rainbow is simply an intermediate in a long causal chain. If this is so, then a rainbow penetrates the future as an ordinary cause, one designating its own effect. From this it follows that it is not a sign, because signs do not designate their effects. Aquinas at once draws the obvious conclusion suggested by his analogy. "It is impossible to acquire foreknowledge of the future from an observation of the stars, *except* insofar as effects can be foreknown from their causes."

These homely but powerful examples are now allowed to lapse. They have served their purpose and they have done their work. Divination in general and astrology in particular reacquire their pride of place. Aquinas reminds his secretaries what is at issue: "*Some have stated that the stars signify rather than cause.*" It is this thesis that Aquinas is finally prepared to rebut. What, he demands, do the *stars* do? They are the causes of further effects and the effects of prior causes. They may thus be either causes or effects. There is nothing more they might do because there is nothing more they can do. If they are signs, they must either designate their own cause or designate their own effects. In the first case, they cannot penetrate the future; in the second, they are not signs. It follows that, insofar as the stars are signs, they do not penetrate the future and insofar as they penetrate the future, they are not signs.

The secretaries have finished scribbling. The argument has been concluded.

AQUINAS HAS ADDRESSED an ancient astrological thesis, and he has shown that it is empty. He has done more. He has, in fact, come very close to a series of radical propositions. Nature is an impersonal system, Aquinas suggests, one in which causes give way to effects, which are in turn causes. The astrologer or astronomer who grasps this remote system *does* have access to the future—this Aquinas never doubts—but it is access achieved only by means of an entry forced into a causal sequence. Seeing smoke rising from his stall, the butcher may infer fire; seeing a rainbow, the prelate may predict good weather. If Saturn is a malefic planet, as astrologers have argued, then Saturn in crossing the night sky acts as an ordinary cause, bringing ruination to kingdoms or disaster to individuals in just the way that fire causes smoke or rainbows good weather. *In exactly the same way.* There are no *signs* in nature pointing toward the future, no hints, intimations, indications, pointers, magical markers, or literary revelations. There are no signs in nature because nature is not a sign-like system. It is otherwise. It is this idea that is radical, and it is new.

And like any radical idea, it invites objections. Aquinas certainly knew that in addition to signifying fire, smoke can signify other things. On the election of a new pope, the modern papal curia sends up a puff of white smoke, one designating the selection of a pope as well as the modest paper fire that prompted it. For that matter, ordinary words and letters have a two-fold role to play, acting both as physical objects and as symbols or signs, their peculiar shapes playing a role in various symbolic systems, as when the sign "dog," to take a simple case, is used to refer generally to dogs.

In order to signify, signs require an immersion in a world in which things are noticed, intentions formed, plans made, ideas conceived, and symbols assigned meaning. This world exists, it is close to our hearts, and without it we would be lost, but it is not the world in which the celestial objects turn in the night sky. For the first time, one sees in outline the strange, disturbing double system at work in the modern soul, that hard, dismaying distinction between the material world in which causes chase their effects through space and time, and the symbolic world in which material objects briefly acquire the ability to transcend themselves.

If the conclusions toward which Aquinas is tending are radical, they are also dangerous. The idea that the stars are *signs* signifying, but not causing, future events—the idea that Aquinas rejects—was accepted gratefully by Augustine, as he found himself at war with himself, his Roman nature in conflict with his Christian faith. Church officials thereafter regarded this idea as the compromise making free will possible. Marcilio Ficino, the Renaissance philosopher writing two hundred years after Aquinas' death, accounts for astrology by quoting Plotinus: "We may think of the stars as letters perpetually being inscribed on the heavens,... and those who know how to read this sort of writing... can read the future from their patterns." This view goes back to the scribes of the *Enuma,* and after bypassing classical Rome, where a good many men had the toughness to look fate in the face, it goes forward to Galileo, who described nature as a book, one written in the language of mathematics.

In developing his argument, Aquinas has had no reason to question the astrological idea that the stars influence human events. Something does, after all. But in rejecting the idea that they influence human events as signs, he has accepted the thesis that stars influence human events as causes. Causes are uncompromising. Given a cause in nature, its effect must follow. Why else call it a *cause?* Aquinas has come very close to the forbidden affirmation that the stars *determine* human behavior. Augustine had seen clearly that in this way lies the ultimate denial of Christian truth. A world in which human behavior is the necessary effect of some material cause cannot be a world in which there is contrition, repentance, and salvation. This is something that Aquinas understood.

There follows a certain amount of anxious backtracking as Aquinas searches for a way to enlarge his argument without compromising his principles. There are two sorts of events or effects, Aquinas decides, which cannot be understood in terms of ordinary causal sequences. The first are events that occur by chance. About these he has nothing of interest to say. The second are events in which "acts of free will, which is the faculty of will and reason, escape the causality of heavenly bodies." The intellect is not a body, nor the act of a bodily organ, and neither is the will. It follows that their operation cannot be the effect of a body in motion, or of *any* corporeal substance, for that matter. The conclusion Aquinas draws from this claim is a masterpiece of equivocation:

> Hence the heavenly bodies cannot be the direct cause of the free-will's operations. Nevertheless they can be a dispositive cause of an inclination to those operations, in so far as they

make an impression on the human body, and consequently on the sensitive powers which are acts of bodily organs having an inclination for human acts. Since, however, the sensitive powers obey reason,... this does not impose any necessity on the free will, and man is able, by his reason, to act counter to the inclination of the heavenly bodies.

These remarks suggest that, in some unforeseen way, the argument that Aquinas has advanced has proven too explosive for the good it may have done. Cosmic determinism is an unhappy doctrine, one reducing human behavior and human beings to a fixed place in an endless pattern. What is worse, since the stars and planets are in periodic motion, cosmic determinism may quickly lead to the view that human history is an endlessly recycled drama, the same acts succeeding the same acts for all eternity. Not only is this "horrible," as Albertus Magnus remarks, it is incompatible with Christian doctrine. The crucifixion, Church fathers taught, was a *unique* event. But Aquinas cannot bring himself to rebut determinism by striking at its fundamental assumption. The proposition that men are free because *nothing* acts to cause their behavior—the perfect truth, it would seem—lies beyond the margins of his sympathy.

It is this circumstance that prompts Aquinas to espouse the oddly familiar doctrine that the stars, in governing human affairs, *incline but do not compel.* If he accepts the idea, it could not have been with enthusiasm. Aquinas is simply too fine a philosopher not to have seen the obvious difficulty with this position. If *inclination* is anything like cause, his formula—*incline but do not compel*—involves a contradiction in terms. How can a cause or cause-like event incline without compelling? If *inclination* is nothing like cause, what role do the stars play in getting anything to get going?

Still, it must be said that for all its philosophical defects, the idea that the stars incline but do not compel points the astrologer, and the rest of us, as well, to very familiar experiences. The human voice, asking, demanding, wheedling, urging, affirming, adverting, boasting, pleading, or commanding, is very often a force that inclines but does not compel. And so are the gestures of the human face.

Did at least one of those bright, able secretaries ask Aquinas *whose* voice might be murmuring through the haze of stars, and did he wonder how ever it was heard?

THOMAS AQUINAS DIED IN 1275. Medieval culture was yet at its height, its institutions in the full power of their glory. His way of life was about to end and his way of thinking fall into decline. In the years before his death, he had been vouchsafed certain visions, the contents of which he could not convey. He would stare raptly at church windows, pause in mid-speech or mid-lecture, his heavy, noble face consumed by an expression of beatitude. He had been a man of exceptional religious sensibility, but nothing in his life of devoted and massive intellectual labor had prepared him for these visions. On December 6, 1273, while attending mass, he fell into a prolonged and evidently rapturous mystic state; and thereafter he ceased to write. When urged by officials of the Church to continue his work on the *Summa Theologica,* which despite its length he left unfinished, he replied, "I can do no more. Such secrets have been revealed to me that all I have written now appears to be of little value."

⌒

WHEN LAST SEEN, the footloose Michael Scot was at the emperor's side, or whispering in his ear. Sometime later, he was in Paris again, lecturing at the university, offering courses on astronomy. They must have been dreadful, those courses. Like so many of the lesser medieval thinkers, Scot had the habit of organizing his thoughts into numbered lists. There are four things that make a man wise, nine ways to true learning. Twelve things are required in the arts. There are four definitions of the word "horizon," seven regions of the air, and twenty-eight mansions of the moon. The universe is divided into four sub-universes. The first day of creation was the eighteenth of March. A rainbow has two names but the sun has seven. There are ten orders of angels, but one has fallen. The remaining nine angels are divided into groups of three. There are four elements, four cardinal virtues, four points of the compass, four seasons of the year, four evangelists, four angels at the throne of God, and four principal parts of the human body. Seven is the chief cosmic number, since there are seven planets, seven firmaments, seven abysses, seven ages, and seven human actions, this particular list ending finally with seven cells found in the human womb.

Scot's reputation precedes him. He is known as a very competent astrologer. There are inevitably troubling rumors about a book of secrets, fatal to those attempting to open it. Then he is in Sicily once more, attending again to the emperor. Benvenuto tells the following story.

> Michael is said to have forseen his own death, which he could not evade: he had forseen himself dying from the impact of a small stone of an exact weight which was to fall upon his head. He took precautions by always wearing an iron skull cap beneath his hood. But just once, when entering the Church for the feast of Corpus Domini, he took off his skull cap with his hood, more so as not to be remarked by the crowd, I believe, than for love of Christ, for whom he cared little.

This scene is superbly set, the narration itself intimating its own inevitable conclusion:

> And suddenly a small stone fell upon his naked head, slightly wounding his scalp. After picking it up and weighing it, Michael discovered it was exactly the weight he had

predicted, and now certain of his death, he ordered his affairs and died of that wound.

In the twentieth Canto of the *Inferno*, Dante, in a wonderfully biting and malicious passage, considers the punishment of those who "presumed, while living, to predict future events." It is, Virgil reveals, "to have their faces reversed and set the contrary way on their limbs, so that, being deprived of the power to see before them, they are constrained ever to walk backward."

Amphiaraus, Tiresias, Aruns, and Manto are included in this group, "each wonderously seem'd to be reversed/At the neck bone," and so is Guido Bonatti, "an astrologer of Forli."

And so is Michael Scot.

♎

THE ASTROLOGERS had been right. A planetary conjunction was in prospect. Astrological predictions in the twelfth century had their origin in the Moslem world, if only because no European astrologer possessed the skills that would have enabled him to do more than affirm with confidence that the sun would rise, the moon set, and the stars twinkle. Transits and conjunctions were a Moslem astrological specialty, the provenance, in fact, of Abu Mashar, whose voice may well have been conveyed from Baghdad to Toledo by Michael Scot. In a tract entitled *On Historical Astrology: The Book of Religions and Dynasties*, and subtitled *On the Great Conjunctions*, Abu Mashar considered the role that planetary conjunctions play in human affairs. His general interest in the matter notwithstanding, he did not discuss the consequences of a grand conjunction in which all seven of the planets are lined up in one sign.

Modern astrologers must therefore follow the fate of each planet as it enters Libra—the fateful sign in September of 1186—and piece together a general doctrine from various indirect clues. No doubt this is what the Toledo astrologers did as well.

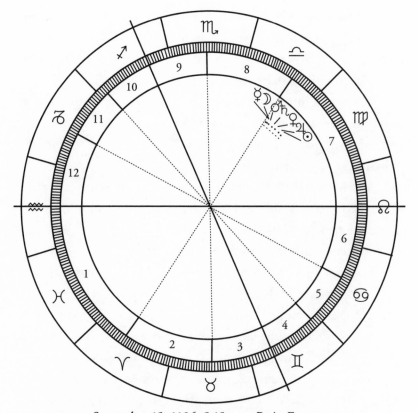

September 15, 1186, 5:15 P.M., Paris, France.
The ominous prospect indicated by a planetary conjunction.
Even today, those planets stolidly occupying the same region of the
heavens seem to suggest bad news in prospect.

When Saturn is in Libra, Abu Mashar writes, and the latitude
is northern, "this indicates the frequent blowing of winds, and
their raging." If Jupiter or the moon are in aspect, he goes on to
say—and in 1186, both were—"this indicates the darkness of the
atmosphere; [and] that the air is muddy; and raging winds, an intensity of heat, many separations of men from their wives, and a
scarcity of food, juice, and oil."

Jupiter is next. A continuous blowing of winds is anticipated.
Then Mars. Winds again. If Mars is near Saturn, as it was in

1186, then there will be "many deaths, the raging of thieves, and fears and epidemics...together with an abundance of rain, fog and clouds." This is very grim. Abu Mashar also predicts "an abundance of fears, false rumors, and evil among the people."

Venus in Libra suggests little by way of disasters: quite the opposite. Dry winds are set to blow and the air will be fresh. And yet, Abu Mashar insists, there will be "confusion and oppressive false rumors among the people."

And Mercury? "A large number of winds." If Venus is near, as it was in 1186, this indicates "that wars will break out in the west, and that people [will] kill each other." It indicates as well that "confusions [will] occur to the common people."

The moon in Libra is not a good sign. "A battle between leaders" is in prospect, and there will be "mental disorders in the country, fear, death and grief occurring to the people, a large number of riots, an attack of the locusts, and a decrease in drink." There is the inevitable "blowing of winds," cold now and desolate.

And finally the sun in Libra indicates "a large number of harms occurring to the king of Babylon, the occurrence of plague in that country, and the death of horses and camels, together with riots occurring in the land of Byzantium."

The easily panicked Christian letter writers of the twelfth and thirteenth centuries must have known these predictions. How else would they have conceived their dread of planetary conjunctions? With some margin allowed for experimental error, the position of the sun in Libra could well account for Corumphiza's prediction of disaster falling over the Arab world. The position of the other planets in Libra suggest uniformly that a cold, dark wind is about to blow.

But there remains Mercury, Mars, and Venus, and while their entry into Libra is a sign now written on the wind, they reveal another message as well: Whatever the winds, the cold, the fog, or the darkness attending a planetary conjunction, the chief effect is likely to be panic.

For all that, September of 1186 passed uneventfully.

But gathering itself over the Aral Sea or sweeping through the plains of central Asia, another harder wind was blowing.

CHAPTER EIGHT

SCORPIO
♏
THE STINKING WIND

O RIGINATING IN central Asia or in western China and then following the old caravan routes and sea lanes out of Asia, the thing had made its way to Europe. It must have arrived in the early 1340s. In England the point of entry was the busy port of Bristol, and on the continent, one of the Italian trading cities such as Genoa. In both cities, harbor life was much the same, workmen offloading ships that had arrived from African and Mediterranean ports carrying spices, silk, salt, hemp, cedar, and grain. The single-masted ships were hardly models of cleanliness, and the harbors were themselves filthy, filled with debris, garbage piled carelessly along the wharves, a deep, ineradicable reek in the humid air. The men clambering down wet wooden ladders and then hauling crates up to the deck from the ship's cargo hold were stained by toil, their fingernails black, their hair matted and stringy, the sweat of long hours of labor forming a salt scab over their skins.

If in the next day or week or month, one of the workers was found dead in an alleyway, or in a harbor tavern, that was hardly surprising. Life in the fourteenth century was not cheap—it is never cheap—but it was short, and heavy labor was difficult, dangerous work. The inevitable ghastly accidents were commonplace. *Vulnerant omnes, ultima necat,* as Latin writers said. Every hour wounds, the last one kills.

But this death was different. No one had ever seen anything like it. The man's body had been covered with dark, swollen buboes, the line of eruption following the path of his lymphatic nodes. Some had erupted before his death, releasing a purulent fluid.

City officials were called to examine the corpse. Local physicians were consulted. They concurred gravely. Some swift savage *thing* had overtaken the poor wretch, but it was not typhus, which they could recognize, nor cholera, nor any of a dozen or so infectious diseases; and it was definitely not the pox. The more perceptive among them shivered in apprehension.

Within two years, the plague—for that was what it was—swept through England, Italy, France, Germany, and the Netherlands; it reached as far east as Hungary and as far north as the Baltic states. It devastated the Scandinavian countries and was carried by Italian merchants to the eastern Mediterranean. It was relentless in its effects but by no means uniform in its course. Villages and cities would become infected; but for reasons that no one could determine, some people survived, others succumbed after prolonged suffering, and still others collapsed and died within hours after symptoms appeared. Physicians perished with their patients, and the good with the bad. Peasants were struck down in their fields, princes and princesses in their castles. Dynasties foundered. Edward III of England had carefully arranged the marriage of his daughter Joan to Pedro, the heir to King Alfonso of Castile; the union was intended to be the foundation of an Anglo-Spanish alliance. Young, radiant, and devout, Joan died in Bordeaux, en route to Spain, the treasures of her trousseau wasted. "But see with what intense bitterness of heart we have to tell you this," King Edward wrote to King Alfonso. "Death has lamentably snatched from both of us our dearest daughter."

♏

AN IMMERSION in the ignoble is now in order. Bernard Tornius, a medieval physician of the late fifteenth century, is about to conduct an autopsy. It is his autopsy report that has side-slipped into the stream of history. A professor of medicine at the University of Pisa, Tornius was a practicing physician as well as an academic, a man occupied with the burdens and demands of a busy practice. Born in 1452, he died in his forty-second year. His autopsy report, written in a vigorous medieval Latin, conveys some of the directness of a man persuaded of his own importance.

The victim is a young man, and Tornius begins his report by expressing his sympathies to the boy's father. It is difficult to lose a child to disease, especially one, Tornius adds with rare humility, "not understood by doctors."

Tornius proceeds to cut open the body. He is, of course, not using gloves, and if the smell has not discouraged him, this is owing only to the fact that after conducting hundreds of autopsies, it is now familiar. "The belly," he writes,

> appeared quite swollen, although the abdomen was thin. But after dividing... the abdomen and peritoneum, we saw the intestines and the bladder, which was turgid and full of urine.

The autopsy continues in a systematic manner:

> Removing further the colon and the caecum, there appeared in them more gross wind than filth. Then when the ileum and jejunem and duodenum were removed, two worms were found, quite large and white, showing phlegm rather than any other humour.

The internal organs are examined one after the other, until the liver provides the crucial clue:

[T]here appeared around the source of the emulgent veins in the hollow of the chilic vein an evident obstruction by which the whole cavity was filled with viscous humour.

Tornius now concludes that his work is done:

Having seen this much, I did not examine further concerning anything else, since the cause of death was apparent in my judgment.

There follows an obligatory coda, as Tornius imposes on the victim's father the weight and majesty of his own immersion in an ancient medical tradition. Although Tornius saw that "evident obstruction" with his "own eyes," Galen, writing in the second century A.D., had remarked in the sixth book of his *Therapeutic* that "those matters which require consideration should be considered," a declaration hard to fault even today, and it is this citation from the medical literature that gives Tornius confidence in the plain evidence of his senses.

Whatever his need to cite authority, Dr. Tornius, it is quite obvious, knew his way around the human body. Careful observation is in evidence throughout his report, and a very deliberate effort made to place the awful result in the context of a plausible chain of causes and their effects. If what Tornius is doing is not science, then nothing is.

Another medieval physician, Jean Ganivet, has left a strikingly different account of his art, a death foretold, rather than explained. Like Dr. Tornius, Dr. Ganivet was a professor, but he held a chair in theology and not medicine, lecturing at the University of Vienne in southwestern France. His interests in medicine were theoretical as well as practical, and like so many physicians throughout history, he came early to the conclusion that his clinical experience was too valuable to be wasted on his patients. He determined to write a book. The result was the *Amicus Medicorum* (Friend of Doctors). Published in 1496, it quickly became a leading medical text, a connecting link between medicine and astrology and so between the corruption of the body and the course of the stars. In his treatise, Dr. Ganivet writes often about difficult matters on which other physicians required his counsel, but unlike Dr. Tornius, his point of view and the focus of his deliberations is purely astrological:

> In the year of our Lord Jesus 1431 and on the seventh day of the month of August, which was the day of Mars, with seven hours completed from the middle of the night, in the hour of the Sun, a certain master in arts and doctor in medicine named Henry Amici, a native of Brussels in the Brabant, asked on behalf of the lord dean of Vienne, who was ill, whether he would survive or not. It happened that the figure of the heaven above Vienne at that hour was shown.

These words suggest that Dr. Amici, the physician of record, was managing a patient whose prognosis is uncertain. He has his hands full; he is asking for help, but *not* in order to treat his patient better. No remedies are cited, no therapies discussed. At issue is the solemn issue of survival. Very much like an internist sending the details of a difficult case in which the liver is at issue to a great liver specialist, Dr. Amici has consulted an expert.

The figure that Dr. Ganivet is considering is not a horoscope. It answers to a single question: Will this man (the lord dean of Vienne) live or die? The chart has been cast for the moment the question was posed, the stars interrogated from that point of view. By long tradition, the querent, or the questioner, is assigned to the ascendant. The analysis is methodical, Dr. Ganivet going through the chart in steps, and at each step searching for the symptoms that it suggests, its secrets and its signs.

> I looked at this figure or question and I have the Ascendant and Moon to the ill dean and saw that the Moon was applying to the conjunction of the Sun and was already under the Sun's rays. This was one testimony of death.

The passage of the moon underneath the sun's rays has always been considered an ominous astrological sign; Dr. Ganivet is appealing to a tradition stretching back to the oldest astrological authorities.

Dr. Ganivet next considers four further astrological signs, all of them entirely traditional and all of them grave:

> I considered that the Part of the Killing Planet in the 14th degree of Leo between the Moon and the Sun and within the rays of the Sun at the beginning of the 12th House to be a sign of the evil tormenting the patient.

> I considered in the third place that the Part of Death in the 26th degree of Virgo in the Ascendant, the House of Life, was an evil testimony.

> Fourthly, I considered the Part of Life of the present figure in the 26th degree of Aries, in the House of Death; so that there was a certain evil combination, i.e. life or the Part of Life in the House of Death, and the Part of Death in the House of Life; both in the same number of degrees in each Sign, which degrees are the terms of the malefics.

> Furthermore, the Part of Fortune was in the 7th degree of Virgo in the 12th House, with Mercury at the end of its direct motion coming to the beginning of its retrogradation and corrupting the Ascendant.

These signs point uniformly toward one conclusion. "I judged," Dr. Ganivet soberly remarks, "that the patient would come to delirium within one natural day at the latest, no matter how prudent he was, and so it happened that he became delirious before one natural day and died before two."

Like any physician, Dr. Ganivet is, of course, offering a record of his successes and not his failures; but the case he presents is unusual in that the astrological signs are uniform. No astrologer could miss them. In 1555, more than a half-century after Ganivet lived and worked, an astrologer named Andrew Dygges published a text entitled *A Prognostication, Manuscript on Medical Astrology.* The treatise suggests in more vivid detail the system of medical interpretation to which Jean Ganivet appealed.

Each of the organs of the human body is associated with a sign of the zodiac. Mercury is given command of the brain and nerves; Jupiter is assigned the liver, and so down to Saturn, then as now the province of the orthopedic surgeons, commanding the bones and the skeleton. The system then divides itself further into diagnostic categories that are also based on the signs of the zodiac. A facial complaint, such as trigeminal neuralgia? Aries is to be consulted. Virgo is pertinent to the patient presenting symptoms affecting the heart, the spine, or the lower part of the liver. Pisces gets the feet and the toes. There follows, finally, an assignment of symptoms that are organized by sun signs. Taurus assembles what might be called the diseases of gluttony: overindulgence and a weakness for comfort. Leo, on the other hand, handles overexertion in individuals who simply cannot slow down and rest. Dygges' manual concludes with a very sensible pharmacopoeia, one primarily herbal in nature. The various diseases are grouped by astrological signs and so, too, are their various herbal and floral remedies.

That there was a discernable connection between the cosmological and the biological order was widely believed throughout the high Latin Middle Ages. A physician of the thirteenth century published his thoughts on the two chief diagnostic indicators of medieval medicine: the pulse and the urine. Dr. X—for the man has vanished in the shadow of his book—considers the role of the heart and the liver, two of the four chief organs of the human body. "The heart and the liver," he writes, "fill the same place in the microcosm as the sun and the moon do in the greater world." The metaphor is not dead: it contains a living scientific hypothesis. "Just as innate heat," Dr. X affirms, "passes from the sun through the air as a gift to all living things on earth, so too the heat progresses from the heart, its source, via the vital spirit... And the liver is analogous to the moon: for just as the moon communicates moisture to the regions next to it...just as the liver generates humors and bestows a suitable humor on every member."

These cosmological considerations explain the great importance of the urine and the pulse: The first indicates the state of the liver, and the second, the state of the heart.

But cosmological considerations do more: They provide an immensely sophisticated diagnostic technique. Living and working in the early part of the twelfth century, the physician known as William of Marseille composed a text entitled *De Urina non Visa* (On Unseen Urine), a title still capable of provoking a certain reluctant curiosity among contemporary readers. A patient's urine is of crucial diagnostic value, he argued, but there are times when the physician must achieve his diagnosis at a distance, the patient's urine unavailable because the patient is in another city, unable or perhaps even unwilling to urinate on command. The superior physician must nonetheless be able to evaluate the missing urine by casting the patient's chart. It is possible to see in such charts the forerunner of such diagnostic devices as CAT scans and positive emission tomography.

The fact that physicians must resort to astrological charts in order to establish their conclusions is also an explanation for the limitations of their skill. Medicine is an art of succor, a human bond; but it is also a rational exercise, and as such, committed to forecasting accurately the course of disease. How else might a physician devise a remedy for an affliction but by considering its natural progression? But a perfect penetration of the future is possible, William argues, only when the physician's attention is confined to the celestial sphere, where effects follow from their causes with unbroken regularity and the past, the present, and the future are all equally accessible to the astrologer's eye. The causes that sustain the movement of the stars certainly have an effect on human well-being: They are, indeed, its *ultimate* causes, if only because the earth lies at the center of the universe, powerful lines of force all converging on a single point.

But from the same heavenly causes, quite different terrestrial effects might follow. Practical predictions in medicine, or in any other human science, William observes, can never be completely accurate, the accidents of life and the contingencies of matter so varied and so random as to defeat every predictive scheme.

This doctrine serves, of course, to excuse the failings of a science by explaining its errors in advance. William, we are inclined to say, has simply made it impossible to put his views to the test. If an astrological prediction is confirmed, well and good, and if it is not, well and good as well. This is a doctrine too rewarding to be true. But before indicting William too strongly, it is worth recalling how very often contemporary physicians offer the same excuse to their patients, or their living relatives, as when they explain that although the tests were negative, the patient died.

♏

THE PLAGUE WAS frightening—it was *terrifying*—in the implacable way it killed so many. In a society disposed to search for significance in the routine affairs of life—a climbing rose suggesting the bliss of the incarnation, its thorn calling to mind the crucifixion—disease ordinarily carried a symbolic message, but the message conveyed by the plague lacked all symbolic structure. It punished the good and the wicked, the young and the old, and from time to time it whimsically spared the miscreant or the misanthrope. It did not so much punish as *annihilate*. The living were hard pressed to bury the dead.

In his *Historia de Morbo* (History of the Illness), the Italian attorney Gabrielle de Mussis left an account of the plague matchless in its capacity to evoke a sense of overpowering dread. The report begins by assigning the ultimate provenance of the disease to God's punishment. A righteous God having warned the human race to repent, "disease was sent forth, [and] the quivering spear of the Almighty was aimed everywhere and infected the whole human race with its pitiless wounds." These stern sentences suggest a sense of moral clarity nowhere in evidence in de Mussis' factual account, for the plague broke carelessly every bond of human sympathy: "When one person lay sick in the house," de Mussis writes, "no one would come near. Even dear friends would hide themselves away, weeping. The physician would not visit, [and] even the priest, panic stricken, administered the sacraments with fear and trembling." The plague broke with equal measure the bonds between husband and wife and parents and their children. "And when the sick were in the throes of death, they still called out piteously to their friends and neighbors." To no avail. Their cries provoked their neighbors to "keep their distance, [and] the houses of the dead shut up."

"I am overwhelmed," de Mussis admits, "I cannot go on."

What made the plague so deeply perplexing was just that its symptoms signaled a course that, although almost invariable in its end, was maddeningly variable in its means. The physician and surgeon Guy de Chauliac, and the author of a very comprehensive treatise on surgery *Ars Chiurgicalis Guidonis Cauliaci Medici*, offers this account of the plague as it invaded Avignon in January of 1348. The epidemic appeared in two forms. The first, lasting for two months, "was characterized by a continuous fever and a spitting of blood," and killed within two days. The second stage, lasting for five months, "was characterized by apostemes [i.e. buboes] and carbuncles and tumors in the external parts, mainly the armpit and the groin, and men died of it within five days." The infection was horribly contagious, de Chauliac observes: "One man caught it from another not just when living nearby but simply by looking at him."

Writing in Montpellier, an anonymous practitioner was even more emphatic in assigning terrible powers to what was in effect an evil eye: "The most virulent moment of this *epidemia*," he wrote, "which causes an almost sudden death, is when the air spirit emitted from the sick person's eyes, particularly when he is dying, strikes the eyes of a healthy man nearby who looks closely at him."

Like Thucydides recounting the plague in Syracuse, these men have plainly witnessed something beyond their comprehension, devastation so extensive "that it left scarcely the fourth part of the population alive." In absolute numbers, the Spanish flu epidemic, which in 1918 killed more than sixty million men and women worldwide, was a heavier blow, but in numbers relative to the population, the Black Death was worse. It was, in fact, the greatest single catastrophe in human history, overwhelming all medical, moral, and literary resources, and confounding the best minds in Europe.

No remedies were known to be effective.

♏

SOMETIME IN THE late summer of 1348, when the plague had already killed in the thousands and then the hundreds of thousands, Philip, the King of France, asked the masters of the medical faculty of the University of Paris to explain the catastrophe unfolding throughout Europe. The medical faculty complied, issuing their report in October of the same year. These were not men responding simply to some theoretical question.

They were themselves at risk of death. Chronicles kept by the monks at the Abbey of Saint Denis suggest that the plague had entered Paris from the north, near the town of Roissy early in 1348. Within a year, fifty thousand people had died in Paris. At the height of the epidemic, Jean de Vanette, a Carmelite friar, writes, more than five hundred corpses were removed daily from the Hôtel Dieu, then as now a leading Parisian hospital.

As they began their deliberations and considered their charge, the masters of the medical faculty could *see* the tragedy gathering force, as the disease spread through the city like a cold, sinister cloud. Houses were shuttered throughout the narrow, close lanes of the *quartier latin,* the student quarter; carts loaded with the dead made their way down the hillside toward outlying cemeteries, the mules' feet clacking along the streets. Members of the faculty of medicine were all physicians, and they had all passed through a course of study placing astrology and Aristotle at the center of their concerns. It is within the pages of their report that astrology as a system of belief finds itself promoted to a position of intellectual authority at the very moment it was most challenged by events.

The first sentences of the report convey its tone. "Seeing things which cannot be explained," the masters wrote, "even by the most gifted intellects, initially stirs the human mind to amazement; but after marveling, the prudent soul next yields to its desire for understanding, and anxious for its own perfection, strives with all its might to discover the causes of the amazing event." There is within the human mind, the masters add, "an innate desire to seize on goodness and truth." Although obviously true, this sentiment is rarely expressed and almost never expressed by scholars.

The plague, the masters write, represents a complex phenomenon, one with two separate but related causes. Its ultimate causes lie with the heavens and the dispositions of the stars. "We say, that the distant and first cause of this pestilence was and is the configuration of the heavens." It is here that the medical faculty reaches not only for the astrological tradition, but also for theses that by the fourteenth century had become canonical *within* that tradition, matters of common sense. "In 1345," they observe—correctly, of course—"at one hour after noon on 20 March, there was a major conjunction of three planets in Aquarius." The planets were Saturn, Mars, and Jupiter, and their conjunction had *always* been regarded as an ominous sign. "The mortality of races and the depopulation of kingdoms," the masters add, "occur at the conjunction of Saturn and Jupiter." Writing some years *before* 1345, the astrologer Jean de Murs had predicted that the planetary conjunction would have evil consequences, mentioning the destruction of sects, changes in government, the appearance of prophets, popular unrest, and most ominously of all, winds of terrifying power.

And yet planetary conjunctions are not rare events, and in 1325, Mars, Saturn, and Jupiter had *also* been conjoined in Gemini. No epidemics followed. No winds arose. This is not a point discussed by the medical faculty, perhaps because they thought the relevant details obvious, but it is one addressed by the astrologer Geoffrey de Meaux. The medical faculty thought Jupiter played a crucial role in the unfolding plague, and so it did, Geoffrey de Meaux agrees. But Saturn, which the masters assigned an ancillary role, was in fact *exalted* in Aquarius in 1345 and *not* exalted in Gemini in 1325. This is an important distinction. It explains why a planetary conjunction might be innocuous in one year and devastating in another. And there is a second and even more important distinction. A lunar eclipse, Geoffrey de Meaux notes, occurred in 1345 precisely when Saturn, Mars, and Jupiter were conjoined in Aquarius. Such events dramatically increase the power of various planets. "For when the sun is directly opposite the moon," he writes, "then the power of each of them reaches the earth in a straight line, and the mingling of influences of sun and moon with that of the superior planets creates a single celestial force." The planetary conjunction of 1345 thus has a violence denied the planetary conjunction of 1325.

The masters now give content to their views by endowing them with detail.

> These effects [of the planetary conjunction] were intensified because Mars—a malevolent planet breeding anger and war—was in the sign of Leo [a fire sign, and so an influence that intensified the influence cast by Mars] from 6 October 1347 until the end of May this year, along with the head of the dragon, and because all these things are hot they attracted many vapors, which is why the winter was not as cold as it should have been. And Mars was also retrograde, and therefore attracted many vapors from the earth and the sea which, when mixed with the air, corrupted its substance. Mars was also looking toward Jupiter with a hostile aspect, that is to say in quartile, and that caused an evil disposition or quality in the air, harmful and hurtful to our nature. This state of affairs generated strong winds . . . which gave rise to excess heat and moisture on the earth.

Astrological analysis thus served to fix the outbreak of the plague in a universal scheme of causes, the disposition of the planets acting as the distant initial condition by which the catastrophe was set in motion. But astrological analysis did more. It suggested to the medical authorities that by means of an auxiliary *medical* hypothesis, they could coordinate in one intellectual figure those distant causes and their ultimate effects. That medical hypothesis they in turn derived from the long empirical tradition of medicine.

♏

WHEN DR. TORNIUS justified his fifteenth-century opinions by citing Galen, he was doing nothing more than lawyers might do

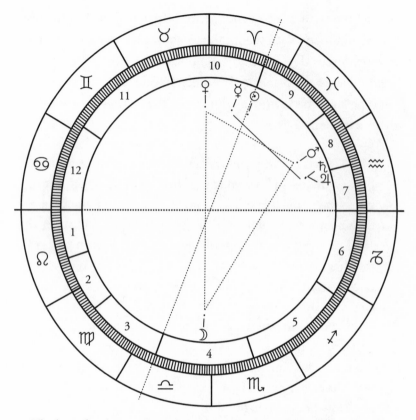

The basis for the astrological explanation of the plague offered by the masters of medicine at the University of Paris. The astrological signs are clear enough—those planets *are* bunched together, a fact as suggestive to medieval astrologers as facts about global warming are to us today.

in quoting Blackstone—appealing to the field's leading historical authority. In this, he was drawing a connection between astrological and empirical medicine. Galen was born in roughly 130 A.D. during the reign of the emperor Hadrian and he died seventy years later, Septimius Severus on the throne. Although he was Greek, and born in Pergamum, which is in Asia Minor, he passed his life during the long period at which the Roman Empire was at the height of its power. If, in his medical philosophy, he stressed balance, order, sobriety, and nuanced judgment, this might perhaps reflect the unusual circumstances in which he lived.

Galen was an able pharmacologist and a canny diagnostician. And he was superbly educated in the classics, philosophy, and logic, a master of the Greek rhetorical style, a finely finished man. Chinese mandarins, with their exquisite manners and refined sensibility, are his next of kin.

Living systems are unusual, Galen taught, in one important respect. Like things made of stone or metal, they may be analyzed in terms of their constituents. The dissection into constituents proceeds downward, the organism revealing itself to be made up of or composed of various organs, muscles, bones, and fluids, and these in turn may be dissected to the level of various *tissues*. It is with tissue as a fundamental substance that the analysis must stop.

A metaphysical doctrine, and so a large general claim, now supervenes on this biological insight. Aristotle had taught that things on earth, whether inanimate or animate, were compounded of the four elements: air, water, earth, and fire. These elements are distinguished by contrary pairs of properties: hot and cold, wet and dry. The juxtaposition of these contraries runs up the scale of creation, from the terrestrial dust, which Aristotle shook from his sandaled feet, to the planets themselves. The malefic Saturn and the war-like Mars are both dry, but Saturn is cold and Mars hot.

Like ordinary material objects, living creatures are composed of fire and air, earth and water. They are, after all, material objects and so a part of the grand tapestry of creation. But if human beings are alike in their constituents, they are different in the way those constituents are blended. In some men, fire predominates; in others, it is air, water, or earth. The precise composition of the elements determines a man's *complexion*, and this is fixed by the stars at the moment of his birth. With the complexions organized systematically in terms of contrary qualities, the result is the doctrine of the four humours. A man in whom cold, dry humour predominates is melancholic; cold, wet humour gives rise to men who are plodding and phlegmatic; hot, wet humour produces men who are sanguine; and choleric men are formed by their hot, dry humour.

The humours are further identified in Galen's system with four bodily fluids: black bile, phlegm, blood, and yellow bile. It is precisely the role of the humours to nourish the various tissues of the body. When they are not properly balanced, disease is the result.

This is not a crude doctrine. It rests on a sympathetic appreciation for the anomalous status of living tissue in a world of matter; and it accounts for the fact that health and disease lie along a continuum from excellent health to morbid infirmity. Modern medicine has tended to treat disease as a discrete state caused by an invasion of the organism by some foreign entity, or a specific lesion or growth, or a catastrophic accident, and so it has been unable to explain satisfactorily why a man might feel unwell when he is not ill.

♏

THE DOCTRINE OF the humours, passed down from Galen's hand, allowed the masters of the medical faculty at Paris to unify their inferences, drawing a seamless connection from the planetary conjunction of 1345 to the outbreak of disease three years later. Disease, Galen had taught, was primarily hydrodynamic, the humours fluid-*like* and, as such, needing to be balanced as water might be balanced by an adjustment in a lock. But the humours were located within the human body and there, concentrated in the liver or the gall bladder, they should presumably be in balance quite on their own. And yet disease and so *im*balance was common. Causes must be sought, and given the barrier of the human skin, those causes could only evoke their effects by being taken *into* the body. Food and drink thus played a crucial role in Galenic medicine. A man might eat and drink himself into disease, a doctrine known to have currency even today, but by far the most important element influencing the balance of the four humours was the air itself. "Although major pestilential illnesses may be caused by the corruption of water or food," the Paris masters wrote, "yet we still regard illnesses proceeding from the corruption of the air as much more dangerous. This is because bad air is more noxious than food or drink in that it can penetrate quickly to the heart and lungs to do damage."

With this observation, the connection between astrological and medical matters emerges. The stars had had an influence on the air, raising foul vapors from the ground; the air had had an influence on public health, corrupting the humours by changing their balance. This hypothesis served various scientific ends. It explained *how* the plague spread and *why* it spread so quickly. Nothing in the fourteenth century moved faster than the air, and so only the air could account for the plague's monstrously rapid dissemination. And it explained how the ominous distribution of the planets could come to have such a devastating effect on human health. The causal chain, the masters at Paris might have said, was too elegant and too obvious to be false.

We believe the present epidemic or plague has arisen from air corrupt in its substance, and not changed in its attributes. By which we wish it to be understood that air, being pure and clear by nature [i.e. in the sense that it is one of the four elements], can only become putrid or corrupt by being mixed with something else, that is to say, with evil vapours.

What happened was that the many vapours which had been corrupted at the time of the conjunction were drawn up from the earth and water, and were then mixed with the air and spread abroad by frequent gusts of wind in the wild southerly gales, and because of these alien vapours which they carried the winds corrupted the air in its substance, and are still doing so. And this corrupted air, when breathed in, necessarily penetrates to the heart and corrupts the substance of the spirit there and rots the surrounding moisture, and the heat thus caused destroys the life force and this is the immediate cause of the present epidemic.

In the three thousand years before the fourteenth century A.D., astrology had flourished and it had lain fallow. With these words, it reached its supreme moment. The astrologers had done what they had been asked to do. In confronting an unprecedented human catastrophe, they had so arranged their art as to resolve, if only briefly, its contradictions. Once the influence of the stars had been accepted as an axiom, every other part of their causal chain obeyed the maxim, so cherished by Albertus Magnus, that there is no action without contact.

Their scientific deliberations complete, the masters remind themselves of the obvious:

> We must not overlook the fact that any pestilence proceeds from the divine will, and our advice therefore can only be to return humbly to God.

♏

FOR MANY YEARS, the explanation offered by the faculty at the University of Paris stood as a textbook example of what one might call scientific superstition—scientific because members of the medical faculty, unlike the clergy, were searching for something like a natural explanation of events, one that eased the mind while confining it within a circle of physical concepts. And a superstition because the germ theory of disease, advanced six centuries later, indicated clearly that the causative organism of

the plague was the bacterium *Yersinia pestis.* The plague is primarily a disease of wild rodents. Its vector of transmission in crossing from the rodent to the human population is the rat-flea
Xenopsylla cheopsis, but once the bacillus has been established in a
given human population, it spreads by human-to-human contact
as well.

The plague originated in central Asia, epidemiologists now
believe, where the local population of rats had for many years
harbored the bacillus without transmitting it to human hosts.
The long-standing ecological balance was then upset. Islamic
scholars mention famine, floods, and earthquakes. The disease
managed to leap between species, and thereafter men with poi-
soned blood traveled to infect the cities of the west. The fleas
carried their infected blood to other human victims, either regur-
gitating blood into the new victims before beginning to feed, or
depositing their plague-loaded feces near a scab, a cut, or a blis-
ter. In this way the first step in a fatal transmission route was
taken.

But the epidemic that struck medieval Europe was more
than just an outbreak of the bubonic plague. The disease, it
turned out, did not require the rat-flea as a vector of transmission; it did not require a vector of transmission at all. In certain
of the plague's victims the focal point of infection proved to
be the lungs and *not* the lymphatic system. The lungs are wet
and they are rich in mucus, and so ideal places in which a bacillus might breed. Those infected with *pneumonic* plague were
both the source and the vector of its transmission. Coughing
wretchedly after infection in a doomed effort to clear their own
lungs of blood, they would spray the bacillus into the air,
promptly infecting those attempting to relieve them, the contents of their coughed-out lungs adhering to their clothing and
so infecting those who, after their death, were forced to dispose
of their effects.

In a number of respects, the modern epidemiological view is consistent with the assessment offered by the masters of Paris. The cause of the disease was some sort of dislocation. The masters assigned the dislocation to the planetary conjunction of 1345, modern researchers to some ecological disturbance in central Asia. Flooding, famine, and earthquake are possible sources. These are precisely the consequences of the planetary conjunction predicted on astrological grounds, and virtually every astrological authority makes the point quite specifically.

The astrologers imagined that the effects of the planetary conjunction would be to pollute the air by releasing foul vapors from the bowels of the earth. Their imagination did not extend to rodents and their fleas, if only because they could not observe the bacillus that they carried. But they had quite grasped the fact that, considering the magnitude of the disaster, the vector of transmission would have to be fast moving and wide ranging. They erred only in assigning that vector to the circulating air. It was an honest mistake.

In the end, neither the views of the masters of Paris nor the views of modern epidemiologists are entirely satisfactory. There is much about the plague of 1348 that remains mysterious.

The idea that the Black Death represented an outbreak of *bubonic* plague is hardly a model of consistency. For one thing, the disease spread throughout Europe at a speed far in excess of known rates of transmission by rats or fleas. Rats are not in any case migratory animals, and it is simply not clear why pockets of infection, if they were indeed restricted to rodent hosts in various cities, should suddenly spread to far-distant cities, when distance is measured by the inclination and ability of an ordinary rat. Scurry? Yes, these creatures could scurry. And perhaps even saunter defiantly, as anyone who has observed a rat well knows. But they could not cover long distances.

For another thing, death rates did not seem to vary with the seasons. But both fleas and rats are seasonal creatures, cold ordinarily killing fleas and sending rats into isolation. The pneumonic plague may have conveyed the bacillus from one person to another during winter months, but then epidemic rates should have changed dramatically with the coming of spring. They did not.

And finally, modern bubonic plague, although contagious, is nowhere near as contagious as the Black Death, the disease very often guttering out after a few isolated cases have been reported, as in the American Southwest. And by the same token, modern bubonic plague, although virulent, is nowhere near as virulent as the medieval plague, mortality rates in modern societies roughly half the reported mortality rates in fourteenth-century Europe. While symptoms reported by medieval physicians are similar to symptoms reported by Indian physicians treating known cases of bubonic plague, there are differences as well. The plague has a very predictable course; the Black Death did not. Men could die within hours of exposure, or after weeks; and occasionally they could recover from one episode of the disease only to succumb to another. And there is the odd, poignant fact that the medieval plague spread as rapidly among domestic animals, especially dogs and cats, as among men. Andronikous Palealogous, a librarian at Constantinople and the author of a fourteenth-century chronicle of the plague, reported that birds were dying in large numbers, the image of a flock of birds wheeling in the sky and then falling stricken to the ground remarkable in its bleakness. Neither dogs nor cats nor birds are particularly vulnerable to modern bubonic plague. They should not have succumbed in the fourteenth century.

No contemporary epidemiological account ever explains with any plausibility the feature of the medieval plague that seemed most striking to contemporary chroniclers: that it was initiated by some vast disturbance of the atmosphere and conveyed by corrupt, indeed, foul, air. Louis Heyligen, a musician at the papal court in Avignon, writes that the plague was spread by "the stinking breath of the wind."

What none of these conjectures begin to address is the very question that tortured the best minds at the University of Paris. Whatever its proximate causes, why did the Black Death strike when it did and with the force that it had?

And to this question, in an age when the entire sequence of the human genome is known, we have collectively no better answer than the one offered by the faculty of medicine at the University of Paris.

♏

THE BLACK DEATH darkened the human heart. In Petrarch, the affliction found a poet of elegiac power. In letters to his friend Louis Heyligen in 1349, Petrarch found the tone appropriate to the events:

> What are we to do now brother? Now that we have lost almost everything and found no rest. . . . Time as they say has slipped through our fingers. Our former hopes lie buried with our friends.

And in a second letter:

> Where are our dear friends now? Where are the beloved faces? Where are the affectionate words, the relaxed and enjoyable conversations? What lightning bolt devoured them? What earthquake toppled them? What tempest drowned them? What abyss swallowed them? There was a crowd of us, now we are almost alone. . . .

The great love of Petrarch's life was a young woman named Laura, and through Petrarch's art, she has become one of the sublime romantic figures in western history, running through the lilac fields at Vaucluse, her golden hair streaming behind her and her lithe twelve-year-old body ravished by the wind. She is never mentioned in Petrarch's letters to Louis Heyligen, but she, too, died in the catastrophe unfolding all around them.

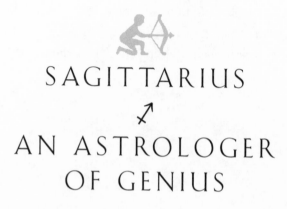

CHAPTER NINE

SAGITTARIUS

♐

AN ASTROLOGER
OF GENIUS

D INNERS AT THE Benatky Castle must have been an ordeal. They began late and they lasted a very long time. There were typically a dozen or so men in attendance, and on some evenings twice that many: astronomers and astrologers, of course, clerks, scribes, instrument makers, mathematicians, merchants, weedy *gräfin* with a touch of the diseased Danube in their veins, and members of the emperor's entourage, there to pay their respects or pass along gossip. Dogs wandered in and out of the echoing, candlelit hall, fighting over scraps, their indignant growls giving way every now and again to high-pitched yelps as they were kicked away from the table. No forks, still widely regarded as an effeminate Italian contrivance. Men ate with their knives, slicing slabs of meat and then spearing them. Bad wine in pitchers, questionable water in jugs, and good sound Bohemian beer in tankards. A huge roaring fire making the near side of the company drowsy while keeping the far side chilly. Shivers up and down various spines. And outside, the snow piling up on the exterior stone windowsills and sifting through the cracks between the mullions and the heavy flowing glass, the wind moaning. Benatky Castle is in the open country, twenty-two miles outside of Prague, and the central European winters are hard and dark.

The Imperial Mathematician Tycho Brahe sat at the head of the great table. A man of medium height, with narrow shoulders, a notable paunch, and short legs, he was nonetheless an imposing figure. Born into the Danish aristocracy, his easy self-assurance showed in the way he carried himself, and in the way he talked, and in the way he expected the table's conversation to flow unfailingly toward him. He had wonderful manners, the gift of putting other men at ease, but the manners did not conceal his self-assurance, and so they carried a subtle suggestion of menace. He was a better man than the men he fed, and, knowing this, the men he fed were eager for his approval. A duel in his youth had sliced away a portion of his nose, which he covered with a metal shield, and the shield, by hiding his face, uncovered his personality.

Born on December 14, 1546, Brahe was educated at the University of Copenhagen, and then sent wandering throughout Germany by his indulgent parents. Universities at Leipzig and Wittenburg applied an invaluable central European polish to the patina of his Danish education. He was passionately interested in the stars. As a young man, he had already done important observational work, coolly calling the appearance of a supernova to the attention of an astronomical community persuaded on Aristotelian grounds that nothing new could arise in a perfect universe. He was at ease in learned circles, lecturing in Latin and mingling with philosophers, mathematicians, and theologians. Throughout his young manhood, he managed to secure the allegiance of the aristocratic class to which by birth he belonged while remaining indifferent to its traditional pursuits of hunting, fornication, and political intrigue.

In 1574, King Frederick II of Denmark presented the island of Hven to Tycho Brahe as a gift. The island is on the Sont, the narrow body of water that flows past Copenhagen from the Baltic Sea. Brahe at once began construction of his own astronomical observatory. He had been profoundly influenced by Nicolas Copernicus; he became a Copernican, one of a small group of men who sensed the full intellectual power that would be required to displace the earth from the center of the universe. The Castle Uraniborg that had long stood on Hven was gutted. Rising four or more stories into the frigid night sky, Uraniborg had resembled Brueghel's tower of Babel in the way it conveyed mass while suggesting incoherence. Now it was transformed. It helped immeasurably, of course, that Brahe was well off. He could conduct his research as he wished and so he could think as he pleased. Brahe filled the place with exquisite astronomical instruments of his own design: sextants, astrolabes, and devices for plotting solar angles by means of solar shadows. He supervised everything, sending his own detailed drawings to various European smiths, nagging them and supervising their work. He was a remarkably effective pest. Brahe taught a generation of astronomers how to observe the night sky, how to record their observations, and how to keep careful accounts of their experiments, and such was the immense force of his personality that he succeeded in creating on that remote island, which was, after all, cold, dark, and wet, a glorious scientific enterprise. Perched there on the open waters of the Sont, the island became well known, and then it became famous, acquiring in cultivated circles a reputation for enchantment, its garden emptying into a menagerie through which elegant young men dressed in red silk hose and suede boots would wander.

What things they saw, as the old, worn, weary stars proceeded across the sky.

At roughly the same historical moment that Brahe's observatory was rising, Turkish naval forces were busy shelling into smithereens the Moslem Royal Astronomical Observatory at Istanbul. The story is told in a Persian manuscript, the *Shaninshahnama*. Written in verse by the poet Ala al Din al Mansur, the *Shaninshahnama* chronicles the reign of Sultan Murad III, the ruler of the Ottoman Turks from 1574 to 1595. The poem itself, Mansur solemnly notes, was completed on October 28, 1581, the last day of Ramadan.

The story that it tells is as blunt as a blow. Summoned to the sultan's presence, the director of the Royal Observatory, Taqi al-Din, is asked to explain its purpose. He responds in the way scientists always respond. The Royal Observatory exists to advance knowledge.

And at once, history is broken in two. With neither an explanation nor an excuse, the sultan demands that his admiral promptly "wreck the observatory, and pull it down from apogee to perigee." Taqi al-Din's reaction, al Mansur neglects delicately to record. "Nothing remains of the observatory," he writes, "but a name and a memory."

The wheel of time had come full circle.

In 1592, Tycho Brahe quit Uraniborg after an incomprehensible quarrel with his patron, King Christian IV of Denmark. Ever resourceful, Brahe struck a deal with the dreamy, pathologically shy Bohemian emperor, Rudolf II, and with his usual decisiveness moved his instruments, research documents, and entourage from the island of Hven to the Benatky Castle outside Prague. The emperor, mindful of Brahe's genius, and, as ever, careless of his own purse, promoted him to the position of imperial mathematician, his salary a princely 30,000 gilders a year. Tycho Brahe had been in command on Hven; he would be in command in Prague.

———

A Turkish scholar's guide to astronomy, composed just years before the great Moslem observatory in Istanbul was reduced to smithereens at the instigation of Moslem theologians.
(*courtesy of the Bibliothèque Nationale de France*)

JOHANNES KEPLER had come to Benatky Castle at Brahe's invitation in January of 1600. A few years before he had sent Brahe a copy of his book, the *Mysterium Cosmographicum* (Mystery of the Universe). Just twenty-eight, his career as a provincial teacher of mathematics in the Austrian village of Graz had been brought to a close by the cold Catholic waters of the Counter-Reformation. His life had not been in danger, but civil authorities had demanded that he publicly renounce the Augsburg Confession, the doctrine that defined his Lutheran faith, and he had refused. Now he was seeking employment as a mathematician. Virtually penniless, he carried the double burden of late marriage and early fatherhood on his back. Word of his remarkable intellectual powers had preceded him, however, and Tycho Brahe, with all the generosity of a nature that could afford a careless gesture, welcomed him to the castle. He saw in the young man a feel for the far away. Kepler could be put to work. Astronomy was young. There was dog work enough to keep a hundred mathematicians busy.

Johannes Kepler had imagined himself as Tycho Brahe's close collaborator, the two of them working intimately and working as equals. His dismayed discovery that at the Benatky Castle he was instead one man among many clamoring for Brahe's attention did nothing to ease his sense that a world prepared to use his genius should take better pains to recognize it.

♐

JOHANNES KEPLER was born January 6, 1572, in the free Swabian village of Weil-der-Stadt, which borders the Black Forest. It is even today a charming place, the village mummified in a comfy late-medieval winding sheet of gables, gabble, and geese; the countryside beyond is dotted with small, neat farms where farmers tramp about in knee-length *lederhosen* and hay is piled on gated horse-drawn wagons, the great somber beasts standing placidly in the golden fields. Beyond the farms there is the smooth, green, polished expanse of the *Schwartzwald,* a marvelously manicured old-growth forest of copper beech, European oak, and ash, enchanted but not dangerous, except for the occasional wild boar, a delicacy in the local *stuberl,* where it is served with black currant jam.

Kepler had been born into a family with no aristocratic connections, his grandfathers craftsmen and furriers, men who could turn a lathe or trim a lynx. His father, Heinrich, who had by profession been involved in estate management, was by inclination a vagabond, and by turns a soldier, a freebooter, and a thug. "Criminally inclined, quarrelsome, liable to a bad end," Kepler had observed in casting his horoscope, and faithful to his astrological inclination, *treue* Heinrich several times left his family to join various military campaigns. One day in 1588 he signed on with a group of Belgian mercenaries and never returned. His mother, as one might imagine, was left a difficult, disappointed woman.

His family pinched financially, Kepler made his way through a clerical school system in which students with nothing to say were taught to say it in Latin. He compiled a flawless academic record, his intelligence flowing like spring water from some hidden but natural source. He was fractious with other students, the rich stuttering bubbles of his speech the natural overflow of a mind too excited by itself to keep still or stop fidgeting. At the same time, Kepler was by nature willing to please his teachers and eager to avoid controversy. "I like to be on the side of the majority," he remarked as an adult, expressing a sentiment that is as commonly felt as it is rarely admitted. Kepler is eternally endearing just because he embodies so perfectly a classical figure and so recognizable a type, the earnest and intelligent, but boastful and insecure boy we all knew.

Or were.

There followed a sound university education in the classics at Tübingen, and employment in the Austrian city of Graz, where he served as an instructor in mathematics at the *stifsschule*, the local high school, and as the district's mathematician and calendar maker. He was expected to issue astrological forecasts with his calendars, and when he correctly predicted a winter of uncommon severity, peasant uprisings, *and* the invasion of Austria by the Turks, his reputation was secured. For the rest of his life, and especially during financially difficult times, he maintained a sideline in practical astrology, composing all in all more than eight hundred horoscopes. When skeptics challenged Kepler's willingness to crank out the charts, he replied with disarming frankness that, all things considered, it was easier than work and superior to begging, words that even today cannot fail to inspire.

Johannes Kepler was small, and somewhat slight; portraits depict a sensitive face, with thick, wavy hair passing backward from a high forehead, and draping itself languorously over his ears. He wears the obligatory expression of sadness in his eyes, which are focused thoughtfully at the far distance, suggesting the preoccupations of a man eternally concerned to keep his wife at peace and his creditors at bay. Although he suffered a variety of ailments, most notably mysterious fevers, some lasting for months without relief, and a spastic stomach, he had the sort of toughness that is very often characteristic of small, wiry men; and when his complaints are matched against the record of his travels throughout central Europe, an admirably stoical character emerges. He was tough. Throughout his life, he maintained "a dog-like aversion to bathing," and I mention this curious point to draw a sympathetic connection between Kepler and Ptolemy, the two greatest astronomers of the western world spiritually united by their indifference to personal hygiene.

From the first moment of intellectual self-awareness, Kepler defined himself as a mathematician, and among mathematicians, as a rhapsodist. He was indifferently disposed toward numbers, although necessity forced him to become a superb calculator; geometry had seized his soul and he very early came to the conclusion that "geometry is one and eternal, a reflection out of the mind of God."

♐

AS THE SIXTEENTH century broke over Europe, the celestial sphere still circumnavigated the earth. Ptolemaic astronomy and Aristotelian cosmology were taught in every European university, and this by men who must have felt oppressed by its venerability, the more so since every attempt to evade its conclusions seemed to end in observational inadequacy. The Ptolemaic system had itself been endlessly and ingeniously refined by local adjustments, small contrivances in its various eccentricities and epicycles. It

was now of very considerable accuracy, its predictions widely verified and its intuitive appeal so obvious as to seem indubitable.
For all that, the system seemed overly ornate, even baroque in the
years before the baroque became a style. An armillary sphere constructed by the great Flemish artisan Gualterus Arsenius in 1568
shows why. It is a model of the solar system, one made of inter-
locking brass and polished copper rings. The burnished ball
of the sun lies hidden in its interior; thick metal loops crisscross
the sphere's six concentric shells, each hinged and ratcheted to
enable the astronomer to mimic the movement of the planets by
waggling its rings. Although beautifully made, the sphere fails to
achieve an appropriate artistic effect. It is simply too complex. In
this it resembles the Standard Model of particle physics.

Alone among the astronomers of Europe, Nicolas Copernicus had argued that the sun and not the earth stood at the center
of the solar system. He had seen that the complexity of the Ptolemaic system was ineradicable and that in the end it would re-
semble a map as large as the country it was meant to describe. A
few perceptive mathematicians and astronomers had grasped the
percussive implications of Copernicus' work; but his thesis was
framed in the same odd evasive terms that Ptolemy employed in
the *Almagest.* The great turning spheres of Ptolemaic astronomy
were in some sense mathematical fictions. They were meant to
explain what astronomers could see. Their ontological status—
were the damn things really real and so really there?—was un-
clear. In a phrase that has forever infected his reputation, Ptolemy
argued that the elaborate machinery of the *Almagest* was intended
only "to save appearances." Copernicus had taken Ptolemy at his
word, creating over the course of hundreds of densely reasoned
pages a mathematical fiction to rival Ptolemy's own, the sun placed
at the very center of the universe, the planets turning around the
sun in neat, perfectly linked circles. But they were not really *real,*

those neat circular orbits, and not really *there*. In matching *his* fictions against the masters', Copernicus had concluded only that his worked better. They were more refined, their agreement with observation more extensive, his account of the heavens simpler.

This synopsis hardly suggests the imaginative difficulties of the work that Copernicus had undertaken. Facsimile copies of his handwritten text may be found in the Bibliothèque Nationale in Paris. The handwriting is firm, small, and elegant, slanting downward and to the right, and it is easy enough to read. Great care has been taken to present the text artistically. Copernicus arranged his large diagrams of the solar system so that the text flowed gracefully around them, text and diagrams forming a miniature heliocentric system of their own. Even so, there are ink blots here and there on the page. They do not suggest haste so much as weariness, Copernicus shaking his cramped hands and stiffened fingers, and as a result splattering ink on the page. This is plainly a work that has eaten up a man's life. The effort required a profound act of self-destruction. Ptolemaic astronomy had been so well-entrenched in the consciousness of astronomers as to seem less an artful theory than an inescapable fact. There it was—the celestial sphere revolved around the earth. Just *look*. Copernicus had forced himself to look and then to cancel what he thought he saw, and in this, he cancelled a layer of his own convictions. For many years, everything was hopelessly confused, strange, odd, singular. He had seen the truth emerge in small, painful stages, but he had not seen the whole of the truth, never once realizing that planetary orbits might not be circular but elliptical. In January of 1543, Copernicus lay on his sick bed, a stroke having destroyed a part of his brain. He had run a long race, but for the most part, he had run the race alone. He took his breaths in long, slow, wet, ragged gasps, a bubble of pale phlegm forming on his lips. Doctors placed the first printed edition of his masterpiece,

On the Revolution of the Heavenly Spheres, in his hands. He stroked the book's burgundy leather cover, grunted, and then died.

⚹

IDEAS IN THE twenty-first century travel at the speed of light, one reason, perhaps, that they often seem to have so little mass; in the second half of the sixteenth century, ideas traveled more slowly, drawn by leisurely hansoms, carried in coaches over rutted roads, or passed from one man to another over elegant meals, so that even austere physical theories found themselves embedded in a slow swirl of gossip. After his death, Copernicus' theories made their way to a few ears that had been receptively cupped. There were not many. Some sixty years later, his wonderfully illiterate informant having drawn his attention to this "Ipernic, or whatever his name is," Cardinal Robert Bellarmine could still regard the Copernican revolution as a *new* threat to Catholic dogma, taking the occasion of its triumph among the best minds of Europe to observe that it had still not proved persuasive among the worst.

Like Tycho Brahe, Johannes Kepler had heard the gossip and then acquired belief. The earth was in revolution around the sun. He had been exposed to the new astronomical theories as a young man, well before his resistance might have been stiffened by habit or his enthusiasm compromised by indolence. Tycho Brahe had embraced Copernicus with gusto, but not with all his heart. He found himself unable to let go completely of the doctrine that the earth was at the center of the universe. He had lingered too long in all the old Ptolemaic corridors of power. Attempting to preserve something of the Ptolemaic scheme in his own theory, he placed the sun at the center of the solar system, as Copernicus had demanded, but the solar system in an odd revolution around the earth. Sixteenth-century illustrations depict an unwieldy celestial contraption, with Tycho Brahe beaming beneath the universe, his drooping white moustaches and merry eyes lending him the air of an improbably amused Chinese mandarin. Kepler's enthusiasm for a heliocentric system was neither corrupted by doubt nor troubled by regret. He took Copernicus at his word. The sun stood at the center of the universe. It *really* did. The planets were in revolution around the sun. They *really* were.

If Kepler found in Copernicus a radical, sharp, clear, clean new system, it was a system yet raw in places, the details unfinished and even some of the architectural principles left in obscurity. The earth had been displaced from the center of the solar system. Questions never before asked now demanded a voice. They hammered insistently. Like Einstein dismissing the universal ether, Copernicus had allowed the celestial sphere to disappear. In a flash, it was gone, leaving the world without its struts. But if the planets were in revolution around the sun, the earth revolving on its own axis, and revolving moreover in empty space, then just why should the *distances* between planetary orbits have the numerical value that they did? Why, for that matter, should there be just six planets, as Kepler believed, and not ten or twenty-seven? And what impelled the planets to keep going indefatigably in their revolution? Before Kepler, it was not possible to ask such questions, and after Kepler, not possible to evade them.

It was not observations that were lacking, but theory. Observational astronomers in the sixteenth century had already determined the distance between planetary orbits, Tycho Brahe and his assistants compiling a matchless series of numbers, dates, and times marching up and down unlined foolscap, the stiff pages piling up on splintery boards in observatory rooms overlooking the sea. But no observations, Kepler understood, could explain the *why* behind these numbers.

The series of inferences that Kepler invoked in the *Mysterium Cosmographicum* to answer these questions is anything but obvious, and it is difficult even today to grasp the pattern of tension and relief that Kepler was plainly struggling to control and then express. "Almost a whole summer was lost in agonizing labor," he writes.

> At last on a quite trifling occasion, I came nearer the truth.
> I believe that Divine Providence intervened so that by
> chance I found what I could never obtain by my own ef-
> forts. I believe this all the more because I have constantly
> prayed to God that I might succeed if what Copernicus said
> was true. Thus it happened [on] July 19th, 1595, as I was
> showing in my class how the great conjunction [of Saturn
> and Jupiter] occurs successively eight Zodiacal signs later,
> and how they gradually pass from one trine to another, that
> I inscribed within a circle many triangles, or quasi-triangles,
> such that the end of one was the beginning of the next. In
> this manner a smaller circle was outlined by the points
> where the lines of the triangle crossed each other.

What Kepler *did*, evidently while doodling, was inscribe a series of triangles on the interior of a circle, one that in this case represented the zodiac. What he *saw* was something else, a second
circle emerging, its circumference determined by those points
marking the intersection of adjacent triangles, base points just
touching base points.

The inferential link connecting this example to the solar system Kepler traversed in a single ecstatic experience. He is teaching a high school class; he is facing the blackboard, his precise
hands holding the chalk, and there are the snoring donkeys behind him, dutifully copying his lucid diagrams into their copy
books. Quite suddenly there is an immense intellectual gush.
"And then it struck me," and "in memory of the event, I am writing down for you the sentence in the words from the moment of
conception," he writes.

> The earth's orbit is the measure of all things; circumscribe
> around it a dodecahedron and the circle containing this will

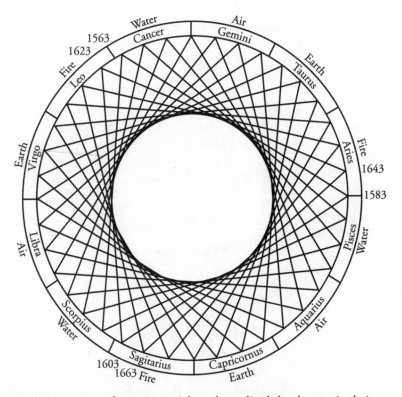

Kepler's moment of supreme insight as he realized that by manipulating the Platonic forms he could go on to create precise geometrical relationships between two circles that represented planetary orbits.

be Mars; circumscribe around Mars a tetrahedron, and the circle containing this will be Jupiter; circumscribe around Jupiter a cube, and the circle containing this will be Saturn. Now inscribe within the earth [i.e. the earth's orbit] an icosahedron, and the circle contained within it will be Venus; inscribe within Venus an octahedron, and the circle contained within it will be Mercury.

The shapes that Kepler cites in this quotation are the regular Platonic solids. In Euclidean geometry, there are just five such solids. But there are also *six* planets, Kepler notes, and *thus* a relationship between Platonic solids and planetary orbits. If the

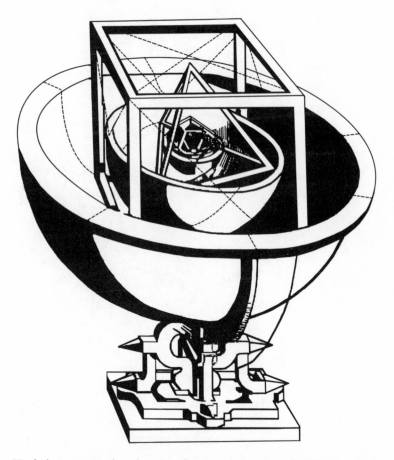

Kepler's geometrical explanation for the relationship of planetary orbits.
Kepler accepted the earth as the fundamental unit of his system, its
relationship to its own Platonic solid unexplained. The rest of his system
then follows. Kepler did not assume that the Platonic solids occupy
regions of space between the planets. They have no independent physical
existence. They are artifacts of explanation. Kepler evidently had
ambitious plans to construct a mechanical model of his system and fill
the various solids with punches of different colors.

earth's orbit *is* accepted as the measure of all things—its fundamental *unit*—then the ratio of the remaining planetary orbits
may be *completely* determined by Kepler's construction.

"You now have the reason," Kepler concludes, "for the number of planets."

He was mad with excitement; he was just twenty-three.

♐

JOHANNES KEPLER had come to the Benatky Castle hoping that Tycho Brahe would open the treasure chest of his astronomical observations, collected patiently over the course of twenty-five years. He knew that only meticulous, comprehensive, and accurate observations could enable him to verify his theories. He was at once disappointed. Brahe dribbled out information at his dinners, tantalizing with hints, but divulging few details. He proposed that Kepler occupy himself with a problem of his own devising, telling the young man to get busy with the orbit of Mars. It was not by any means a trivial problem. Whenever seen, Mars is seen at a moment and it is seen only for a moment, the popular impression that planetary orbits simply display themselves largely derived from slow-motion photography. Brahe's observations marked a series of discrete point in the sky. The geometrical shape connecting these bright data points remained hidden behind the veil of ignorance. While the problem that Brahe had set Kepler was challenging, it was the fact that the problem had been *set* that Kepler found galling.

Looking over the men assembled at the long table, Tycho Brahe must have observed, as the candlelight winked from the metal plate covering his nose, that all that he saw and all that he had amassed, these treasures, were his creation. He was the force that had made them possible, and if he did not choose freely to share what he had learned with the entire world, who could blame him?

He owned the night sky.

And now this *odd*, remarkably *persistent* little man—Johannes Kepler—was sitting at *his* dinner table, eating *his* food and drinking *his* wine, and, far from being either awed or appreciative, he seemed determined chiefly to insist on the one fact that Tycho Brahe had already generously acknowledged, namely, that he was a man of genius.

It was inevitable, of course, that the men would quarrel. Ever mindful of his difficult position, Kepler had attempted to place his life on a secure financial basis. A letter was composed and, as always happens, shown to men who could not be trusted to guard its confidences. Intrigues multiplied. Demands were made injudiciously. Kepler asked Brahe to provide his family with so many bushels of wheat, so much by way of bread, cheese, eggs, butter, sausages, wine, beer, and lard. And would he be permitted to work as he saw fit, indeed, as he pleased, with *no* vexing schedules to meet? He did not care to rise early or retire late. Dinners at the castle? He thought not. And for that matter he would not care overmuch to work *with* Tycho Brahe if that meant living *near* him. And could these matters be put in *writing* and solemnly sealed, Kepler demanded of the discomfited Brahe, adding that he could not *possibly* accept his general assurances that all would be well.

In the course of these negotiations, Kepler, it would seem, lost his temper, wounding Brahe with his impertinence; and then Brahe lost *his* temper in turn, offending Kepler with his hauteur. Both men stomped off in a fine fury, each arguing to friends that the other had behaved badly. Given time for reflection, Brahe came to treat the argument with his habitual generosity. He was able to wipe himself free of resentment. Kepler wrote Brahe a long, weepy, contrition-filled letter. A few months later, the men officially reconciled. *Schnapps* all around. Kepler returned to his work. No further fireworks were reported, but both Brahe and Kepler must have had the uneasy sense that, like two elephants in one cage, their personalities were just a little too large to occupy any kind of intimate space.

Tycho Brahe fell ill in the autumn of 1601, his affliction evidently the result of a bladder infection, one proceeding ignominiously from dining and drinking to discomfort and then disaster. He summoned Kepler to his deathbed and begged him to complete the *Rudolphine Tables* of planetary motions that he had himself accepted as a commission from the emperor, Rudolf II. And would Kepler complete *his* account of the heavens according to *his* astronomical scheme—the sun at rest, the planets somehow conspiring to retain at least some of their ancient Ptolemaic movements?

Tycho Brahe died on October 24, 1601. The observatory at Uraniborg had been emptied of the last of its treasures.

Johannes Kepler was promoted to the post of imperial mathematician days later.

♐

JOHANNES KEPLER has entered history as a great observational and theoretical astronomer; he was as well an outstanding mathematician and, as any number of astrologers now remind me, a capable astrologer, a practitioner of the art. The geometrical objects that Kepler introduced for astronomical purposes in the *Mysterium Cosmographicum* thus served astrological purposes as well, an interesting example of the virtues, and dangers, of intellectual thrift. In Kepler's scheme, each planet except the earth is assigned a solid as its tag:

Saturn—Cube
Jupiter—Tetrahedron
Mars—Dodecahedron
Venus—Icosahedron
Mercury—Octahedron

Astrological consequences now follow in the way they have traditionally followed astrological premises, that is, largely by confabulation. "In the case of Jupiter first, of Saturn next, and lastly of

Mercury," Kepler writes, "their calm and the steadiness of their character are the result of the fewness of their faces." With Venus and Mars, it is the other way around, the many faces of their associated solids giving rise to their "changeability and turbulence." Since women are "always fickle and capricious," it stands to reason that Venus is the most capricious and variable of all the planets. Just consider the number of her faces! The conclusion of this argument, representing a poetical intelligence in the process of mathematical free association, will seem to many somewhat arbitrary.

Nevertheless, the strange conclusions multiply. Are Jupiter, Venus, and Mercury represented by solids with triangular faces? They are. This is the reason, Kepler affirms, for their friendship. Their friendship as *planets*. Why those triangular faces should signify friendship among planets and not undying enmity, Kepler does not say. Nor, for that matter, does he indicate why friendship among planets should signify amity among men.

His treatment of Saturn and Mercury, which are busy sharing various squares, proceeds from the same psychological space in which anything goes because anything may be said. And then there is Saturn, a lonely, singular, solitary planet, one deriving its character from the stringency of the right angles making up a cube. Jupiter, by way of contrast, is altogether more congenial. No wonder. The angles in a tetrahedron are all acute. Friendship is assured.

IN A NUMBER OF tracts written during and after his stay in Prague, Kepler organized his mature reflections on astrology in the form of polemics conducted against two helpful stooges, a Dr. Philip Feselius and a Dr. Heliseus Röslinus. Feselius was an opponent of astrology, an opponent, indeed, of Copernicus, and his criticisms, turning on the concept of action at a distance, are interesting in that they concentrate a sense of unease that has always been a part of the astrological tradition. Astrology's chief claim is false, Dr. Feselius had argued, because there is no physical medium between the stars and the earth.

Dr. Röslinus, on the other hand, was passionately committed to astrology. Like Feselius, he rejected the Copernican solar system, perhaps from an obscure sense that if the earth were no longer the center of the solar system, astrology would become impossible. This is a spectacular example of a scientific inference exploding indecorously in precisely the wrong place. Kepler answered Röslinus in a polemic entitled *Antwort auff Röslini Discurs* (The Answer to Röslinus' Discourse). There is a note of measured skepticism throughout. "That the heavens do something in people," he writes, "one sees clearly enough." And there follows the profound reservation: "But what it does specifically remains hidden."

Kepler the Skeptic is in short order followed by Kepler the More Measured. In a pamphlet entitled *Tertius Interveniens,* for which the phrase "man in the middle" might be a colloquial translation, Kepler addresses a warning to certain theologians, physicians, and philosophers, and especially to Dr. Feselius, that by precipitously denouncing the astrologer's superstitions, "they do not end up throwing the baby out with the bath water." These words have provided comfort to astrologers ever since.

Kepler's defense of astrology begins with a sharp dismissal of a great many ancient astrological doctrines. The zodiac is the first to go, and then the ecliptic, and with it the system of houses. Kepler does not make the argument explicitly, but he does suggest that if Copernican theory is true, both the zodiac and the houses must be rejected as artifacts.

But having gone this far toward skepticism, Kepler goes no farther, going backward instead and then re-entering again the warm bath of belief. A man's horoscope is not a trivial document, he insists, and the ascendant is not an irrelevance: It has a special force in shaping human character, and so does the geometrical relationship among the planets at the moment of birth. These are communicated to an individual by means of "rays falling to the earth." Patterns in the sky leave "traces in the formation of the countenance and of the remaining shape of the body." They affect a man's "business affairs [and] his manners and gestures," and these characteristic traces of celestial geometry in turn are imparted to other men. The enormous variety of human types are reflections of "the lovely and exact, or the extensive and ungainly configuration [of various celestial objects], and ... the colors and movement of the planets."

♐

JOHANNES KEPLER had never been completely at home in Prague. There was something in the city's wistful aristocratic beauty that failed properly to satisfy his temperament. His wife, Barbara Müller, a Kepler by virtue of double widowhood, was especially unhappy. Her complaints expanded to fill her time. She disliked the weather, the seasons, the language, and the food. Nonetheless, Prague had been a refuge, and Kepler imagined himself making his peace with the city's dark streets, the winter snow sifting over the steepled churches or falling soundlessly into the Vlatva, the hooded night watchman waving his lamp in a little arc and calling out the hours in Czech. Kepler had work to do. He was after all the *imperial* mathematician.

Misfortune then enveloped him. Tinder for the Thirty Years' War had begun to accumulate in central Europe, each party to the conflict concerned to blow on its freshening twigs in the foolish expectation that others would be discouraged from blowing harder. Soldiers entered Prague, their great, wet tramping boots leaving mud in all the exquisite medieval courtyards. The city became a gathering point not only for diplomats and hard-eyed rascals, but also for devastating microbes that had been piggybacked across Europe by men-at-arms. Kepler's wife fell gravely ill, coughing weakly in the night. His shy, lonely patron, the Emperor Rudolf II, was forced to abdicate his throne in favor of his stepbrother Mattius II. Rudolf II had spent days and weeks in his chambers, refusing to see visitors or diplomats; but if he had ruled without authority, he had also ruled without rancor. Now he was gone.

Kepler's years in Prague were at an end. The evenings at dinner and those nights in which Kepler sat shivering in his unheated chambers, the lavish meals and those Bohemian tankards twisting his tender stomach into knots and the privies a cold exposed walk in the woods away—they were over.

With some difficulty, Kepler managed to secure employment as a provincial mathematician in Linz. He regarded the prospect of a return to his own country with satisfaction, if not for his own sake, then for his wife's. Lonely and afraid, she longed for the warm, burbling sounds of the German language, and the familiar organization of German life. Barbara Müller died in July of 1611. She had been infected by spotted typhus. Darkness overcame Kepler. The occasion of her death prompted him to compose a few lovely Latin lines in her memory: *Sic nunc inanes cernis imagines, Si functus aevo ipisimma lumina Cernes; quid haec amittere horres, O Ocule, et meliora apisci?*

With a courage all the more admirable for being so hard won, Kepler carried on, his greatest work still before his soul's dancing eyes.

♐

THE *HARMONICUM MUNDI* (Harmony of the World) is Johannes Kepler's masterpiece. It is far-reaching in scope and rich in mathematical invention. And it is a work of astrology, the greatest ever written, if only because it is the only work of astrology written by a man of genius.

Kepler's aims in this book are inseparable from his means, and his means are geometrical. In the *Mysterium Cosmographicum,* he had heard a melody rustling throughout the cosmos; he had explained one part of the melody by an appeal to the five regular Platonic solids. In the *Harmonicum Mundi* that melody becomes contrapuntal.

There are two forms of harmony in the universe, Kepler reasoned, one musical, the other spatial. Musical harmonies proceed by means of the division of a straight line into ratios, spatial harmonies by the division of a circle into sections. Musical harmonies yield consonances, spatial harmonies aspects, and, in particular, they yield *astrological* aspects.

Kepler the mathematician now takes over from the other murmurous and exigent Keplers—the physicist, the grieving husband, the suppliant, the astronomer, the mystic, and the astrologer. Kepler regarded the straight line and the circle as his fundamentals, shapes given in nature and so shapes resident in the human soul.

Here are a few necessary definitions, a way to watch a subtle mind at work. A polygon is a plane figure with a certain number of sides—the triangle, three; the square, four; the pentagon, five; and so on to shapes that have thousands of sides. The *regular* polygons are those whose sides are equal in length—equilateral triangles, *yes,* isosceles triangles, *no;* squares, *yes,* rectangles, *no.*

Some regular polygons, Kepler observed, may be constructed by ruler and compass, the classical measure of Euclidean geometry. Such polygons are *knowable,* all others *un*knowable. The knowable polygons, Kepler believed, are pivots of the world order, placed in the plane by God.

If polygons may be classified by what they *are,* they may *also* be classified, Kepler next argued, in terms of what they *do.* The geometrical plane is by itself completely lacking in pattern. It has length and breadth but no interior detail. But given an endless supply of squares, the mathematical decorator may cover the mathematical plane completely simply by placing one square next to the other. No part of the plane need be left exposed. With the squares in place, the result is a *tessellation* of the plane. The pentagon, by way of contrast, cannot tesselate the plane. No matter how its five sides are adjusted, some part of the plane will always peek through.

It is this circumstance that suggested to Kepler a second scheme of classification, and so a second division of the regular polygons. Those polygons that could be slotted together to form plane tessellations, Kepler called *sociable;* the rest are *un*sociable. Only three regular polygons are sociable with themselves or *self*-sociable, to coin a phrase. They are the equilateral triangle, the square, and the hexagon.

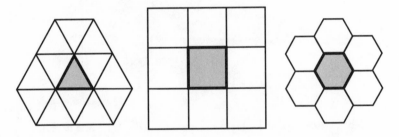

Tessellation of the plane by triangles, squares, and hexagons.

But by the same token, *different* self-sociable polygons may combine with one another to form tessellations of their own—squares with triangles, or hexagons with squares. The result is a *semi-regular* tessellation of the plane.

There is a further level of complexity, but it is the last. It is not only the plane that may be tessellated. The Platonic solids fill up a portion of space and so exist in three dimensions. But each Platonic solid is made up of faces that are themselves regular polygons. What is a cube, after all, but six wandering squares that have met at eight expectant vertices? Solids formed in this way are called uniform polyhedra, and their covering by regular polygons is again a tesselation. The Platonic solids may all be constructed from their respective regular polygons in the square-to-cube fashion. But the tesselated polyhedra go just a little beyond the Platonic solids to include three spectacular star-polyhedra that Kepler discovered. These are again solid shapes whose faces may be completely covered by an arrangement of regular polygons.

Kepler discovered three fabulous star polyhedra. The one depicted is the simplest. The entire polyhedron can be tessellated by regular plane figures—in this case, triangles.

And thus to the crucial concept—*sociability*. A polygon's sociability is a measure of the number of ways it might interact with other regular polygons *either* to tessellate the plane *or* to tessellate a uniform polyhedron.

The definitions have been concluded and Kepler's classification is complete.

ENTER NOW THE astrologers. Aspects have played a role in astrology at least since the time of the Greeks. The zodiac is, after all, a giant circle surrounding the earth, and as two (or more) planets travel the circle on its circumference, the arc between them changes at every moment. Ptolemy introduced five important aspects in the *Tetrabiblos,* corresponding to angles of 0, 60, 90, 120, and 180 degrees. When planets are found in *these* positions, Ptolemy claimed, their influence is very considerable. Having advanced his claims without argument, he expected astrologers to accept his conclusions without demurral. As they, in fact, did.

In the *Harmonicum Mundi,* Kepler brought eight additional aspects into astrological thought. *His* aspects, however, were derived from an underlying geometrical theory, and they arise by means of an argument that, while never quite rational, is also never wholly arbitrary. Both of Kepler's geometrical hierarchies play a role in Kepler's astrological theory.

The zodiac is in place, and two planets, let us imagine, may be found in revolution on its circumference. They are for a moment frozen in their rotation. A straight line is drawn connecting each planet to the pinpoint of the earth lying at the zodiac's center. The astrologer now constructs a third straight line, one directly connecting the two planets, and so forming a chord cutting the zodiac. That chord represents one side of a polygon. To complete the polygon, the astrologer need only to specify its interior angles. It is this that the original angle between planets provides. An inscribed polygon now occupies the interior of the zodiac, an artifact of an astrological inference.

There is in this nothing that would have been alien to traditional astrological thought. Two planets *do* have an angular relationship to one another. The aspects had a sound basis in visual geometry. But inasmuch as there are 360 degrees available for aspects, and so *infinitely* many possible angular relationships between planets, the astrologer, Kepler argued, requires some scheme for distinguishing aspects with the power to affect human beings from all the rest.

It is this that Kepler's scheme of classification provides. An aspect is astrologically powerful, Kepler argued, if it corresponds to an inscribed polygon that is *both* knowable *and* sociable. The sextile is, for example, a classical Ptolemaic aspect. Planets separated by a sextile aspect find themselves at the vertices of an inscribed hexagon, and hexagons are both knowable and sociable. The sextile is thus an astrologically powerful aspect: It commands attention because it controls events.

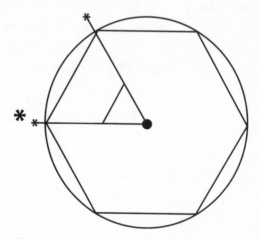

The angular aspects arising from the sextile between planets inscribed, in this case, within a hexagon.

These arguments, when extended, lead to a classification of astrological aspects on the basis of their knowability and their sociability. They do more, bringing about a *ranking* of aspects in terms of their power, or "nobility," as Kepler termed it. The most powerful aspects are opposition and conjunction; the weakest are aspects lying between eighteen and twenty-four degrees.

Whatever judgments one might make today about Kepler's theory of the aspects, it is clear, in terms of the theories *he* had inherited, that he succeeded in bringing a certain degree of mathematical plausibility to what is, after all, an entirely whimsical doctrine.

♐

JOHANNES KEPLER spent the next fourteen years of his life in Linz, a city now well known for its chocolates. He remarried and he endured. His biography reveals a man harassed by petty inconveniences: incompetent printers, financial difficulties, and the intolerance of other men. He was denied Communion in Linz for reasons of doctrinal deviation so slight as to appear virtually invisible.

But in addition, his mother was accused of witchcraft. The news, he recounts, "nearly caused his heart to burst from his body." Although forced to leave Prague, Kepler had retained his position as the imperial mathematician. It was necessary to use his prestige to rescue his mother from the stake. The story is both terrible and poignant. Kepler himself believed in witches, and like the most primitive of German peasants believed in malicious or diabolical spirits. These views were common among both Catholics and Protestants, and the more vigorously they were held, the more obvious they had seemed. Kepler was psychologically unable to journey to Wurtemburg and declare in outrage that the proceedings against his mother were absurd. He could argue only that his mother was innocent. The trial dragged on for more than a year, and in the end, Kepler's mother was released on a legal technicality.

In these very difficult circumstances, he brought to completion the second half of his vast astrological scheme.

KEPLER'S THEORY of astrological aspects offered an account of certain spatial harmonies among the planets. But Kepler's ambitions overflowed the aspects, and during the long years in which he gave himself over to visions of cosmic harmony, he found himself driven to an even more audacious effort, a scheme to coordinate musical and celestial harmonies directly. Ptolemy had recognized musical harmonies by successively dividing a string into sections; he had used his ears to pick the divisions that corresponded to something that sounded good and affected him pleasantly. Kepler found this a dismayingly indifferent procedure. Any mathematician would.

The concept of knowability came to dominate his mind and served to concentrate his attention. The beloved string of Ptolemaic theory is curved to form a circle, and so a link to the zodiac. Kepler now imagined every possible knowable polygon inscribed within the circle, their vertices matched to its circumference. This is not a pencil and paper exercise. There are infinitely many knowable polygons. Polygons tumbled in Kepler's consciousness without measure. Let us track Kepler tracking an inscribed six-sided polygon within a circle, a knowable *and* a sociable figure, as it happens. The hexagon divides the circle where it touches its circumference. Very well. So it does. Kepler now suggests to himself—one can almost hear his pleased mutter drifting upward through the centuries—that he should attend to the ratio of part to whole defined by this division. There is a mental flicker, akin actually to the combined sound and flash of a match being struck. The ratio just discovered corresponds to a *knowable* regular polygon quite on its own. There now follows the flash. The divisions of the circle creating precisely such knowable regular polygons are the requisite harmonic ratios.

Geometry, existing as a thought in the mind of God, has yielded the secrets of harmony, existing as a song in the mind of man.

In developing his elaborate harmonic theories, Kepler's aim was to place his mind in contact with the very sources of the cosmos, the geometrical principles by which the great celestial panorama was organized. The musical harmonies are there; they sound like the Tibetan chant of creation, the *Monolem Chelmo*, but they are not confined to string instruments or the human voice. The eye must withdraw from the earth to an imagined place on the sun; and it is from the sun that Kepler is prepared to survey the solar system, and so the universe as he grasped it. The planets are in motion, swift in the case of Mercury, slow in the case of Saturn, and Kepler proposed to compare their speed at perihelion and aphelion with his own harmonic ratios. There is a rough correspondence. It is enough. He begins to hear a fantastic celestial harmony. It is largely dissonant since the planets travel at different rates of speed, but Kepler can imagine their coincidence, placing the moment of perfect harmony at the beginning of creation.

His soul swoons.

♐

KEPLER DIED IN 1630 in the city of Regensburg, still medieval today, still quaint. He had suffered a fever; but he had his whole life suffered fevers, and he had no reason to suspect that this one was unusual. His strength ebbed. He had time to order his affairs and write a few Latin verses. He did not suffer false modesty: He knew his worth, but he also knew his place in the grand scheme of things. He met death without fear. Contemporary physicists honor Kepler for his discovery of the laws of planetary motion, adding, of course, that they follow mathematically from Isaac Newton's far more comprehensive law of universal gravitational attraction. That business about astrology and its aspects? It is what one might expect. Contemporary astrologers, on the other hand, honor Kepler for his work on the astrological aspects. They recognize the importance of his work in pure physical theory. But the aspects are where his heart lay. His heart and theirs.

In some respects, Kepler's dearest doctrines have been unjustly neglected. The idea that the geometry of the planets has an effect on the human soul is odd, but it is not irrational. Writing at roughly the same time as Kepler, Galileo argued that nature is like a book, one written in the language of mathematics. The metaphor feeds on itself. If nature is like a book, then it is a book expressed in a thousand ways, nature grunting and babbling, affirming itself in the course of the stars or the way in which rivers flow. This metaphor has proven inspirational for more than four hundred years. It is now a target for analytic philosophers who pay the metaphor the respect of bothering to dispute its validity. Is this noble metaphor in any appreciable way different from Kepler's metaphor of a world in which geometrical relationships influence the human soul? Kepler was not able to say *how* the aspects affected the soul, but, of course, Galileo was unable to say *how* the book of nature affects the mind.

There is one respect in which Kepler's astrological ideas were prophetic. Only mathematical ideas, he believed, could illuminate a series of physical facts. In this he was correct. As a young man of twenty-five, Kepler had once had occasion to cast his own horoscope. It is a charming document, one that reveals a man with a rueful sense of his own limitations and an honest appreciation of his gifts. Mercury was in the seventh house at his birth, he writes, and as a result, he "devoted himself passionately to playing." He is talking, of course, of his childhood, recalling the boy that used to be. In playing, Kepler had discovered the low, small place in the garden wall through which a man might wriggle, coming out on the other side to what would become modern science itself.

CHAPTER TEN

CAPRICORN
♑
THE ASTROLOGER'S
LAST DINNER

I N 1665, THE PLAGUE that had devastated Europe in the four-teenth century was observed again in London. Riddled with buboes, a seaman's corpse had been discovered not far from Drury Lane; additional corpses were found near the waterfront, a chain of contagion leading like rat droppings back to the trading vessels that had sailed up the Thames. Fear was widespread, but not panic.

By the seventeenth century, few of England's intellectuals be-lieved that the plague was a sign of divine displeasure. Medieval modes of thought had by no means disappeared, but in matters of health, they had lost their power to command. The plague was contagious. Safety could be purchased first by flight and then by isolation. Such was the counsel of common sense, even if com-mon sense might have recalled that in the fourteenth century the plague often overran those running from it. Not that many people fled London, but Oxford and Cambridge emptied them-selves as university communities.

Two men may now be observed in flight, their hobnailed shoes clanking briskly on various country roads, a cloud of dust behind them. They are the astrologer and physician William

Lilly, and the mathematician and physicist Isaac Newton, Lilly fleeing from London and Newton from Cambridge. There are other men and women on the high roads, and it is a relief to notice that they are not pausing to whip themselves, as fourteenth-century penitents had done, or scourge their flesh with their lamentably filthy fingernails. An urgent but controlled exodus is in progress, but the diapason of life has changed, the men and women now shuffling or surging along the various highways and byways almost modern in their sense of alert self-interest.

Lilly was at the time sixty-three, two years younger than the century, and slight of figure. His face was elongated in an oval, and his somewhat asymmetrically set eyes, wispy beard, and small neat features suggest a personality cunning enough to conceal his cunning and not quite cunning enough entirely to succeed. Newton was forty years younger. Portraits of him at this age made later in his life, when he had already become famous, depict a face of great sensitivity, his suspicious eyes never losing their fixed stare. Newton grew into his dignity, his face softening with age, and I imagine that if anyone were much disposed to study his features as he tramped away from Cambridge, their most obvious effect would have been the impression they conveyed of rawness. Newton's and Lilly's paths did not cross. That would be asking too much of fate. But their lives were nonetheless bound by the curious universal joint connecting the end of one era to the beginning of another.

ॐ

WILLIAM LILLY WAS born on May 1, 1602, and at the age of thirty he was, if not without promise, at least without prospects. On an odd Sunday sometime in 1632, he fell into conversation with the clerk to the local justice of the peace in Diseworth, Leicestershire, the place of his birth. The men were "discoursing on many things," as Lilly recalled in his autobiography, *History of His Life and Times.* The clerk happened to mention "one Evans in Gunpowder Alley, an excellent wise man . . . [who] studied the Black Art," and "a great scholar" as well. Lilly was intrigued.

The helpful clerk made the necessary arrangements, and the next week, Lilly and the clerk set off to meet Mr. Evans:

> When we came to his house, he, having been drunk the night before, was upon his bed, if it be lawful to call that a bed whereon he lay; he roused up himself.

The disheveled house and that drunken master have long since become stock fixtures in various trite melodramas, the master revealing in short order a heart of gold in addition to a stomach of iron; it is satisfying to learn from Lilly's memoir that *his* mentor was rotten all the way down:

> [He] was by birth a Welshman, a Master of Arts, and sacred orders; he had formerly had a cure of souls in Staffordshire, but now was come to try his fortunes in London, being in a manner enforced to fly for some offences very scandalous, committed by him in these parts, where he had lately lived; . . . he was the most Saturnine person my eyes had ever beheld, either before I practiced or since; of a middle stature, broad forehead, beetle-browed, thick shoulders, flat nosed, full lips, down-looked, black curling stiff hair, splay-footed; . . . very much addicted to debauchery, and then very abusive and quarrelsome seldom without a black eye, or one mischief or other.

Whatever his fondness for drink, or his generally debauched state, Evans agreed to tutor Lilly in the astrological arts, a course of study that occupied six weeks. Lilly set up shop as an astrologer, and within a few years became a figure of great importance, the most influential astrologer of his age. By the time he took to the high road leading away from London thirty-five years later, he had become famous as the author of *Christian Astrology*, a three-volume treatise on his own methods in astrology.

Scurrying away from the plague-infected city, he carried not only his own personal concerns on his somewhat stooped shoulders, but the dignity of his art as well.

WILLIAM LILLY was born into the lower gentry just a year before Queen Elizabeth I died, and so a year before James VI of Scotland became King James I of England. His father was sent to debtor's prison when Lilly was eighteen. Lilly received no formal education beyond grammar school. His Latin was evidently excellent, Lilly going so far as to claim that he spoke it as well as English. At the height of his success, he was known among other astrologers for his mathematical ineptitude.

In 1620, Lilly set off on foot for London, and thereafter his feet seem to have carried him securely every additional step of his way through:

—service to a wealthy salt merchant;

—lessons in astrology;

—marriage to a wealthy woman, who on her immensely convenient death in 1633, left the lucky Lilly a fortune of nearly one thousand pounds; and

—marriage to another well-provided young woman, Jane Rowely, who entered his bed after first placing a dowry of five hundred pounds in his hands.

Thereafter Lilly occupied himself first with real estate and then increasingly with astrology, casting horary charts and horoscopes, talking with other astrologers, and serving on occasions as an instructor in the astrological arts.

There follows in 1636 an odd interlude, the only one that Lilly records, of "hypochondriack melancholy," a sudden and unexpected crisis so pressing that Lilly burnt his astrological texts and retired to the countryside at Surrey for more than five years.

Whatever his afflictions, Lilly returned to London in 1641, "perceiving," in his own words, "that there was money to be got," greed proving a remarkably effective, if seldom utilized, antidote to spiritual torpor.

His personal interests and professional identity merged completely. He appeared in London as he has appeared in history—as William Lilly, the astrologer.

WHEN THE FRENCH REVOLUTION broke out in the late eighteenth century, English political philosophers, such as Edmund Burke, regarded the chaos across the channel with the quiet satisfaction of men possessing short memories. The English Civil Wars began in 1642 and were cruel, bloody, and often savage. Lilly was a Puritan; he allied himself with the forces of the English Parliament, and in the three years that followed published a number of startling horary charts. He assessed the armies of the king and queen; he anticipated the outcome of the siege of Reading and the final illness of John Pym; and he correctly analyzed the battle of Alresford. No doubt with satisfaction, he predicted the catastrophic consequences attending the Earl of Essex's western campaign. On December 3, 1644, he published his horary predicting the death of Archbishop Laud. On June 14, 1645, he published *The Starry Messenger,* its charts predicting a Roundhead victory. On the day of publication, news reached London of the king's defeat at the battle of Naseby.

The first English Civil War came to an end with the surrender of Charles I to the Scots in 1646, Lilly taking the occasion to begin work on *Christian Astrology,* which was published to wide acclaim the following year. But civil wars very rarely end amicably, and Charles I, although defeated, nonetheless regarded himself as king by divine right. It was his disgruntlement that precipitated the second English Civil War in 1648. In some respects, Lilly's keen sense of the future seems to have suspended itself during the year. In his autobiography, he claims to have supplied a hacksaw to Charles I at Carlsbrook Castle, hardly a device likely to have enabled the monarch to escape from his well-guarded captivity, and later that summer to have encouraged Parliament's troops at the siege of Colchester with predictions of victory. If he had distributed his sympathies by suspending his judgment, Lilly might well have argued that, in times of turmoil, even unusually gifted astrologers are required to make compromises with their convictions. The king lost his head along with his claims to rule by divine right; Lilly was awarded an annual pension of one hundred pounds for his service to the Roundhead cause. If he had not accurately foreseen every political turn in the road, he had seen them sufficiently well to emerge from a period of political chaos with both his head in place and his future in hand.

There followed ten years of tumultuous political and astrological activity, with Lilly falling variously out of favor with powerful politicians, and then managing to clamber back into their good graces. A number of astrological predictions were defeated by events, Lilly's serene confidence that Richard Cromwell would succeed Oliver Cromwell at odds with the restoration of Charles II as England's monarch.

But at some time in the early 1660s, the lines of fate that would send Lilly and Newton scuttling to the countryside had already crossed and recrossed themselves.

LILLY'S INTELLIGENCE, while sensitive, was not large; but like Samuel Pepys, he had an incorrigible taste for gossip, and in his account of "some minor London astrologers" he offered a portrayal of the profession in the decades just before it disappeared.

There was Alexander Hart, a former soldier who specialized in astrological forecasts designed to help young men succeed in gambling. Lilly recalled posing three questions to Hart, and re-counts with pleasure that "he erred in every one." In addition, "he was a cheat." Sentenced to the pillory, Hart managed to flee to Holland. Hart's loss was Lilly's gain. On the hastily arranged sale of Hart's library, Lilly managed to pick up a copy of Argol's *Primum Mobile* for fourteen shillings.

Or there was Captain Bubb, another specialist in horary as-trology, and thus a rival of sorts to Lilly. "A proper handsome man," Lilly remarks, "but covetous and of no honesty."

> A certain butcher was robbed, going to a fair, of forty pounds. He goes to Bubb, who for ten pounds in hand paid would help him to find the thief; appoints the butcher such a night precisely to watch at such a place, and the thief should come thither; commanded him by any means to stop him. The butcher attends according to his direction. About twelve in the night there comes one riding very fiercely upon a full gallop, whom the butcher knocks down and seized both the man and the horse. The butcher brings the man and the horse to the next town—but then, the person whom the butcher attacked was John, the servant of Captain Bubb; for which the Captain was indicted and suffered upon the pillory, and afterwards ended his days in great disgrace.

Or there was Jeffrey Neve, a young man and "a student of Physick and Astrology." Neve, Lilly admits, was "a very grave per-son, laborious and honest, of tall stature and comely features." And the characteristically spiteful note:

> He had a design of printing 200 verified Questions, and de-sired my approbation ere they went to press, that I first would see them and then give testimony. When I had pe-rused the first 40, I corrected thirty of them, would read over no more. I showed him how erroneous they were, de-sired his emendation of the rest, which he performed not.

Or there was William Poole, "a nibbler at astrology," best remembered, by Lilly, at least, for having "discharged his belly" on the grave of one of his enemies.

Or there was Doctor Ardee, an astrologer and physician, to whom an angel had appeared promising him long life.

Or there was William Bredon, the vicar of Thornton in Buckinghamshire, "who was so given over to tobacco and drink that when he had no tobacco, he would cut the bell ropes and smoke them." Lilly described Bredon as "strictly adhering to Ptolemy," one of the very few references indicating the persistence of Ptolemaic thought in the first half of the seventeenth century.

There is in these biographical sketches of flawed but not disgraceful men a current of warm sympathy, one that Lilly evokes but does not endorse. They got by, these astrologers. They struggled, schemed, lived, and died.

Newton, too.

THE BATTLE OF ALRESFORD was fought on the afternoon of March 29, 1644. It was one of the minor battles of the English Civil War, and much about the battle, including its precise location, is not known with any certainty. The armies represented the forces of Parliament and the fortunes of the Crown, Charles I, who was soon to lose his life, prefiguring his own fate by losing this battle. The commanders on the field were respectively Sir William Waller and Sir Ralph Hopton, neither man leaving an impression in history of overwhelming military competence. It is this battle that Lilly chose to illustrate his astrological method, and his account of the figure that he constructed, which is contained in *Christian Astrology,* says much about the nature, and the limitations, of his technique.

The figure, or chart, is a standard description of the houses, numbered from one to twelve. It is *not* a birth chart or horoscope; its purpose is horary (or judicial). The chart has been

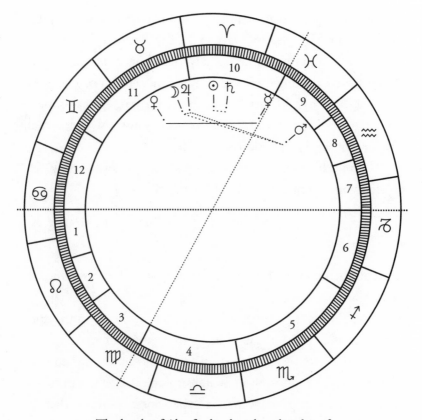

The battle of Alresford reduced to the play of
planetary forces in two dimensions.

drawn to determine "whether Sir William Waller or Sir Ralph
Hopton should overcome, they being supposed to be engaged
near Alresford." It is the time the question is posed that governs
the chart, just as the time of birth governs a horoscope.

The first house is fixed at the nine o'clock position on the
chart, and the successive houses occupy slots in a counter-
clockwise direction. Presumably it is Sir William Waller who is
the "querent," the man asking the question. Waller's fate is bound
to the ascendant, which represents the first house, and Sir Ralph
Hopton's fate to the seventh house, which is directly diagonal to
the first. The placement of Ralph Hopton in the seventh house

follows from principles of horary astrology. It is invariably the querent who takes pride of place in the first house. If his question involves a relationship, whether adversarial or amicable, his antagonist must occupy the seventh house by definition. There is a crude algebra at work here, of course, with geometrical opposition along a diagonal (in the chart) standing for physical, moral, amatory, or legal opposition in real life.

With both generals confined to astrological houses, Lilly's interpretation commences, my comments following.

> The Ascendant is for our army, the Moon, Jupiter and Venus for our General.

The ascendant, as it happened, was Leo. "If your Significator or Lord of the Ascendant," Lilly writes in *Christian Astrology,* "be in Aries, Taurus, Leo, Sagittarius, Capricorn, there's in the condition of that party something of the nature of the Beast... which represents the sign he is in." The association of Leo with strength, vitality, and power is an astrological given, a part of a tradition stretching backward to the Babylonians. To say that the moon, Jupiter, and Venus are *for* the General simply means that on the time given—*the time the question was asked*—these planets were found in Leo. This, Lilly would have been able accurately to compute.

> Sir Ralph Hopton is signified by Saturn, ruler of the seventh, his army by Capricorn, in the descending part of the heaven. There is only Mars and the dragon's tail in the 9th House, so that by this it appeared that Sir Ralph had no supplies ready to attend to that day's success.

It is not entirely clear why Lilly draws a distinction between Sir Ralph and his army, but whatever his reasons, he finds it of astrological importance that Saturn is the ruler of the seventh, and that Sir Ralph's house designates Capricorn, so that Leo and Capricorn are in conflict.

Still, the fact that Lilly draws a connection between the appearance of Mars in the *ninth* house and a lack of provisions is strange. Mars in the ninth house may mean many things: an interest in travel, a willingness to take risks, a certain inflexibility in mind and character; but I have not been able to determine the connection Lilly thought he saw between these common characteristics and military provisioning.

> From the existence of the Moon in her exaltation, and in the eleventh house with Jupiter, she being the ruler of the Ascendant and having principal signification for us and our army engaged for the Parliament, I concluded that all was and would be well for our side and the victory ours.

Here Lilly is on firmer astrological ground. The moon plays the same role for Sir William Waller as Saturn does for Sir Ralph Hopton, and when found in the eleventh house signifies emotional bonding. But Jupiter—*ah*, Jupiter—in the eleventh house governs people who achieve their goals, men of decisive action, successful military men.

Lilly's analysis goes further, but what is clear is only that what he claims as conclusions go considerably beyond what anyone could reasonably infer from his assumptions. Beyond appealing to certain established astrological categories, such as the ancient idea that Mars is warlike or Jupiter resolute, Lilly does not offer much by way of interpretive assistance to his readers.

It is not a matter of candor. Lilly was more than willing to share the secrets of his art. He was, in fact, effusive. No one reading *Christian Astrology* could possibly wish it longer. The trouble is elsewhere. The historian A. L. Rowse has written that seventeenth-century astrologers shared a common methodology and appealed to commonly held principles. It is hard to believe that he has studied their charts. The reverse is more nearly true. Lilly was a necromancer, someone who charmed life out of platitudes. We can read what he says, and follow what he claims, but where we see an inferential trail guttering out inconclusively, *he* sees it going on through the tangled brush, into the forest, and then out beyond the meadow. What would his chart have predicted, for example, had Sir Ralph Hopton and not Sir William Waller been the querent? Nothing in the sky would have changed, and yet Hopton's ascendant would have been Leo, and Waller's Capricorn. Had Hopton thought to put *his* question first, Lilly would have assigned him a lion's steadfastness on the field of battle. This is reason enough to suppose that whatever was essential in Lilly's art he did not reveal, just possibly because it lay below the threshold of his consciousness.

Twentieth-century scholars studying *Christian Astrology* have always found it difficult to reconcile the fact that Lilly was good at astrology with the question what he was good *at*. Lilly was widely admired, and a great many men and women paid well for his services. It is very hard to credit the hypothesis that all of them were fools, or that Lilly was simply a rascal. His predictions are too specific to be immune to failure. The social historian Ann Geneva has suggested that Lilly was in his own way "a genius at judicial astrology." This is a description masquerading as an explanation, but it does provoke an interesting idea. No set of principles, whether in pure mathematics *or* astrology, ever suffices to explain itself. Even a recipe must be interpreted and complicated recipes interpreted by a community, men and women capable of explaining to one another what various terms mean and how certain rules are to be applied. The rules, in turn, are part of a still wider interpretative community, the regress moving backward and expanding without limit. Lilly, we know, was a member in good standing of a guild of sorts, and members of the guild exchanged cases, discussed difficult issues, and even swapped clients. The London astrologers disappeared shortly after the interregnum. They took their secrets with them. It is for this reason that we can make so little sense of what they wrote. The rules are there in plain sight; their interpretation is a mystery. This elegant hypothesis is lacking in only one respect. It does not explain why a community so successful should have vanished.

For all that, Lilly was right, as he so often was. Sir William Waller and the parliamentary forces under his command prevailed.

LILLY'S ART WAS NOT always pressed in the service of great political causes. He was a consulting astrologer, one of a group of raffish men that had risen from the lower gentry. There was not much by way of university education in any of them, but an obvious shrewdness in all. During the years just before and after the interregnum, they established themselves as a professional presence in London, their clientele drawn from every level of society. Their professional success often was more impressive than that of physicians, who in the mid-seventeenth century still could offer suffering patients little more than a course of leeches, lavish bloodletting, or a round of purges—treatments that made the sick worse, and the well, ill.

The astrologers were especially good at finding things: lost jewelry, stolen household objects, misplaced keys or trifles. They were called in to adjudicate domestic tragedies, wives begging the astrologers to track down errant husbands, or asking for news of ships long overdue at sea. They gathered in offices on streets with names like Hogsbreath Lane or Pig and Pudding Alley, and settled at old oak desks with parchment and inkwells to wait for their first clients of the day. Outside, rain drizzled. This was, after all, London. But the weather notwithstanding, there was the usual commotion on the streets, sheep being marched to market, merchants hawking their wares, and housewives scurrying about. The shops were open for trade, carriages clattered over the cobblestones, men dressed in silk waistcoats visited their tailors, women met their lovers, beggars, cripples, and urchins scuttled about, and light-fingered pickpockets sifted through the crowds.

Clients begged for appointments by leaving their visiting cards. Proper married women consulted Lilly—*Dr.* Lilly—on matters of personal hygiene. Their menstrual cycles were irregular or heavy; a pregnancy was inconvenient; a husband could not be satisfactorily aroused or snored after intercourse. A young woman "had permitted a Lord to have the Use of her Body." She required Lilly's assistance in gaining admittance to the lord's chambers. Lilly persevered and he succeeded. Other clients queried Lilly, and so the stars, about a pair of missing silver candlesticks, keys that had been misplaced, or a servant seen smiling inappropriately on Lent. Long-nosed and long-necked aristocratic women consulted Lilly on how best to conduct themselves in the swirling intrigues of upper-class adultery, where men and women ardently pursued one another, falling in love and falling promptly out of love, pursuing pleasure as an agenda with the same diligence that members of the lower gentry pursued financial stability and the peasantry food and shelter.

Lilly must have had that curious ability, characteristic of great astrologers and physicians, to see past various verbal subterfuges into a patient's unrevealed agenda. He often listened for no more than a few minutes. He asked few questions, soliciting, if available, accurate information about his client's date and place of birth. He quickly jotted down his client's name and problems in something like a physician's log. Nothing more.

The same evening he would quickly draw up a chart, scan it to get its sense, and draw his conclusions.

These brisk, often hurried consultations went on all day, Lilly drawing up some three thousand charts in the course of a working year. His reputation grew by word of mouth; he was considered an astrologer of remarkable accuracy. On occasion, he used his art to help himself, tracking down a lost fish together with the man who stole it by means of a judicial chart he cobbled together. Like virtually every one of his charts, this one indicated a method without ever revealing it.

He was widely appreciated. We have no reason to doubt these reports and no explanation for them either, for the fact of the matter is that William Lilly was an uncommonly successful astrologer.

♑

WHEN THE PLAGUE STRUCK, William Lilly retreated from London to take up residence in Hersham, and in due course became churchwarden at Walton-upon-Thames. Isaac Newton retired from Cambridge to his mother's home in the manor of Woolsthorpe. Unlike Lilly, who was by then an established figure, Newton was quite alone, a dark, solitary, brooding young man of great intellectual power. Within the space of the next fifteen months, Newton discovered the calculus, proved and expanded the binomial theorem, played brilliantly with infinite series, and for the first time entertained the astonishing conjecture that "the force of gravity might extend to the orb of the moon." Asking no one's permission, he had opened the door of European science and mathematics, entered into the stately chambers beyond, and, within the next few years, made himself their master.

Nicolas Copernicus, Tycho Brahe, Johannes Kepler, and Galileo Galilei had, by the first quarter of the seventeenth century, completed a collective reassessment of the ancient and durable Ptolemaic system. Myth has it that they noticed what astronomers had for more than fifteen hundred years ignored, the fact that the earth is not the center of the solar system. But this myth is more moth-eaten than most, the neat impression of decisive progress at odds with the facts at almost every turn.

The Ptolemaic and Copernican systems are, to begin with, observationally equivalent to at least a first-order of approximation. If Copernican astronomy had made great strides in the sixty years since Copernicus' death, so, too, had Ptolemaic astronomy. Gualterus Arsenius' armillary sphere depicts the Ptolemaic universe in three dimensions of brushed and beaten brass or copper. The artifact is a masterpiece of intricacy, an ingenious and highly detailed quantitative model of the Ptolemaic universe. It is plainly a work of art, fully comparable to the statuary masterpieces of the High Renaissance, but it is also a scientific instrument, a working model of the heavens. The various spheres rotate on a number of separate axes, each movement precisely calibrated so that observational astronomers using the armillary sphere could calculate eccentrics and ecliptics.

The sphere reveals, of course, what Kepler suspected. The Copernican system is simpler. But simplicity is one thing, and accuracy another. The Ptolemaic system was as accurate as the Copernican system, and for all practical purposes it could be used *today* to forecast eclipses, track the phases of the moon, plot the orbit of the planets, or send a man or a spaceship aloft and keep them fixed in a geocentric orbit.

The Ptolemaic and Copernican systems are, in the second place, roughly comparable in *computational* complexity. Ptolemaic astronomy required epicycles and contrivances; but then again, so did—so *does*—Copernican astronomy. The radical simplicity inherent in the heliocentric view could not emerge until Newton demonstrated that Kepler's laws of planetary motion could be compressed to fit neatly on the head of a mathematical pin.

And there is a third place. The Copernican system is physically counterintuitive. It fails to explain the fact that the earth's rotation is never locally observed, objects failing conspicuously to sail off into space as they would were they perched on the rim of a spinning merry-go-round. It was again Newton who provided the correct explanation for these oddities in the heliocentric system, addressing not only his distinguished predecessors but Aristotle and the Greek astronomers as well.

♑

AT SOME TIME in the summer of 1684, the astronomer Edmund Halley traveled to Cambridge to discuss certain questions with Isaac Newton. The mathematician Abraham de Moivre has provided a very well-known account of their exchange:

> In 1684, Dr. Halley came to visit him [Newton] at Cambridge, after they had been some time together the Dr. asked him what he thought the curve would be that would be described by the planets supposing the force of attraction toward the sun to be reciprocal to the square of their distance from it. Sir Isaac replied immediately that it would be an ellipsis, the Dr. [Halley], struck with joy and amazement, asked him how he knew it, why saith He, I have calculated it.

William Lilly died on the morning of June 9, 1681; he died a second time when these words were uttered, and with him died the astrological tradition as a living intellectual force. I should say at once that this is by no means a judgment endorsed by social historians. But the fact remains that before Newton's birth, London was crowded with astrologers and after his death, emptied. This may not prove Newton's influence decisive, but it is surely enough to establish the suspicion. What Newton had offered Halley revealed an intellectual method so powerful that it would sweep away every countervailing current, astrology and the astrologers included.

No one knew this at the time. We know it now. It is sobering to wonder whether a similar drama is taking place unacknowledged before our eyes today.

ISAAC NEWTON PUBLISHED the *Principia Mathematica* in 1685. The book made him famous, not only in England but also in Europe, and it established his reputation for all time.

The *Principia* had its origin in thought experiments that Newton had conducted more than twenty-five years earlier; the story of those experiments is now a part of the great mythological history of western science. William Stukeley, Newton's biographer, conveys this account of Newton's discovery. The two men are in a garden, drinking tea:

> Amidst other discourse, he told me, he was just in the same situation, as when formerly, the notion of gravitation came into his mind. It was occasioned by the fall of an apple as he sat in a contemplative mood. Why should that apple always descend perpendicularly to the ground, he thought to himself. Why should it not go sideways or upwards, but always to the earth's centre?

Now apples have been falling to the ground since time immemorial, and every one of them has fallen toward the center of the earth. Why is an explanation needed? That is where they go, if they are disposed to go anywhere at all. But where apples have gone says nothing at all about *why* they go there and not some other place. Nor does it say much about just why apples fall to the earth in a straight line, rather than descending in a spiral, or falling at a shallow angle. Once these questions were asked, and accepted *as* questions, the world suddenly seemed arbitrary to Newton, as arbitrary as it had seemed to Johannes Kepler asking himself just why there should be six planets and not more.

We have a better idea now why apples fall downward than anyone born before 1685 ever did, and a better idea than William Lilly had. Apples fall downward because they are controlled by gravitational attraction. *Controlled,* meaning that they respond to a precise mathematical specification, one coordinating mass, acceleration, and force. Their descent is governed by that relationship. Newton's universal law of gravitation places a halter on disorderly concepts; but far from making the unfamiliar familiar, it serves only to make the arbitrary necessary.

The climactic section of Newton's masterpiece is entitled "The System of the World," the title suggesting something of the scope of Newton's efforts. The system of the world is governed by Newton's universal law of gravitation. All material objects, Newton asserted, whether on the surface of the earth or in the most remote reaches of the universe, attract one another with a force that is proportional to their mass and inversely proportional to the square of the distance between them. The law is quantitative, its fundamental units expressed in terms of mass, length, and time. And the law is universal. Its scope is the cosmos itself. The ancient astrologers had written that the "heavens and earth form a unity." Newton had for the first time demonstrated that this was so. In a mathematical demonstration that even today seems a masterpiece of difficult and close reasoning, Newton showed that he could derive Kepler's three laws of planetary motion from the single assumption that the planets rotated in their orbits in response to the force of gravitational attraction. What is more, he could demonstrate the reverse. Nothing like this had ever appeared in western science before, and nothing like it has ever appeared since.

♑

ISAAC NEWTON AND William Lilly may now be allowed to recede, the one man dead, the other still living, Lilly's descent into desuetude the simple consequence of Newton's promotion to immortality. It is a natural part of our own scientific culture to accept this relationship as obvious. It is a great deal more difficult to quite see why it was necessary.

Astrology has always proceeded by means of a number of hidden assumptions, and even if these assumptions prove false, they are not obviously false and so have a certain lingering claim on our attention. There is action at a distance. The stars and the planets exert an influence on terrestrial affairs. They do so at a distance and they do so without an intervening medium. In answer to the question *how* they do this, the astrological answer is that they just do.

As it happens, this is also the answer given by Newton's theory of gravity, which affirms that objects in space attract one another through the intervening medium of nothing whatsoever. It is in some sense the answer given by modern theories of gravity as well. And action at a distance is the dark force from which physics has been fleeing at least since the seventeenth century, and fleeing with no great success.

Newton provided a mathematical law that describes with remarkable precision the quantitative gravitational relationships between objects of varying mass. The trajectory of a falling object, whether the moon sailing above the earth or a ballerina soaring into space, is completely determined by Newton's law. Action at a distance is in force. Gravitational attraction between objects determines how they will move. This the mathematics describes. What the mathematics does not provide is an account of *how* the thing is done. The force of gravity acts at once, and it acts at a distance and it acts over the intervening medium of nothing whatsoever.

It is interesting to wonder whether this mystery might be minimized by introducing an *intermediate* modality of action, something like al-Kindi's stellar rays? It is not obvious that, even if successful, this tactic would do much good. Intermediates themselves require intermediates—two, in fact, for each new intermediate. At some point, one must run out of intermediates, no? And then the dreaded *it just happens* must logically reappear. The problem is built into the very notion of a world of objects. If the relationship between any two objects must be mediated by a third object, then either there are infinitely many objects loitering about, intermediates multiplying just when they are needed, or some relationships between objects must be unmediated and hence direct. But, of course, as soon as some unmediated relationships are introduced, intellectual indignation tends to lapse. If some, why not others? As long as two distinct objects are exerting an influence on one another, in whatever fashion, action at a distance reappears. If the objects are *distinct*, there must be some distance between them—otherwise they would occupy the same place at the same time—and if their relationships are unmediated, they proceed over that distance by means of no intervening medium whatsoever.

On the other hand, if various objects are not distinct, they must be the same, and the effort to resolve all forms of cause in the natural world to things that cause themselves does not seem to improve our understanding. Ultimately, and at some level of analysis, the idea of causal effect collapses into the idea of causal succession, just as al-Ghazzalli had argued. One thing follows another. There is a line of inference that proceeds inexorably from our innocent assumption that there are things in the world to the altogether more disturbing conclusion that, in the end, cause and effect must leap over the void in one way or another.

There is no escape from this conclusion. It is built into reality.

If astrology is a form of magic, inasmuch as astrologers have never been able to specify the modality of the effects that they anticipate, then so is Newtonian mechanics. Science has by no means severed its connection to magical thinking. It has simply brought magical thinking under the control of powerful intellectual constraints. Newtonian mechanics is the very model of action at a distance domesticated by—and here the intellectual irony is rich—words, in this case words that are mathematical. When all is said and done, it is the capacity of Newtonian mechanics to subordinate the force of gravity to a mathematical form of expression that accounts for its radical and striking success.

And for reasons that we are very far from grasping, this seems to make all the difference in the world.

Sixty years before Isaac Newton published the *Principia*, Johannes Kepler had demonstrated the extent to which a natural scientist of great sensitivity and mathematical talent could shape the traditional materials of astrology. In Kepler, the rich baroque structure of traditional astrology dwindled almost to the vanishing point. Kepler's theory of the aspects remained; it was the treasure of his heart. In coordinating astrological aspects with tessellations of the plane, Kepler had closed one door and opened another. And yet no one had followed him through.

The mathematical culture that might have informed astrology, as the calculus informed Newton's mechanics, did not exist in the sixteenth or the seventeenth century. But in the eighteenth and early nineteenth centuries, mathematicians discovered hyperbolic geometry and complex analysis and they dramatically improved their understanding of spherical geometry. One hundred fifty years after Lilly's death, these tools were used by physicists, and never by astrologers. I am not sure why.

Newton's system of the world succeeds, of course, by virtue of its radical simplification of experience. Lilly's system, by way of contrast, involved the coordination of nine planets, the moon, the sun, and, in the example I have analyzed, two or more contending personalities, and beyond these personalities at least two armies poised to battle one another in crude combat. Newtonian mechanics is still incapable of analyzing completely the behavior of *three* bodies moving under the force of gravity, and the presence of additional bodies makes the problem even more intractable. No wonder Lilly's project lapsed. Together with every other astrologer, both ancient and modern, he had set himself too difficult a problem.

But then why didn't the astrologers do what Newton did and strike the mass of complicated details from their system?

Perhaps it is a matter of something so simple as the truth? Newtonian mechanics is a magnificently successful system, its accuracy verified under every conceivable circumstance, except when objects are accelerated to very high speeds. Astrology, for all of its long, active life, has depended on an intimate association between a geocentric universe and various astrological doctrines. The whole of astrology's intellectual force has been expressed in the ancient picture of the earth at the center of a sphere, the sun, the moon, and the planets all directing their energies *toward* the earth, even if by means that were never clear and could not ever be explained. Modern astrologers claim that with the sun and not the earth at the center of a celestial sphere, astrological calculations may be made as before. In this, they are correct. But it is one thing to do a calculation, quite another to make it live. The plainspoken hypothesis that astrology is simply *false,* while leaving many questions unanswered, explains the most obvious of facts.

Having said this, it is worthwhile to say as well that certain problems that astrologers faced with some diligence of mind have not disappeared from the intellectual scene. Force is the central idea in Newtonian mechanics, and influence the central idea of astrology. In an especially perceptive study of Newtonian mechanics, the physicist Max Jammer compared the traditional concept of a soul with the new concept of a force introduced by Newton. He asked the obvious question, the one that could be asked only by a very competent physicist:

Does this really involve a considerable change? Soul is an unknown *agens,* the existence of which is assumed in order to explain a particular behavior of animate bodies. Force is an unknown *agens,* the existence of which is assumed to explain a particular behavior of inanimate bodies. The only thing that is established with certainty in both cases is the behavior. One does not gain a deeper understanding if one gives a name to the unknown cause of the behavior. In another sense the change is very great indeed. When one proceeds to attribute the motions of the planets to a force instead of a soul, this implies that one wishes to consider them as inanimate bodies.

This is very perceptive, inasmuch as it reintroduces a distinction in thought that the Newtonian revolution is widely thought to have abolished. If influence becomes a legitimate concept only when celestial objects are considered *inanimate,* it is not only astrology that stands threatened, but every inquiry into life itself. The unification of experience promised by the advent of mathematical physics now lapses, another distinction at once replacing it. There is the world of matter and the world of life. In one there is force; in the other, influence. In the three hundred years since the *Principia,* this has remained a distinction that no theory has been able to efface.

♑

IN THE YEARS BEFORE the restoration of 1652, a group of some forty astrologers, calling itself the *Society of Astrologers in London,* gathered several times a year to celebrate one another's company, pass around professional tidbits, troll for clients, and, of course, stuff themselves with food and drink. Sermons were given. Elegant and well-appointed or down-at-the-heels and somewhat shabby, the astrologers were all there. Dinner guests included men of great raffishness who, with a wink and a nod and a certain suave charm, managed to persuade wealthy aristocrats or credulous London merchants that they had in hand a system for predicting the proper time in which to propose a marriage, conduct an affair, disguise an embezzlement, or win at whist without seeming to cheat. There were men like William Lilly and Elias Ashmole, who had achieved their reputations by means of their uncanny ability to control the flux of time. And there were men whose genius ran in reverse, their every prediction, however unobtrusively made, falsified by events so that their careers acquired a certain lonely grandeur.

One dinner was held at the Painters-Stainers Hall in Little Trinity Lane. The precise menu has been lost, but something very much like it can be reconstructed from a dinner that the astrologer Elias Ashmole gave some twenty years later. The first course consisted of Haunch of Venison and Cawley Flowers, Batalia Pie, Ragowe of Veal, Venison Pastry, and Chyne of Mutton and Chyne of Veal in a dish. The *first* course. The second course included chicken, duck, turkey, fried salmon and sole, kidney beans, imported ham and beef tongue, and jowl of sturgeon. The third and blessedly final course consisted of fruit.

It requires a certain stoicism of spirit to undertake a meal of this sort, and, after a dinner held on August 14, 1651, Ashmole evidently became indisposed, the result, he conjectured modestly, of drinking too much water after eating too much meat. He reported himself "greatly oppressed in [his] stomach." No doubt. The assistance of his physician proved unavailing. The next day, "Mr. Sanders, the astrologer, sent me a piece of bryony root to hold in my hand," Ashmole reported. His stomach was directly thereafter freed of its considerable oppression.

Within a few years, the dinners would cease, the astrologers would one by one die off, and the splendid tradition that they represented would nearly vanish. The Royal Society replaced the Society of Astrologers at the center of serious intellectual life. In the thousands of charts these men prepared, documents dealing with every human contingency, not one predicted the eclipse of their way of life.

The haunches of venison are cleared from the table. The candles begin to gutter. A tankard is banged one last time. Someone says *to your health, gentlemen, to your very good health.*

And then there is nothing as the eye of history winks shut.

CHAPTER ELEVEN

AQUARIUS

∿

SHOW ME THE MEN

S HOW ME THE man," Lavrenty Beria once remarked to Josef Stalin, "and I will show you his crime." It is a fine if chilling sentiment, and since we are all guilty of something, a universal truth as well. In October of 1975, 186 scientists used the pages of the *Humanist* to focus the wandering searchlight of their indignation on astrology and astrologers:

> Acceptance of astrology pervades modern society. This can only contribute to the growth of irrationalism and obscurantism. We believe the time has come to challenge directly and forcefully the pretentious claims of astrological charlatans. It should be apparent that those individuals who continue to have faith in astrology do so in spite of the fact that there is no verified scientific basis for their beliefs, and, indeed, that there is strong scientific evidence to the contrary.

Shortly after this document became widely known, the philosopher Paul Feyerabend asked why, if the declaration contained an argument, 186 names were necessary to enforce its statement, and if it did not, whether those 186 names were sufficient to disguise its absence? Reasonable questions. But, of course, beside the point. A scientific anathema is not a rational document. Whatever the sources of their vexation, the scientists adding their name to this indictment of astrology were simply restating a point of view that had long been the common property of the scientific community.

A proud old discipline has fallen on hard times.

〰

GERARD ENCAUSSE WAS born in Spain in 1865, but he was educated in France and in all respects became completely French. He was round-faced as an adult, with chubby cheeks, small, flat eyes, and a full beard. Deeply interested in mystical mumbo-jumbo of all sorts, Encausse studied the Kabbalah, consulted the tarot, joined the French theosophical society, and listened gravely to Madame Blavatsky, who held séances in Paris in which she communicated with the dead. Together with friends, Encausse founded the Kabbalistic Order of the Red Cross, a society whose chief aim was to admit members eager to exclude others. Encausse fought two duels with various rivals over obscure matters of magical interpretation. The duels have become a part of nineteenth-century French folklore. A number of spooky events were recorded. Otherwise responsible horses bolted on their way to the dueling grounds. Pistols mysteriously misfired. Strange mists were seen. No one was hurt and, with the disputes resolved, Encausse later formed a close friendship with his antagonists. He led a blameless life, but he associated with shady characters, such as the writer J. K. Huysman, the author of *Là-Bas,* a novel proposing to investigate the lower depths and succeeding entirely. In 1891, Encausse founded a mystic society called *L'ordre des supérieures inconnues* (the Order of the Higher Mysteries) which was based loosely on Masonic rites. Members wore rosettes in their lapels and greeted one another by secret signs and handshakes.

Encausse wrote widely. His *Astrology for Initiates,* published under the name Papus, is a straightforward, clear account of classical astrological principles. The text is still in print today and still very much worth reading. It is, of course, not written for initiates at all but rather for beginners, and although Encausse acknowledges the fact that the earth is not at the center of the solar system, the book's text and diagrams are thoroughly Ptolemaic.

Encausse was an astrologer by night, and a physician by day, keeping a busy office on the *rue* Rodin. He had in his youth written a dissertation on anatomy, and while in the late nineteenth century he could effect very few cures, he was well regarded by other physicians and respected by his patients.

Dr. Gerard Encausse perished in the First World War, like William Lilly the victim of another double death, for Encausse took with him the last lingering traces of a sweet mystical strain in astrological thought. "For the anti-scientific astrologers," his contemporary Paul Choisnard wrote in his own treatise on astrology *L'influence astrale* (Astral Influence), "astrology only consists of applying—with more or less skill—the incoherent aphorisms found in ancient texts." The ancient texts now repose in bookstalls along the Seine—just where I found *Astrology for Initiates*. The secret societies have long since disbanded.

And thereafter the trail becomes tangled.

CONSIDER, FOR EXAMPLE, Erik Jan Hanussen, his name, chosen carefully to suggest Danish aristocracy, a cover for one Herman Steinschneider. Whether called Hanussen or Steinschneider, the man himself is quite unknown in the English-speaking world, and no one without an indirect connection to Weimar Germany—due in my case to my father—can appreciate the extent to which his personality played a lurid role in the life and death of its culture.

Hanussen was, in part, a charlatan. He specialized in psychic performances before very large audiences. He seemed to possess remarkable powers of divination and character assessment, but, as he himself acknowledged, the greater part of his success depended on gossip that he had previously obtained, or a very shrewd version of twenty questions in which a sequence of forced guesses invariably would be interpreted as a series of forceful insights. He also used a number of adroitly placed plants in his audiences, men who could provide Hanussen with information by means of pre-arranged signals.

He was a great success, his performances throughout central Europe sold out, and a notorious womanizer with a trail of outraged husbands lumbering in his wake, their embarrassed wives sniffling into dainty lace handkerchiefs just behind. He was a hypnotist and a mind reader, offering private consultations to the wealthy and tidbits to gossips. And he maintained a sideline in blackmail, never the most prudent of professions. He was a practicing astrologer, and his newspaper, the *Berliner Wochenschau*, published a series of astrological predictions in the 1920s that were widely read and often accurately fulfilled.

Hanussen was hardly unique. Astrology flourished in Weimar Germany, the very center of the world's most powerful scientific culture, with Albert Einstein in residence in Berlin and David Hilbert in Göttingen. Elspeth Ebertin, who had early on become the leader of a devoted cult, secured her reputation when, on being sent Hitler's birth date, she reported that "he could expose himself to danger by lack of caution." Her prediction seemed to her followers to describe Hitler's recklessness during the 1923 Munich putsch.

For all his tricks, Hanussen, at least, seemed more than a shrewd stage magician. Like William Lilly, and like so many other astrologers in history, the man had a disturbing ability to sense out the currents of history and to see the pattern of their flow. He lived dangerously. In 1932, his newspaper flatly predicted that Adolf Hitler would within the year obtain the position of Reichschancellor. This was hardly the popular view. The

Nazis had lost ground in parliamentary elections held in 1932, and snickering in various Berlin cafes, a great many intellectuals had come to regard Hitler as a buffoon. Hanussen thought otherwise, and he was right. It is often forgotten that Hitler did not achieve power by democratic vote but by means of a sordid backroom deal engineered by the odious Fritz von Papen.

Hanussen had close ties with members of the Nazi party before they assumed office, and he maintained those ties after they acquired power. He was knowledgeable about their homosexual orgies and gross appetites, and he seemed to understand their curious sense of prissiness. And he was a Jew, a fact that he did not flaunt but did nothing to hide.

Sometime in the late fall or early winter of 1932, Hitler demanded an audience with Hanussen at the Hotel Kaiserdorf in Berlin. After losing ground in the most recent parliamentary elections, Hitler was depressed and anxious. The two men met in Hitler's rooms, which served as the headquarters for the Nazi party. It is not clear what took place. Both men were clairvoyant in some way, their power to penetrate the future resembling two searchlights sweeping different parts of the same ocean.

Hanussen may have cast a chart, or laid his hands on Hitler's head; he seems to have fallen into a trance. When he had quite finished, he assured Hitler that his promotion to power was assured.

"I see victory for you," he said. "It cannot be stopped."

The story grows progressively more lurid. Hanussen played some role in the Reichstag fire. Well in advance of the dreadful events, in language vague in its formulation, but nonetheless clear in its import, he predicted Kristalnacht, the outbreak of war, and Germany's destruction. He based this last prediction on a horoscope that he had himself drawn up, and which, years later, fearful Nazi officials, mindful of enveloping military disaster, made every effort to suppress.

He courted disaster at every turn. At some point he seems to have realized that he had purchased his influence at the cost of his life. In a letter written shortly before his death, and said to be written in invisible ink, Hanussen remarked to an old friend, "I had always thought that business about the Jews was just an election trick of theirs."

In March of 1933, he was arrested by the SA (the forerunner to the SS), and summarily shot, his body buried in a dismal field on the outskirts of Berlin.

LIKE AUGUSTUS, high Nazi officials viewed astrology as a presumption, but whatever their official views, they found the presumption tempting in the best of times and irresistible in the worst. Dr. Karl-Gunther Heimoth was, as his name suggests, an astrologer who fluttered just a little too closely to the flame of power. In this he resembled Ascletario, Domitian's doomed astrologer. The author of an astrological treatise on homosexuality, he found occasion to explain his research to Ernst Röhm, well-known in Nazi circles as a man able neither to control nor to conceal his appetites. In time taken from leadership duties as the head of the SA, Röhm was very much in the habit of repairing to various country hotels in the company of a number of young men. Their orgies were notorious. When Röhm was forced to shoot himself, Heimoth was shot as well, Nazi officials drawing no distinction between the crime and its chronicler.

Karl Ernst Krafft did better, if only because he placed his unwavering devotion to Hitler at the center of his concerns. A noted astrologer, a disciple of Paul Choisnard, in fact, as well as an unrelieved sycophant, the Swiss-born Krafft predicted on November 2, 1939, that Hitler would be in danger of assassination between the seventh and tenth of November. He specifically warned that the attempt on Hitler's life would use "explosive material." Hitler

very narrowly escaped death when on November 9 a bomb ex-
ploded shortly after he had left the Burgerbrau Beer Hall in Munich. Krafft took the occasion to call attention to his prediction,
going so far as to send a telegram to Joseph Goebbels in which he
ostentatiously reminded the propaganda minister that he had
seen the attempt on Hitler's life before it had occurred. Goebbels
was alarmed but not impressed. Gestapo officials summoned
Krafft for a chat. It is still very satisfactory to imagine the fanatical Krafft scanning uneasily the walls of his interrogation chamber as he explained to leather-booted Gestapo officials that gifted
astrologers might well be able to penetrate a plot without in any
way participating in its execution. He must have been a smooth
talker. Astrologers so often are. After clicking their heels and
saluting the open air, his interrogators let him go. When next
seen, the insufferable Krafft was busy interpreting Nostradamus
in a way suggesting the relevance of his verse to the Nazi conquest of Belgium and the Low Countries.

As the war entered its final stages, Nazi officials became
alarmed on comparing notes to discover that astrologers they had
consulted privately were in agreement in predicting what those
officials could have in any case determined by looking at Berlin's
shattered streets—namely, that the war was going badly.

There was Dr. Wilhelm Wulff, for example, Heinrich Himmler's personal astrologer. Altogether more learned than Hanussen,
and altogether less fanatical than Krafft, Wulff had published an
extensive series of astrological essays in the years before the Second
World War. He seems to have been intrigued by Indian astrology,
in part because of its ostensibly Aryan origins. He conducted a
feud with members of an obscure German astrological society
founded by Alfred Witte, and known now among its German
footnotes and American admirers as the Hamburg school. For
reasons that are anything but clear, he was sent to a concentration

camp in 1939, perhaps as part of a general effort by Nazi officials to stamp out forms of irrationalism that they could neither endorse nor control. When word of his talents reached the credulous Himmler, Wulff was taken from one camp and transferred to another, this one devoted to providing comfortable surroundings for various psychic talents. There he was put to work casting charts. When international affairs revealed that the Will had, after all, limitations of its own, Wulff's charts grew gloomy in their character. It is difficult to believe that Himmler accepted Wulff's predictions with gratitude, for as the Russian army advanced stolidly on Berlin, Wulff correctly predicted "*eine grosse Gefahr für Hitler am 20.7. 1944*"—a great danger for Hitler on July 20, 1944. It was, in fact, the date on which Count Stauffenberg attempted, with no great success, to assassinate Hitler at his military headquarters in east Prussia. Wulff went on to depress the thoroughly addled Himmler by flatly predicting "*dass Hitler noch vor dem 7.5. 1945 eines geheimnissvollen Todes sterben werde*,"—that Hitler would die in secret before May 7, 1945.

And so he did.

~~~

THE ENGLISH NEWSPAPERMAN R. H. Naylor now enters this story as a figure that made a stir in order to turn a dollar. In 1930, the editors of the London *Sunday Express* conceived the brilliant idea of asking Naylor to write a regular astrology column. No other newspaper had ever featured such a column, and from the first, it was a great success. Naylor was a competent astrologer with a shrewd, sharp eye for dramatic effect. His columns were far ranging and interesting. There have *always* been astrologers with a certain gift, men whose predictive record suggests something more than a series of lucky guesses. Naylor was one of them. The prediction that made his name may be found in the October 30 edition of the *Express:*

Earthquakes will occur, mostly near deep-sea levels, and affecting peninsulas, in the autumn quarter of 1930. They may not actually occur in October—though from the 8th to the 15th is a real danger point—but they will be exceedingly likely in November or December. British aircraft will be in danger at about the same time.

The British aircraft R101 crashed on approaching the airport at Orly in Paris on October 5, 1930. Many lives were lost. Naylor offers this account of his methods:

> My prediction was based on a very simple observation. It can be proved that, whenever the new moon or the full moon falls at a certain angle to the planet Uranus, aircraft accidents, electrical storms, and sometimes earthquakes follow.

This is interesting; it may well be true. No one, so far as I know, has studied the matter carefully. But what follows is altogether remarkable:

> Now … the configuration referred to occurred on October 7th; the destruction of the R101, therefore prematurely fulfilled the indication.

The R101 crashed on the *fifth* of October. Connoisseurs will quite naturally wish to savor the implications of an astronomical cause that follows its effect. R. H. Naylor's prediction, such as it was, established his reputation, such as it is; and it did something else as well. It created the genre of popular sun sign astrology. Naylor was writing for a wide readership, and the delicacies of time and place needed to construct an accurate horoscope seemed to him an inconvenience. His predictions were large and they were general. On occasion, he set aside his newspaper work to construct discreet horoscopes for well-known figures such as Princess Margaret, this last on the occasion of her birth. Many of those with access to this horoscope came later to remark that it seemed remarkably to fit the princess. When he predicted that "events of tremendous importance to the Royal Family and to the nation will come about near her seventh year," the impression was widespread that the stars had revealed the abdication of one George and the accession of another. For all that, these affairs remained sidelines. Naylor was a newspaperman and his newspaper kept him at his lathe, doing what he did best.

His great rival during the 1930s was Edward Lyndoe, an astrologer recruited by the *People,* a rival to the *Express.* As 1939 began, even the ravens in the English woods could be heard croaking warnings of the war that was coming. Lyndoe demurred, arguing on January 1, 1939, that the stars were decisively in favor of peace. "I see," he said, "no sign of a Great War in 1939." Five months later, he dismissed out of hand the possibility that Germany would attack Britain. Five days before Nazi troops invaded Poland, Lyndoe argued emphatically that "Hitler will not do it." When on September 3, 1939, it became clear that Hitler had done it, Lyndoe affirmed in headlines that "Hitler was a madman against the stars."

If the competition between Naylor and Lyndoe during the 1930s and early 1940s was farcical, it also was fierce. London publications without their own frontline astrologers saw a splendid commercial opportunity in debunking those astrologers with battlefield commissions and the royalties to prove it. On September 6, 1941, three months after the German army had invaded the Soviet Union, the *Picture Post Magazine* commissioned a crude statistical investigation of newspaper forecasts made during the previous ten years. Five astrologers were selected, among them Naylor and Lyndoe. Their columns were weighed against very notable events: the fall of the Spanish Republic, the invasion of Poland, the collapse of France. Far from being right or wrong, the editors of the *Post* concluded, astrologers often failed to "make any reference whatsoever to the events in question," thus suggesting that the newspaper astrologers who had done so much to boost the circulation of their papers were not habitually inclined to read those newspapers themselves. These results were prominently published. They affronted the dignity of still another astrologer, P. J. Harwood, who, directly after the Second World War had begun, imprudently published a book entitled *When the War Will End.* In a letter published by the *Post* on September 27, 1941, Harwood handsomely confessed that "like other astrologers, I have made my mistakes." Nonetheless, he argued gamely, "a large number of close hits have been scored."

He referred the editors to his book. He asked that it be given suitable publicity. Harwood had predicted an invasion of the continent by English forces in May of 1941, followed by a separate peace with Italy in July of 1941. He thought it unlikely that Russia would be involved in war, his letter commending his own book for its "close hits" appearing in print just as German forces were sweeping through Russia and advancing ominously toward Moscow.

His prediction that World War II would end on Christmas Eve of 1941 was not satisfied by events.

≋

MICHEL GAUQUELIN WAS born in 1928, and he received a classical French education at the Sorbonne in psychology and statistics. He was a fine athlete as a young man, with a ranking among the top fifty French tennis players. His game was, I suspect, a graceful, old-fashioned relic, one dominated by long fluid baseline volleys and a few leaping arabesques at the net, but crippled nonetheless by an anemic serve, the kind of accurate but pallid pat that allowed his more aggressive opponents to slam shots to the corners of the court even as Gauquelin, dressed in white flannels and an elegant open-necked shirt, would watch in helpless frustration. A picture published of Gauquelin in middle age depicts an attractive bald man with a somewhat square, froggish face, and what is obviously the well-preserved, rangy body of a young athlete, the torso compact, and his elegant long arms folded in his lap.

As a student, Gauquelin was influenced by Paul Choisnard, and it is Choisnard who has played a dominating if somewhat distant role in what is still a strong tradition in French astrological thought.

Born in 1867 in Tours, Choisnard died in "his famous sixty third climateric year" in Paris, according to Patrice Guinard, who writes often and astringently about French astrology. A graduate of the *Ecole Polytechnique* and so a member in good standing of the French intellectual elite, Choisnard is widely regarded as the founder of a hard-headed, tough, no-nonsense, disciplined empirical school of astrological research. He wrote widely—more than thirty books—and he published with distinguished French houses such as Ernest Leroux and Alcan. He was no fool. In 1913, he founded a review entitled *L'influence astrale* (Astral Influence). The review was short-lived, its first issue in 1913 beginning with a programmatic statement by one Paul Flambart, and its fifth issue in 1914 ending with an essay discussing heredity and astrology, again by Paul Flambart. In between, there are a great many additional articles by Paul Flambart, the pseudonym, as it happens, for Paul Choisnard himself. Like so many other hard-headed men, Choisnard was not disposed to let other men do his talking for him. Skeptical by nature, Choisnard seems to have been a rarity among astrologers in being skeptical about astrology. Although he was himself an indifferent statistician—a journeyman, but not a bungler—he stressed the importance of statistical technique to the astrologers that he taught.

Gauquelin acquired a mentor at a distance. The biographical details now tend to wander, often in opposite directions. His admirers depict him as a statistician persuaded by astrology, and his detractors as an astrologer persuaded by statistics. Gauquelin himself offers this description of himself as a young man. "At the age of twenty," he recounts (in his book, *The Truth about Astrology*), "I was wildly enthusiastic about everything to do with astrology, although I was equally mad about painting and tennis." It is an ardent if somewhat indiscriminate account.

Whatever the truth, Gauquelin was interested in astrology *and* he was a competent statistician, entirely more a fair-minded researcher than his critics, who were very often inclined to dismiss his research without first studying his books or verifying his data.

His work, and the work he inspired, represent the first and only attempt in the twentieth century to place at least certain astrological claims on a secure statistical basis—the only attempt, in fact, to bring astrology in from the badlands and place the discipline within the bounded confines of orthodox scientific thought.

GAUQUELIN'S CHIEF PROJECT has the merit of great simplicity. He wished to test the hypothesis that planets rising at the time of a man's birth influence his life in measurable ways. Two variables require specification: the relevant planets and those measurable ways. Gauquelin's earliest research was devoted to various professions. In looking at the birth date and hour of 508 well-known French physicians, Gauquelin came to suspect that Saturn and Mars were over-represented in their first and ninth houses. The correlation was weak, and the sample small.

In 1955, Gauquelin published his first book, *L'influence des astres* (The Influence of the Stars); and it is there that he made his general claim explicit.

From year to year, it became clearer that this was no mere freak of chance; in every country investigated, the same results appeared. Although they were separated by frontiers and different customs and languages, the newborn who were later to follow a given profession chose to come into the world under the same planet, whether they were French, Italians or Germans. Absurd though it seemed, a closer and closer connection was revealed between the time when certain great men were born and their professional careers. Doctors were not the only example, and Mars and Saturn were not the only planets to follow this rule. Jupiter and the moon appeared to have an equally large importance for other professions.

Gauquelin's research had convinced him that traditional astrological doctrines were very often worthless, and where worthwhile, in need of elaboration. A constellation appears on the eastern horizon, the planets enter their houses, and the sky assumes a complicated geometrical pattern. Powerful but hidden forces, Gauquelin believed, are at work within this traditional but simple model. There are regions of the sky where astrological forces intensify themselves, like pedestrians suddenly forming a crowd. Such are the Gauquelin zones. They are:

—The twelfth House and the ten degrees of the first House adjacent to the ascendant
—The ninth House and the ten degrees of the tenth House adjacent to the mid-heaven
—The sixth House and the ten degrees of the seventh House adjacent to the descendant
—The third House and the ten degrees of the fourth House adjacent to the *Imum Coeli*

It is the first and second zones that concentrate the force of various planets on the human personality; it is there that the astrological connection vibrates and hums. Gauquelin extended this astrological revision to include five planets: Jupiter, Saturn,

Mars, Venus, and the moon, and in a chart, he outlined the association between zones of maximum planetary intensity and personality configurations:

JUPITER	SATURN	MARS	VENUS	MOON
ambitious	cold	active	affable	amiable
authoritarian	concentrated	ardent	agreeable	disorganized
conceited	conscientious	belligerent	ambiguous	dreamer
gay (merry)	discreet	brave	attractive	easy-going
harsh	introvert	combative	beloved	fashionable
humorous	methodical	daring	benevolent	friendly
independent	meticulous	dynamic	charming	generous
ironical	modest	energetic	considerate	good company
lively	observant	fearless	courteous	good hearted
mocking	precise	fighter	elegant	helpful
proud	sad	offensive	gallant	imaginative
prodigal	reserved	lively	flattering	tolerant
show-off	simple	reckless	gracious	impressionable
social climber	somber	spontaneous	juvenile	impulsive
spendthrift	stiff	strong-willed	kind	merry
talkative	taciturn	stormy	obliging	nonchalant
warm	thoughtful	tireless	pleasant	popular
well-off	timid	tough	poetic	socialite
witty	uncommunicative	valiant	polite	spontaneous
worldly	wise	full of vitality	seductive	superficial

The entries in the chart will hardly come as a surprise to students of astrology. The psychological characteristics listed are both familiar and vague, and their planetary associations have long entered the stock of human metaphors. Just as Ptolemy suggested, the Saturnine personality is concentrated, introverted, methodical, precise, reserved, somber, and cold, even as Mars is aggressive, domineering, warlike, and fierce.

The Gauquelin zones represent an interesting addition to the astrological literature, a descriptive ornament. Astrologers are forever refining their systems, charting hidden angles and searching out obscure patterns that even planetary astronomers tend to ignore.

But for all that he may have been interested in doctors, Gauquelin was an athlete, and the long hours spent on the courts watching more powerful and rangier men beat him silly suggested a simple, interesting, measurable standard of astrological assessment. With his zones now available as tools, Gauquelin determined to study the personalities of championship *athletes*. He proposed to ask whether Mars—the planet of war, domination, power, and authority—might have shaped their talent by playing a role at their birth.

It was surely an interesting idea.

In *L'influence des astres,* and in a good many publications thereafter, Gauquelin concluded that Mars occupied certain positions in the sky more often at the birth of great athletes than it did at the birth of ordinary men and women. His statistical sample was not enormous—roughly five hundred cases—but it seemed at the time to be fairly chosen. The astrological influence Gauquelin discerned represented a refinement of his doctrine of intensity. In addition to zones, there are now sectors. In the case of Mars, the first starts at the point Mars rises; the fourth, at the point Mars crosses the line of the mid-heaven; and the sixth at the point Mars descends below the horizon. There are six comparable sectors numbered seven through twelve describing the orbit of the planet when Mars is below the horizon, and so hidden from sight.

His statistical analysis, Gauquelin argued, revealed that with respect to the Gauquelin zones of maximum intensity, sectors one and four are crucial. Roughly seventeen percent of the population at large—the halt, the lame, the merely clumsy, duffers, incompetents, would-be athletes, weekend golfers, and tennis players who poop out after two sets—should be born in the key sectors. This is the normal, the expected, distribution.

But among championship athletes, the relevant figure is *twenty-two* percent. The difference between the base line and test distributions is statistically significant, Mars apparently taking an immensely personal interest in the formation of a champion's personality.

This statistical result is known now as Gauquelin's Mars effect.

THE MARS EFFECT has, of course, elicited an enormous amount of attention from astrologers and skeptics alike, debates taking place in the late 1960s and throughout most of the 1970s, with a number of potshots and scattered exchanges recorded in the 1980s and the 1990s. The editors of the *Humanist* concluded, naturally enough, that Gauquelin's results represented selection bias on Gauquelin's part. Gauquelin listened very courteously to their criticisms, answering some, deflecting others. A statistician, Marvin Zelen, then the chair of the department of biostatistics at Harvard University, was introduced into the controversy in order to provide both camps with an objective protocol. Faithfully following Zelen's recommendations, Gauquelin tracked 16,756 men and women born within three days and in roughly the same place as 303 sports champions. He thus created a test sample against the background of a random population distribution. The test sample itself was drawn from a larger sample of 2,088 championship athletes. By comparing directly a small sample of athletes with a much larger sample of ordinary men and women, Gauquelin hoped to demonstrate that the Mars effect was something more than a statistical artifact or anomaly. Although it was Gauquelin himself who carried out the study, the results were solemnly approved by Marvin Zelen, and, indeed, the diagram illustrating these results is striking.

In 1994, Suitbert Ertel and Henrich Müller revisited Gauquelin's original study and reported that their analysis confirmed his findings. The Mars effect was "significant." Two years later, Ertel and Kenneth Irving published a volume entitled *The Tenacious Mars Effect*. In an article entitled, "Is the Mars effect Genuine?", Paul Kurtz, the editor of the *Humanist*, together with

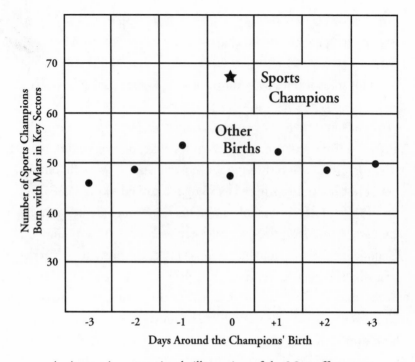

An interesting, very simple illustration of the Mars effect, one
indicating—if reliable—a statistical level of significance.

J. W. Nienhuysm and Ranjit Sandhu, argued that Ertel and Irving had begged a crucial question.

The controversy continues to play on, although with diminished intensity, and like the Pachelbel Canon, seems fascinating
until just that point that it becomes clear that canon and controversy are both unstoppable. Whatever the truth—I do not know
it and I suspect that no one does—the one fact that remains clear
is that the Mars effect, if genuine, represents a very weak signal
spotted against a great deal of noise.

Some years earlier, Ptolemy, writing in the treasure chest of
the *Tetrabiblos,* and obviously anticipating the course of history,
provided astrologers with a supremely versatile explanation for the
fact that astrological predictions, if genuine, are also weak. *Astron-*

omy, he argued, is cold, clear, and precise as a knife blade. *Astrology*, on the other hand, shares in the messiness of human life. Astrologers must inevitably make errors in observations, and these errors ramify through their inferences, often disastrously. Ptolemy compared astronomy and astrology directly: "Everything that is hard to attain," he wrote, "is easily assailed by the generality of men, and in the case of... [astronomy and astrology] ... the allegations against the first could be made only by the blind, while there are specious grounds for those leveled against the second."

Although convenient, the argument that follows is certainly not irrational. The general connection between the position of the planets and various human affairs and relationships, Ptolemy takes for granted. He assumes that as a theory, astrology is true. He means to ask how it is that a theory that is true might nonetheless be false.

> Nevertheless it is clear that even though one approaches astrology in the most inquiring and legitimate spirit possible, he may frequently err... because of the very nature of the thing and his own weakness in comparison with the magnitude of his profession.... It is furthermore true that the ancient configuration of the planets, upon the basis of which we attach to similar aspects of our own day the effects observed by the ancients in theirs, can be more or less similar to modern aspects, and that, too, over long intervals, but not identical, since the exact return of all heavenly bodies and the earth to the same positions... either takes place not at all or at least not in the period of time that falls within the experience of men.... So for this reason predictions sometimes fail.

Political scientists, social psychologists, sociologists, epidemiologists, cardiologists, dieticians, fitness trainers, marriage counselors, criminologists, meteorologists, poll takers, evolutionary biologists, physicians, jury selection consultants, fish hatchery specialists, phonologists, fashion designers, and even certain cosmologists, their success in prediction no better than Gauquelin's, may find in Ptolemy's argument a curious source of comfort.

His research inconclusive, Michel Gauquelin took his own life in 1991.

≈

SOME ASTROLOGERS continue to publish newspaper columns, of course, but I daresay that these columns are seen for what they are because they are what they seem—sheer nonsense. Still other astrologers form institutes and hold meetings. They assure one another that progress is being made and that all is well. Degrees are awarded, some well-known astrologers entering into print with at least thirty glowing letters after their names. A few astrologers lose themselves to mathematical mysticism. Influenced by Kepler's theory of the aspects, the English astrologer John Addey devoted himself to harmonic analysis. He seems to have been obsessed by the number nine. "All things," he wrote, "pass through nine stages." As one admirer reports, "His famous book, *Harmonics in Astrology*, long out of print is now again out of print," a circumstance that seems explicable in something less than nine stages.

A very few astrologers have made out very well. The story of Joan Quigley's influence on President Ronald Reagan has achieved a certain notoriety, although what Quigley actually provided Reagan seems never to have gone beyond advice concerning his schedule. President François Mitterand of France, a far more sinister political figure, had a far more serious relationship with a comely French astrologer, Elizabeth Teissier. French political gossips have been remarkably circumspect about the astrological counsel that he received. Teissier went on to receive a *doctorat d'état* from the Sorbonne's department of sociology. Employing critical standards that they had only recently discovered and never before applied, many French academics affirmed that they were scandalized. Teissier now appears regularly on French television.

These cynical reflections should now be brought to an end. Modern astrological theories have run out over a desert floor. But no culture quite manages to inter its past for long or for good. Despite assurances by the scientific community that we have collectively said good-bye to all that, the fact remains that the system of intellectual impulses that made astrology possible have by no means perished; and having for so long sustained the astrologers, these impulses are now sustaining others.

CHAPTER TWELVE

PISCES
♓
THE RETURN OF
RAWLINSON'S LEOPARD

B UT REALLY, THEY HAD no idea, the astrologers. They were
persuaded that they could peer into the future and manage
the flow of time. Perhaps some of them could; perhaps
some of them did. But what, in the end, did they see? Kings sitting insecurely on their thrones or storms at sea, a ship wallowing
in the waves. The harvest in autumn or snow piling up in gray
fields. The conquest of the Turks. This is all trifling, even if true.
The astrologers could not conquer time in any sense beyond the
trivial. They had no idea of the power and the depth of a profound scientific system.

The great theories of mathematical physics—*these structures
and no others*—have done what the astrologers could not do.
They have conquered time. Under their influence, the physical
universe has become temporally transparent. The laws of nature
specify processes in the world, as when a stone dropped from a
great height accelerates toward the center of the earth, its position
changing at every passing moment. Newton's laws of motion describe the relationship between free fall and free time. The relationship is simple. The position of a falling object near the earth
is *determined* by the time it has been falling. Although simple, the

relationship is nevertheless exact, Newton's laws coordinating position and distance for as far as the mathematician can see. No astrologer's chart has ever contained predictions as powerful.

There have been in all of history only four absolutely fundamental physical theories: Newtonian mechanics, Clerk Maxwell's theory of the electromagnetic field, Einstein's theory of relativity, and quantum mechanics. They stand in thought like the staring stone statues on Easter Island, blank-eyed and monumental. Each is embedded in a continuous mathematical representation of the world; each succeeds in amalgamating far-flung processes and properties into a single, remarkably compressed affirmation, a tight intellectual knot. And each theory contains far more than it seems to state. The theories of mathematical physics are vatic declarations, their ultimate message hidden in their symbols.

Within mathematical physics, predictions command a degree of accuracy that must be reckoned miraculous. Quantum electrodynamics is accurate to something like eleven decimal places. In determining the distance from New York to Los Angeles, theory and experiment diverge by no more than the width of a single human hair, pure thought and physical experience coinciding to a degree that is unprecedented in the entire history of the race, a specification of points and places utterly at odds with our habitual inability to say where our keys may have been misplaced or our hearts irretrievably lost.

X

WHATEVER IS REPRESSED in feeling, Freud memorably remarked, has a tendency to return in sentiment, often in disguise, and often with increased intensity. The astrologers have been driven underground by the contempt and indifference of the scientific community. Their obsessions have survived because they are so entirely human, and the peculiar nature of astrological thought is evident in all the sciences, disguised in form, but the same in spirit.

Throughout the long history of astrological thought, the astrologers have known that they were dealing in dangerous doctrines. Are the stars the *causes* of human action? A cause is a cage and, once in place, it permits no escape. What is known, logic suggests, cannot be changed. "We are all slaves," Marcus Aurelius wrote, "in a great family." Astrologers have made every effort to reject or to compromise this doctrine. And no wonder. It is unbearable. And yet the connection between knowledge and fatalism reappears in modern scientific thought, embedded in the greatest of physical theories, cold, cheerless, and grim.

The mathematician Pierre-Simon Laplace was born on the twenty-third of March, 1749, in Neaumont-en-Auge, and died in Paris on the fifth of March, 1827. He saw the great revolutionary convulsions in French life firsthand and if he was not quite an actor in the drama, he was at least a witness to its history. His youth was spent in a society still ruled by its corrupt aristocratic and clerical classes, and in his middle age he saw that society destroyed by terror. He was a man of considerable political skill, his survival of those political purges that consumed his close friend, the chemist Anton Lavoisier, an exercise in disciplined obsequiousness. Thereafter he was able to accommodate great hustlers like Napoleon and adjust himself to the new hard-edged and competitive version of French society that they had created. Mathematicians have never thought to diminish his reputation because he cared enough for his head to wish to keep it on his shoulders, and Laplace was not simply a mathematician, but a mathematician of remarkable range and power.

In addition to his purely mathematical work, Laplace was Newton's greatest interpreter, the five volumes of his magnificent *Traité de Mécanique Céleste* (Treatise on Celestial Mechanics) summarizing and expanding Newton's *Principia*, and projecting its mathematical program forward into the future.

On one occasion, Napoleon found it amusing to interrogate Laplace, asking questions about his mathematical work. Laplace answered as best he could, knowing that Napoleon's grasp of mathematics did not extend beyond what was necessary to prepare artillery tables.

"And what of God?" Napoleon asked.

"Sire," Laplace answered, "I have no need of that hypothesis."

This answer has come to represent the scientific enterprise itself. Laplace knew, as Newton did not, that the Newtonian system of thought had introduced the world to its material identity. There were no God or gods, as Laplace informed Napoleon, speaking as one blunt man to another, no signs or signals. Newton's laws bind up the parts of an impersonal universe. These coarse considerations led Laplace to a startling and prophetic conclusion. Like the omens of the *Enuma*, the arguments of the *Principia* are expressed as a series of conditional inferences. What material objects do is determined by their initial conditions— *if*—and the laws governing their behavior—*if-then*. When the *if* is given in fact, the future opens by means of a logical inference.

Laplace the mathematician now passes from the particular (falling objects on the surface of the earth, the moon in its orbit) to the general (the *entire* causal stream). "We ought then," he wrote, "to regard the present state of the universe as the effect of the anterior state and as the cause of the one that is to follow." The question that Laplace next asks has come to haunt the physical imagination. How would the universal progression seem "to a sufficiently vast intelligence"? Such an intelligence would find it unnecessary to divide the causal stream into the past, the present, and the future. "Nothing would be uncertain," Laplace writes, "all inferences instantly apparent, and the future, like the past, would be present to his eyes." This is not an experiment in religious thought. The sufficiently vast intelligence to which Laplace is appealing lies at the end of inquiry. When mathematical physics has reached its appointed end, it is the physicists who will see the universe as God might have seen it. They will have become omniscient.

To know everything is to know a universe emptied of its surprises. Things in such a universe do not become, have not been, and will not be. They simply are, available to inspection by the mind before they are available to inspection in fact. Frozen like a vast block of ice, the universe is uniformly accessible, cold, clear, eternal. Human beings reach events in the future by displacing themselves in time, just as they reach places on the earth by displacing themselves in space, but as they do not bring those places into being, they do not create those events. Whatever is simply is, now and forever. It is thus that time dwindles, and thus that time disappears.

Einstein's special theory of relativity is widely thought to support this view. Imagine a group of observers scattered carelessly throughout the cosmos. Each is able to organize the events of his life into a linear order; as a result, each is persuaded that his life consists of a series of *nows,* moving moments passing from the past to the present to the future. This is, indeed, how *we* see things. Now is, after all, now, is it not? *Right* now.

Apparently not. Simultaneity, special relativity revealed, depends on the speed at which observers are moving with respect to one another. Moving at different speeds, one man might conclude that his *now* is another man's past, or his future.

It follows that what is becoming for one observer may have become or may become for another. It is not clear how something can become when it has already been. What is left after becoming is subtracted from the cosmic account is time—that remains as a measurement, a local order imposed upon events; but it is a form of time blanched of meaning. Change has disappeared. And with change, action at a distance. If there is no change, there is no action either.

Writing to the widow of his old friend Michael Besso, Einstein appealed to his theory for comfort in the face of death. "For us believing physicists," he wrote, "the distinction between the past, the present and the future is only an illusion." It is an illusion, he added ruefully, that is rather stubbornly held.

More than two thousand years earlier, the Greek philosopher Favorinus argued that the future could not be known; he argued as well that *even* if it could be known, knowing it would do men little good. What cannot be changed cannot, after all, be changed. Ptolemy grasped this argument and met it by an assertion that he did not defend: The future can be known, he affirmed hopefully, *and* it can be changed.

The Italian astrologer Girolamo Cardano considered this exchange and, in the late sixteenth century, offered Favorinus a retrospective chance at the last word. "If events can be changed," he wrote, "they are not the future." But, of course, events lying in the past cannot be changed either; and since the present has no temporal extent—it is right now right now—it follows again that *nothing* can be changed.

)(

WHATEVER THE AUTHORITY of the scientific system of belief, and its authority is very great, the conclusion that the future cannot be changed has been widely rejected by ordinary men and women, and if not rejected, then resisted in a dull but stubborn way. A ring of iron may enclose the material world. No matter. It has not enclosed *us*. We think, judge, evaluate, and ponder, and we then make decisions as we see fit. We are persuaded that with respect to the spare, precious arena of human life, we are the masters and not the servants of an ineluctable process. Science as it is taught and life as it is lived are in conflict—one reason, I suppose, that the achievements of mathematical physics command respect but rarely elicit affection.

And yet, if it is true that knowledge reveals change to be impossible, the reverse is true as well. To the extent that the world *can* be changed, it is to that extent unknowable. This allows human freedom a small crawl space in which to wriggle, but like a crawl space in an imposing mansion, it is narrow and it is dark, and it is not clear that, crawling as we do, there is any place we may crawl *to*.

In 1900, Louis Bachelier, a student of mathematics, advanced the thesis that short-term price fluctuations on the French stock exchange could be modeled by a random walk. A walk of this sort is meant to evoke the proverbial drunkard, tottering from lamppost to liquor store, his steps moving erratically. For many years, his idea, although supported by a handful of economic studies, remained as an oddity on the margins of economic thought.

But in 1961, the mathematical economist Paul Samuelson demonstrated that Bachelier's hunch could be supported by a mathematical argument. The goal of the rational investor, Samuelson assumed, is to assess future stock market prices. What he has to go on are share prices that have already been set, and so the history of a commodity. This information is fully reflected in the price of the stock. In attempting to determine the future price of such an asset, the rational investor guesses at their expected mean value, with various market guesses and counter-guesses forming a frothing cascade. Nothing in this is meant to suggest the play of chance. Those guesses may be informed by art or science; they may be subtle, shrewd, and well-reasoned; and they may reflect the seasoned professional's long years of experience or the daring first venture of a neophyte ignorant of almost everything but the trade at hand. They are as reasonable and as solid as any estimation of the future beyond mathematical physics might be. And, of course, the guesses are themselves instruments of action. The guessed-at future is brought about by those guesses.

There is nothing in this that is not either obvious or trivial. This *is* how human beings bring about change.

Samuelson was nonetheless able to demonstrate that under these conditions, stock market prices would behave with no statistically significant movement in any direction. This result is now known as the random-walk hypothesis among stock market analysts and traders, and it has a richness of philosophical depth that is more considerable than its uninteresting mathematical character might suggest. Suppose the market replaced by an ordinary human crowd. Men and women are doing what men and women always do: They are thinking things through, weighing their options, sizing up risks, and considering what it is that deep down they really want. They mean to bring about change, and they do.

And *still*, the future must appear to them as if it were described by a random walk. To say this is to admit that the future is impenetrable in any interesting sense, the stock market analyst's frustrated *who knows?*, when asked what the market will do, echoed by our own frustrated *who knows?*, when asked what the future will bring. The doubled expression of uncertainty reflects the general principle that what will happen is anyone's guess. The conceptual connection goes from human choices, made freely, to a general and inviolable failure of prediction. This conclusion holds when the market shrinks to encompass one and only one individual, or when it expands to include the human community at large. The assumptions needed to power this argument forward are very modest: a quantitative measure, such as stock market prices, and perfect information widely distributed, nothing else.

One argument has suggested that, insofar as the future is known, it cannot be changed; it is an argument supported by all of the majesty of a great physical theory. Another argument has suggested that, insofar as the future *can* be changed, it cannot be known. And this argument is supported by the squeak of a small theorem in economics. The two arguments are related; they are, in fact, logically the same. Insofar as the future is known, it cannot be changed, and insofar as the future can be changed, it is not known.

This argument having been grasped, it is entirely possible that nothing of classical astrology remains. But if this is so, much *besides* astrology perishes *with* astrology, and in particular any attempt to bring free human action under the control of a scientific system of belief must be accommodated as an illusion.

)(

AS THE RULER OF THE SOUL, Ptolemy wrote in the *Tetrabiblos*, Saturn "has the *power* to make men sordid, petty, mean-spirited, indifferent, mean-minded, malignant, cowardly, diffident, evil-speakers, solitary, tearful, shameless, superstitious, fond of toil, unfeeling, devisers of plots against their friends, gloomy, taking no care of the body." There is no need to drown the point in words: *Some men are just rotten.* In answer to the question *why* rotten men are rotten, Ptolemy assigned the chief responsibility to Saturn. It is hardly an answer that has received much by way of careful statistical analysis, but whether Ptolemy was correct in the particulars or not, his explanation of human rottenness clearly captured some portion of the truth. It is awfully difficult to accept the thesis that rotten men are rotten because that is just the way that they *are*. It is, in fact, as difficult to accept this thesis as it is to accept the correlative conclusion that objects fall toward the center of the earth because that is just what they *do*. Something gets rotten men to be rotten. In wondering whether this something is Saturn, we are quibbling about the details. If not Saturn, then something else.

Certain explanations that once enjoyed great currency no longer compel our allegiance: the class struggle, early behavioral training, repressed infantile sexuality, the devil and his companions, the stars. Our collective inclination—and *collective* is just the right word, signaling as it does an almost complete consensus—is to assess the human personality in terms of the evolutionary history of the human race. Like the Big Bang, the relevant evolutionary story has acquired the aspect of a contemporary myth, one widely believed because widely told and vice versa.

The explanation's pivot is Darwin's theory of evolution. Only two ideas are crucial: random variation and natural selection. Things in nature arise by chance, and they survive by selection. The beak of the finch, the orchid's blush, the elephant's nose, and the giraffe's neck have all been explained by this simple story, beak, blush, nose, or neck arising by chance and surviving because they have, after all, survived.

Within the past fifty years, the story has been immeasurably enriched by being told at the molecular level. The essential narrative is now familiar, its art enhanced by repetition. Every living creature divides itself into its material constituents *and* an animating system of instruction and information. The material constituents are comprised of the proteins, the fats, and various other biochemical structures. Instruction and information is provided by DNA, a double-stranded molecule, its two strands turned as a helix. DNA is comprised of four elementary biochemical units, which are organized as triplets, and which run up and down the molecule's spine like beads on a string. The beads are in turn organized as genes. The genes handle instruction and information. They are strictly brain workers. Collectively, they control the organism, stamping onto its material constituents the very marks of its biological identity. It is when the genes are scrambled randomly that the result is a change in the genome, and so a change in the organism. Beak, blush, nose, or neck may now be explained on the molecular level, where accidents take place and strange things happen.

And if beak, blush, nose, or neck, why not behavior itself? Why not indeed?

"Beneath the variety of [human behavior]," the *New York Times* science writer Boyce Rensberger has argued, "there [are] common behavioral patterns *governed* by the genes and shaped by Darwinian evolution." Between Ptolemy's declaration that Saturn has the power to govern men's souls and Rensberger's declaration that certain genes have the power to govern men's behavior, there is a gently vibrating chord of sympathy.

SO FORTIFIED, we are returned to the question of old. Just why *are* some men "sordid, petty, mean-spirited, indifferent, mean-minded, malignant, cowardly, diffident, evil-speakers, solitary, tearful, shameless, superstitious, fond of toil, unfeeling, devisers of plots against their friends, gloomy, taking no care of the body?" More than two thousand years have gone by since Ptolemy offered his answer. The stars have withdrawn themselves. They are far away in space and lost in time. Their role has been assigned to other objects. According to views now current, indeed inescapable, some men are "sordid, petty, mean-spirited, indifferent, mean-minded, malignant, cowardly"—*they are just rotten*—because this is the way they have been made, and they have been made this way by their genes. Nothing else, after all, is capable of making a man in the first place. The story now goes backward in time to the Pleistocene Era or Stone Age, that half-mythical, half-real period of time during which human beings lived in small tribes of hunter-gatherers somewhere on the African savannah. A great burst of evolutionary inventiveness is assumed, the genetic apparatus of our ancestors scrambled randomly so that a rich repertoire of behavioral strategies became available for inspection by natural selection. The inevitable struggle for survival ensued, those strategies calculated in the nature of things to improve the representation of a man's genes in the future slotted to survive, the others to disappear.

This account has been used by Darwinian biologists to explain the development of a bipedal gait, the tendency to laugh when amused, obesity and anorexia nervosa, business negotiations, a preference for tropical landscapes, the evolutionary roots of political rhetoric, maternal love, infanticide, clan formation, marriage, divorce, certain comical sounds, funeral rites, the formation of regular verb forms, altruism, feminism, greed, romantic love, jealousy, monogamy, polygamy, adultery, recursion, sexual display, abstract art, and religious beliefs from the doctrine of the ubiquity of the Body of Christ to the deification of the Buddha.

"Who that knew well astrology," the astrologer John Gadbury remarked in 1674, "there is nothing in the world of which he could enquire by reason that he should not have knowledge thereof."

THERE IS A POINT in reading the *Tetrabiblos* when even the most sympathetic of students might well ask the obvious question. *Saturn?* Very well. It is the cause of human rottenness. But how does Saturn, which is, after all, very far away from the sordid locus of human affairs, *get* rotten men to be rotten? Surely it is fair to conclude that Ptolemy does not say because plainly he does not know.

But the simple and unavoidable fact is that if Ptolemy had no idea how Saturn makes men rotten, *we* have no idea how the gene for being "sordid, petty, mean-spirited, indifferent, mean-minded, malignant, cowardly, diffident, evil-speakers, solitary, tearful, shameless, superstitious, fond of toil, unfeeling, devisers of plots against their friends, gloomy, taking no care of the body" gets a man to *be* "sordid, petty, mean-spirited, indifferent, mean-minded, malignant, cowardly, diffident, evil-speakers, solitary, tearful, shameless, superstitious, fond of toil, unfeeling, devisers of plots against their friends, gloomy, taking no care of the body." We have *no* causal account that might tie a man's genes to what he does, if only because we have no causal account tying *any* gene directly to *any* form of biological activity beyond the biochemical.

DNA functions in any number of causal pathways, the tic of its triplets inducing certain biochemical changes and suppressing others. But even the simplest cell partakes in all of the mysteries of life. The bacterium *Escherichia coli* contains roughly two thousand separate proteins, and every one of them is mad with purpose and busy beyond belief. Chemicals cross the cell membrane on a tight schedule, consult with other chemicals, undertake their work, and are then capped in cylinders, degraded, and unceremoniously ejected from the cell. Dozens of separate biochemical systems act independently, their coordination finely orchestrated by various signaling systems. Enzymes prompt chemical reactions to commence and their work completed, causes them to stop as well.

No matter the causal pathways initiated by DNA, some feature of the cell remains stubbornly beyond their reach. Chemical actions are combinatorial in nature and local in effect. Chemicals affect chemicals within the cell by means of various weak affinities in which molecules exchange their parts in an irenic exchange, or like seaweed fronds, drift close to one another and then hold fast. But the activities of the cell are global. The cell is, after all, alive. It exists in time and it moves through space. It creates itself from itself, its constituents bringing order out of potential chaos, rather like a very intricate ballet achieved without a choreographer. We know of no causal sequence originating in DNA that explains this completely.

What cannot be done on the level of the bacterial cell plainly cannot be done on the level of the human being. The length of the path between a rotten man's genes and his rottenness is not only great but *infinite*. Human rottenness is something more than an organization of matter. A plot is not a disposition of material objects. It is a legal, social, and moral construction. How, then, can the biological effect of a gene get a man to be a "diviser of plots"? Although the concept of cause plays a role in our intuitive analysis of plots, the role that it plays does not exhaust the explanations that we seek. What a man does becomes a plot only when he has certain beliefs, is prepared to tell certain lies, exhibits certain convictions, has certain ends, and forms certain human bonds, perhaps with other plotters. If we understood what causes his beliefs, lies, convictions, goals, and all the other aspects of the human soul that are required to comprehend even the most ordinary of polluted political plots, then we might be in a better position to assess Saturn's role in causing rottenness. But if we need *first* to assess these things, then we are very much in the position of a man endeavoring to bail a boat from one end while watching it sink rapidly at the other.

We are thus returned to our original question: how do a rotten man's genes engender his rottenness?

Apparently, they just do.

THE GREAT ISSUES now return in all their disturbing vivacity and force. Darwinists do not think that "genes have a *deterministic* influence on development," the eminent astrologer Richard Dawkins has written. The idea is pernicious. Summarizing his views, his admirer Cosma Shalizi loyally adds that:

> Genes do not determine anatomy or physiology or behavior; genes encode the information to make proteins. Which

genes will be expressed...depends on a very subtle biochemical process, the complexity and intricacy of which is
hidden by the labels "signal transduction" and "genetic reg-
ulation." The idea that once we know an organism's genotype...we could read off its traits is a baseless fantasy
propagated by people who are at best idiots...or at worst
should know much better.

This is forthright, and confidently expressed. But look, every astrologer is now tempted to say with some asperity, either genes
determine human behavior or they do not. If they *do*, then far
from being a "baseless fantasy," the claim that once "we know
an organism's genotype...we could read off its traits" is the inescapable consequence of the idea that human behavior is under
genetic control.

If genes do *not* determine human behavior, then *no* causal
connection may be traced from the supposed sources of action in
genetics to its expression in rottenness. After all, to say that genes
do not determine behavior is just to say that you cannot get here
from there.

And if biologists are determined to have it both ways, arguing that something causes and does not cause human behavior,
we are returned to the astrological doctrine that the stars incline
but do not compel. It is perhaps only now that we can appreciate
the extent to which the astrologer's intuitions reflect a living truth
while failing entirely to embed that truth in a coherent scientific
theory. To a certain extent, we *are* in charge of things, and although there is much even within the perimeters of our own
bodies that we cannot control, much remains subject to our will,
and in the end we do manage to get the great lummoxy thing to
go where we wish, sit when we want, and, even on impossibly hot
days, break into a dogged trot. Our intuitions and the scientific
system of belief are nonetheless in hopeless conflict. There are in

nature no *causes* that incline but do not compel, if only because the concept is incoherent. Inclination without compulsion suggests a cause that is not a cause. The phrase must be discarded, and with it the idea that it prompts.

"Perhaps we should think of socio-biology," Tom Bethell has written sensibly (and not without sympathy), "as the astrology of the modern academy. Just as the mysterious emanations from celestial objects were once thought to shape character (with a role reserved for free will), so today's mysterious emanations from molecular objects are thought to do the same."

)(

FROM THE FIRST, astrologers were unsure whether the stars were causes or signs. It is the dividing point in the astrological system, the place where complicated inferences begin. Thomas Aquinas argued that, insofar as the stars gave access to the future, they did so as causes, and not as signs. This powerful conclusion has commanded the discussion for more than eight hundred years. It is the official doctrine of the Catholic Church *and* the modern scientific system of belief, a point not without its own power to convey a sense of irony. And now it is undergoing a subtle form of interior dissolution.

In advancing his doctrine of stellar rays, al-Kindi remarked that "the will of man is altered by the expression of words." And surely he was correct. Action at a distance lies as close at hand as the words that we speak or write. We respond to the human voice, the meaning and the message it conveys; we are sensitive to the written word; we are moved, whether to action or emotion, by durable pigments on canvas and all the symbolic contrivances of the race. All of this is as mysterious as it is familiar. How do material objects such as words—so much ink, after all, or vibrations in the air—acquire the power to penetrate other material objects? What makes this question both poignant and perplexing is just that, in explaining what words might do, we have only words to play with, rather like those strangely compelling athletes who, when asked the secret of their perfect golf swing, can do nothing better by way of explanation than shrug sheepishly and then demonstrate that fluid enviable stroke again. Athletes of the ordinary—you and I, that golfer too.

The ancient astrologers thought of the stars as the expression in matter of a god's intentions, or his desires; having conceived a vision of the future, whether involving crop failure or the death of kings, the gods made the matter manifest in signs. The ancient astrologers were thus preoccupied with celestial anomalies, irregularities in the heavens, places where the ordinary celestial fabric was, for one reason or another, ripped or torn. It is only there, they reasoned, that they could see into the heart of things, the place where the future stood revealed. What took place unfailingly did not interest them. The regularities of the natural world required no explanation and contained no valuable information. And it is this very old doctrine that has reemerged in modern physical thought.

The laws of physics control the behavior of matter. It is there that necessity rules, its iron fist unyielding. Necessity explains the movement of the sun, the moon, and the planets; it explains the dancing play of atoms and molecules; it governs the very skin of creation. But chance—luck—is also a great governing force. It is chance that accounts for the origin of life, and chance again that has governed the emergence of human beings, with their complicated languages, their insatiable desires, and their doomed sense of curiosity.

The biochemistry of living systems is based on carbon. The periodic table, which begins with hydrogen and then straggles up and down the chart, covers more than one hundred atoms. Among them only carbon can bond with other atoms in four different directions, and so only carbon has the flexibility to create ever larger and more complicated organic structures. As it happens, there is plenty of the stuff around, a state of affairs no less perplexing than the fact that apples unsupported fall downward or that the distances between planets is what it is. Why should these things be so? It is a question that Kepler might have asked, and it is Kepler's spirit that, like a shivery ectoplasm, hovers over this discussion.

In 1946, the astronomer Fred Hoyle published the first of his pioneering studies, *The Synthesis of the Elements from Hydrogen.* With this work, he introduced an extraordinarily interesting countercurrent into prevailing scientific orthodoxy. The rich and complex panoply of chemical elements that is characteristic of the universe, Hoyle argued, must have been forged by a sequential process, one starting with hydrogen and then continuing step by step until the construction of carbon, the universe enlarging itself in stages. The process could not be chemical in any ordinary sense; chemistry leaves the interior of the atom untouched. The creation of matter must thus have been handled within the stars.

If hydrogen is the first step in the chain, deuterium is the next, the fused product of two hydrogen atoms and a vital link in the formation of carbon. There are four fundamental forces in nature: gravity, electromagnetism, and the strong and weak nuclear forces. The fusion that fashions deuterium depends crucially on the magnitude of the strong nuclear force. Like all forces, the strong nuclear force is expressed as a number. The value of that number is critical. Were it weaker than it is, hydrogen atoms would have found themselves unable to fuse; were it stronger, the stars would long ago have burned themselves out.

None of this took place. The strong nuclear force has the value that it does.

The next step is relatively simple: deuterium atoms fuse together to form helium. The laws of physics would normally prevent helium atoms from spontaneously fusing to form anything beyond helium. But two vagrant helium atoms meeting in the interior of a star *can* fuse together to form a beryllium intermediate. It is an intricate celestial dance, and one that is highly unstable because beryllium intermediates are very short lived.

In 1953, Edwin Salpeter discovered that, like an opera singer and the glass she shatters, the nuclear resonance between helium atoms and intermediate beryllium atoms is precisely tuned to facilitate the creation of beryllium. Nuclear resonance is the vibration produced when the frequency of the absorbing nucleus is identical to the frequency of the emitting nucleus. What would otherwise have been a process sputtering into the abyss has now been promoted to a process taking helium into a new element.

There is yet no carbon. Hoyle now entertained his most daring conjecture. Before any evidence was available, he predicted the existence of a *second* nuclear-resonance sounding directly between beryllium and helium, one that would in its turn enable the great stellar furnaces to produce carbon in abundance. This prediction was verified. The steps involved in the construction of carbon lay revealed, and so, too, the path to life.

Hoyle was deeply troubled by the specific nuclear-resonance levels that he had discovered. That they expressed physical properties of material objects was not in doubt. But what explained the appearance of those physical properties in the great causal chain stretching from the Big Bang to the emergence of life? On this point, the laws of physics and the vagaries of chance would both seem unavailing.

"A commonsense interpretation of the facts," Hoyle concluded, "suggests that a superintellect has monkeyed with physics, as well as with chemistry and biology, and that there are no blind forces worth speaking about in nature."

"When I wrote to the King, my Lord," the astrologer Nabu-ahhe-eriba wrote long ago, "saying that 'the gods have opened the ears of the King, my Lord,' I meant that...the gods...send a *message* from heaven."

)(

THE ASTROLOGERS ARE waving from the land of the dead. There are the Babylonian scribes, slapping down wet clay and fashioning their dreaded omens with a sharpened stylus, and there is Balasi and Urad Nanna, anxious both of them about the king's health; Berossos the Chaldean is there and so is Vettius Valens, his financial secrets still a mystery, and austere Ptolemy, lonely in his library; Thrasyllus, Ascletario, and Dorotheos of Sidon ask to be remembered. So do Augustine of Hippo, Alcuin and Abu Mashar, al-Kindi, al-Biruni, al-Ghazzalli, and Michael Scot. Albertus Magnus is there, gentle but confused, and Thomas Aquinas, and the masters of medicine at the University of Paris, and Dr. Tornius, scuttling off to yet another autopsy. There is Tycho Brahe, his nose plate glinting, and Johannes Kepler, and William Lilly. Gerard Encausse, who perished in the First World War, is waving sadly, his hand draped in friendship around Paul Choisnard's shoulder. The sinister Nazi astrologers are busy offering their doomed salutes. The newspaper astrologers are otherwise occupied. And Michel Gauquelin says hello.

Whatever the quirks of their personalities, the astrologers had the gravity of actors in a great and tragic four-thousand-year-old drama. They took their charge seriously. They regarded their powers as a gift. They were conquered by problems they could not solve. They have now disappeared from the stage. The audience has quit the theater. There are peanut shells in all the aisles. Astrology is a failed science. Long live the astrologers, then, and may they flourish, for in their ardor and their innocence they are champions of doctrines that we can no longer fully trust but that we cannot bear to relinquish.

ACKNOWLEDGMENTS

I AM GRATEFUL TO my editor at Harcourt, Jane Isay, for suggesting that I write a book about the history of what she called a "failed science." It was a wonderful suggestion, and following it has introduced me to a landscape I never knew. My agent, Susan Ginsburg, has, as always, provided me sound editorial advice and wonderfully reassuring encouragement. I also wish to thank my good friend, Morris Salkoff, linguist *extraordinaire,* for his meticulous reading of the manuscript.

My greatest debt, however, is to my son, Mischa Berlinski, who served as my research assistant for the entire time that this book was under often laborious construction. This is, of course, a debt that affords a parent intense pleasure to acknowledge. Through fair weather and foul, Mischa trudged with unfailing devotion to various libraries in the United States and Europe, mastering and then poring over their stacks, uncovering obscure documents, tracking down sources, and sniffing out scholarly trails that researchers without his own impeccable classical education would never have been able to follow. Much of the book's organization is due to his sensible advice. In addition to acting as my researcher, Mischa also provided me with superb editorial recommendations, going over the manuscript line by line, and as often as not encouraging me to improve what I had written in haste or written carelessly. If I have, on occasion, decided to go my own way despite his good advice, this must be attributed to a father's effort somehow to hold his own.

Both Mischa and I wish to record our gratitude to the institutions in which the bulk of research for this book has been conducted: The Georgetown University Library in Washington, D.C., The Library of the American University, the Bibliothèque Nationale, the Bibliothèque des Langues Orientales, the Bibliothèque Musée de l'Homme, the Bibliothèque Sainte-Geneviève, and the Bibliothèque de la Maison des Sciences de l'Homme. Although widely derided for its poor architecture, the Bibliothèque Nationale is a splendidly efficient organization, and it contains a matchless collection of classical and modern sources. Working there has been a pleasure for the both of us.

NOTES

To the reader: For reasons of clarity, proper names in ancient languages and Arabic have been spelled without diacritical marks.

The notes that follow are by no stretch of the imagination a complete guide to the scholarly literature about astrology. They serve only to tie quotations in the text to their proper sources. Translations are as cited, but in the case of French, German, Greek, or Latin, all translations have been checked against their originals. Translations from the Arabic have been checked against their originals by Madamoiselle Sabrina Teffahi.

Page   PROLOGUE

3   *Gravely, Maternus considers the question, et. seq.:* Julius Firmicus Maternus, 3.1.9, *Ancient Astrology: Theory and Practice,* translated by Jean Rhys Bram (New Jersey: Noyes Press, 1975).
4   *"Fortune destroys us":* Ibid., 1.8.1.
5   *It was a configuration, Maternus had written, et. seq.:* Ibid., 3.5.23.
5   *And of this configuration:* Ibid., 3.5.22.

CHAPTER ONE

General guides to Babylonian astronomy and astrology:

Michael Baigent, *From the Omens of Babylon: Astrology and Ancient Mesopotamia* (London: Penguin, 1994).

Nicholas Campion, "Babylonian Astrology: Its Origin and Legacy in Europe," *Astronomy Across Cultures,* edited by Helaine Selin (Boston: Kluwer Academic Press, 2000).

For scholars, by scholars:

N. M. Swerdlow, ed., *Ancient Astronomy and Celestial Divination* (Cambridge, Massachusetts: The MIT Press, 1999).

Herman Hunger and David Pingree, *Astral Sciences in Mesopotamia* (The Netherlands: Koninklijke Brill, 1999).

Simo Parpola, *Letters from Assyrian Scholars to the Kings Esarhaddon and Assurbanipal* (in two volumes) (Kevelaer: Butzon und Bercker; Neukirchen-Vluyn: Verlag des Erziehungsvereins, 1970–1983).

9   *The document titles are in English, et. seq.:* Henry Rawlinson, *Cuneiform Inscriptions of Western Asia,* vol. III (London: lithographed by R. E. Bowler, 1870).

10 *"If the Star of Dignity":* Tamara Barton, *Ancient Astrology* (London: Routledge, 1994), p. 12.

11 *"To the King, our Lord":* Parpola, *Letters from Assyrian Scholars,* vol. 1, 51, p. 33.

12 *"May all these gods curse":* Laura Arksey, "The library of Assurbanipal, King of the World," *Wilson Library Bulletin* 51 (1977): 832–840.

12 *"To the King, my Lord":* Parpola, *Letters from Assyrian Scholars,* vol. I, 246, p. 189.

14 *"If an eclipse occurs in Arahsammna":* Francesca Rochberg-Halton, *Aspects of Babylonian Celestial Divination: The Lunar Eclipse Tablets of Enuma Anu Enlil* (Horn, Austria: F. Berger, 1988), VIII.13, p. 147.

14 *"The land of Akkad":* Ibid.

14 *"If the sun is seen":* Wilfred H. Van Soldt, ed., *Solar Omens of Enuma Anu Enlil, tablets 23 (24)–29 (30)* (Istanbul: Nederlands historisch-archaeologisch instituut te Istanbul, Leiden: Nederlands instituut voor het nabije oosten, 1995), vol. VI, tablet 28(29), 74, p. 102.

14 *"If on the first day":* Van Soldt, *Solar Omens,* vol. VI, tablet 28(29), 5, p. 93.

14 *"If Nergal approaches the Scorpion," et. seq.:* Barton, *Ancient Astrology,* p. 12.

14 *"If an eclipse occurs during the morning watch":* Rochberg-Halton, *Aspects,* VII. 3, p. 146.

16 *"Same u ersetim":* Ibid., p. 8.

16 *"Sky and earth together":* Ibid., p. 9.

16 *"The signs on earth just as those":* A. L. Oppenheim, "A Babylonian Diviner's Manual," *Journal of Near Eastern Studies* 33 (1974), p. 204.

16 *"Whoever wrote to the King":* Parpola, *Letters from Assyrian Scholars,* vol. I, 65, p. 43.

17 *"If in the eighth month":* Barton, *Ancient Astrology,* p. 12; but see also Erica Reiner and David Pingree, *Babylonian planetary omens 1, "Enuma Anu Enlil": tablet 63: the Venus tablet of Ammisaduqa* (Malibu: Undena, 1975), p. 29.

17 *"If the Goat star produces":* Hermann Hunger, *Astrological Reports to Assyrian Kings from the State Archives of Assyria* (Helsinki: Helsinki University Press, 1992), 74, p. 43.

18 *"To the King, my Lord,":* Parpola, *Letters from Assyrian Scholars,* 280, p. 229.

19 *"When I wrote to the King":* Hunger, *Astrological Reports,* 63, p. 37.

19 *"Interpretations of [the] omens are like this":* Parpola, *Letters from Assyrian Scholars,* 34, p. 25.

20 *"If Jupiter reaches the middle of the Scorpion":* Erica Reiner, "Babylonian Celestial Divination," in Swerdlow, *Ancient Astronomy and Celestial Divination,* p. 27.

22 *"The situation being one":* George Rawlinson, *A Memoir of Major-General Sir Henry Creswicke Rawlinson* (London: Longmans, Green and Company, 1898), p. 50.

22 *"Lose no opportunity":* Ibid., p. 57.

23 *"Once," his brother recalls:* Ibid., p. 149.

CHAPTER TWO

For scholars and by scholars, but an intensely
interesting human document nonetheless:
Otto Neugebauer and H. B. van Hoesen, *Greek Horoscopes* (Philadelphia: American Philosophical Society, 1959).

24 *"About a small lion":* Neugebauer and van Hoesen, *Horoscopes,* No. L 483, p. 146.

26 *"A most able man," Tatianus remarked:* Tatianus, *Oratio ad Graecos,* 36, quoted in Gerald Verbrugghe and P. Wickersham, *Berossos and Manetho, introduced and translated* (Ann Arbor: University of Michigan Press, 1996), p. 38.

26 *"In Babylonia," Eusebius writes:* Eusebius, *Chronicon,* quoted in Verbrugghe and Wickersham, *Berossos and Manetho,* p. 43.

27 *"Berossos," Seneca writes, "attributed":* Seneca, *Naturales Questiones,* 3.29.1, quoted in Verbrugghe and Wickersham, *Berossos and Manetho,* p. 66.

28 *"Some say she was the Babylonian Sibyl":* Pausanias, *Graeciae Descriptio,* 10.12.9, quoted in Verbrugghe and Wickersham, *Berossos and Manetho,* p. 37.

29 *In the* **Apology:** Plato, *Apology,* 26d, translated by Hugh Tredennick, *The Collected Dialogues of Plato* (New York: Bollingen Foundation, 1963).

29 *Vitruvius credits Berossos with the invention:* Vitruvius, *de Architectura,* 9.8.1, quoted in Verbrugghe and Wickersham, *Berossos and Manetho,* p. 35.

30 *This should come as no surprise:* See Franz Cumont, *Astrology and Religion among the Greeks and Romans* (New York: Dover, 1960).

31 *"The moon in Taurus":* Neugebauer and van Hoesen, *Horoscopes,* No. 15/22, p. 18.

32 *"Nativity of Pichime":* Ibid., No. 283, p. 62.

33 *He sees "well being and an abundance of pleasure,":* Ibid., No. 95, p. 28.

33 *"Another inquiry in Smyrna":* Ibid., No. L 479, p. 144.

36 *"In his 48th year,":* Ibid., No. L 105, p. 103.

36 *The life of Vettius Valens:* Biographical details and quotations from Mark Riley, *A Survey of Vettius Valens,* available online [cited August 18, 2003] at http://www.csus.edu/indiv/r/rileymt/ PDF_folder/VettiusValens.PDF, pp. 1–3.

38 *"The minimum period of the moon":* Neugebauer and van Hoesen, *Horoscopes,* No. L 75, p. 87.

38 *"This person was beheaded":* Ibid., No. L 97, II, p. 98.

38 *"This person hanged himself":* Ibid., No. L 91, p. 96.

38 *"This person burned to death":* Ibid., No. L 97, XI, p. 99.

38 *"This person was banished and committed suicide":* Ibid.

38 *"This person had in the fated places injury and tender feet":* Ibid., No. L 106, p. 103.

38 *"This person was killed by wild beasts":* Ibid., No. L 91, p. 96.

38 *"This person was drowned in bilge water":* Ibid., No. L 88, p. 95.

39 *The horoscope's subject began:* Ibid., No. L 102, p. 101.

40 *"In knowledge of various things":* Pliny, *Historia Naturalis,* 7.123, quoted in Verbrugghe and Wickersham, *Berossos and Manetho,* p. 36.

40 *During the early 1970s:* The existence of such lion sarcophagi was common throughout the classical world. The widespread allusion to lions as pets does raise the interesting question whether they belonged to the same species as the modern African lion.

CHAPTER THREE

41 *At some time between 180:* Aristeas, *Letter to Philocrates,* 9-10, translated by Moses Hadas, *Aristeas to Philocrates: Letter of Aristeas*

(New York, Dropsie College for Hebrew and Cognate Learning: Harper), 1951.

42 *The Greek Egyptian astrologer:* For an excellent general discussion of Ptolemaic astrology, see Mark Riley, "Theoretical and Practical Astrology: Ptolemy and His Colleagues," *Transactions of the American Philological Association 117* (1987), pp. 235–256.

42 *Gossips assigned Ptolemy:* For details of what is probably an apocryphal story, see F. E. Robbins, *The Tetrabiblos,* Cambridge, Massachusetts: Harvard University Press, 1980, p. ix.

43 *In astronomy, he writes,:* Ptolemy, *Tetrabiblos,* I.1.

44 *"The first order of business":* Ptolemy, *Almagest,* I.2, translated by G. J. Toomer, *Ptolemy's Almagest* (Princeton, New Jersey: Princeton University Press), 1998.

45 *"Absolutely all phenomena are":* Ibid., I.3.

48 *"It is clear,":* Ptolemy, *Tetrabiblos,* I.2.

48 *In a section of the* Tetrabiblos: Ibid., III.8.

52 *Conception marks the initial stage:* Ibid., III.1.

57 *There are as many charts:* Ibid.

58 *Some configurations of the heavens:* Ibid., III.13.

CHAPTER FOUR

For a detailed and sober guide to astrology
in Roman law and politics, see:

Frederick H. Cramer, *Astrology in Roman Law and Politics* (Philadelphia: American Philosophical Society, 1954).

60 *"At Appolonia, Augustus and Agrippa":* Suetonius, II.94, translated by Robert Graves, *The Twelve Caesars* (London: Penguin, 1957).

61 *In one of his immensely tiresome speeches:* Cicero, *De Divinatione.*

63 *"Look at Venus," Dorotheos advises:* Dorotheos, *Carmen Astrologicum,* II.1, translated by David Pingree (Leipzig: Teubner, 1976).

63 *"If Saturn is in quartile to Mercury":* Ibid., II.15.

64 *"If Mars is in left quartile":* Ibid.

67 *A bust made of Tiberius:* This bust may be found today in the Hermitage Museum in Saint Petersburg.

68 *Tiberius now subjected the astrologer to an interrogation:* Tacitus, *Annales,* VI.21, edited by Moses Hadas, translated by John Church and William Jackson Brodribb, *Complete Works of Tacitus* (New York: Random House, 1942).

71 *Suetonius tells another story:* Suetonius, XII, and, in particular, XII.15–17.

77 *"For what does this opinion really amount to":* Augustine, *City of God,* V.1, translated by Marcus Dods (New York: Modern Library, 2000).

CHAPTER FIVE

For a valuable introduction to the literature
concerning medieval Islamic astrology, see:
David Pingree, "Astrology," in M. J. L. Young, J. B. Latham and R. B Serjeant, *Religion, Learning and Science in the Abbasid Period* (Cambridge: Cambridge University Press, 1990), pp. 290–300.

80 *This is what Alcuin would have seen:* Yakut, *Geographical Encyclopaedia,* quoted in William Stearns Davis, ed., *Readings in Ancient History: Illustrative Extracts from the Sources* (Boston: Allyn & Bacon, 1912–12), pp. 365–367. This text is also published online [cited August 18, 2003] at http://www.fordham.edu/halsall/sbook.html.

82 *The luscious doctrines and details:* See David Pingree, "Abu Mashar," *Dictionary of Scientific Biography,* vol. 1 (New York: Scribner, 1981), pp. 32–5.

83 *Legends allude to words:* See Claire Fanger, "Things Done Wisely by a Wise Enchanter: Negotiating the Power of Words in the Thirteenth Century," *Esoterica* 1 (1999): p. 103.

85 *"For looking up they saw certain conditions":* Al-Kindi, *De Radiis Stellicis,* translated by Robert Zoller (London: New Library Limited, 2000), p. 30.

86 *The rays arise in the planets:* Ibid., p. 31.

86 *On the surface of the earth:* Ibid., p. 38.

87 *Abu Mashar's services did not come cheap:* See George Saliba, "The Role of the Astrologer in Medieval Islamic Society," *Bulletin d'Etudes Orientales* XLIV (1992): p. 63.

88 *Although Abu Mashar's thoughts:* See Richard LeMay, *Abu Mashar and Latin Aristotelianism in the 12th Century* (Beirut: American University of Beirut, 1962).

89 *If Mars is in Aries:* Abu Mashar, *The Abbreviation of the Introduction of Astrology,* translated by Charles Burnett, Keiji Yamamoto, and Michio Yano (Leiden: E. J. Brill, 1994), p. 15.

90 *But in his hands, Saturn becomes a kaleidoscopic symbol:* Ibid., p. 61.

91 *"When Venus is with Mars":* Abu Mashar, *Libri Mysteriorum,* II.169, translated by Daria Dudziak, available online [cited August 18, 2003] at http://www.cieloeterra.it/eng/eng.testi.metafore/eng.metafore.html.

92 *Whatever the methods by which:* See Lynn Thorndike, "Albumasar in Sadan," *Isis* 45 (1954): pp. 22–32.

93 *"He [Abu Mashar] said the reason":* Ibid., p. 31.

94 *There are any number of standard tracts:* This extraordinary list is drawn from the still more extraordinary list offered by George Atiyeh, *Al-Kindi: The Philosopher of the Arabs* (Islamabad: Islamic Research Institute, 1995), pp. 148–207.

CHAPTER SIX

97 *Whatever the theoretical demands:* The anecdotal accounts of astrological practice in this chapter come from Saliba, "The Role of the Astrologer in Medieval Islamic Society," *Bulletin d'Etudes Orientales,* XLIV (1992), pp. 45–67.

98 *The astrologers, the historian George Saliba writes:* Ibid., p. 56.

99 *Born in Baghdad in 1058:* See Al-Ghazzalli, *The Incoherence of the Philosophers,* translated by Michael Marmura (Provo, Utah: Brigham Young University Press, 1997), pp. xvi–xxvii.

99 *The stars seem small:* Ibid., p. xix.

102 *He served as a jurist:* J. J. O'Connor and E. F. Robertson, "Abu Ali al-Husain ibn Abdallah ibn Sina (Avicenna)," available online [cited August 18, 2003] at http://www-gap.dcs.st-and.ac. uk/~history/Mathematicians/Avicenna.html.

106 *The God of the Koran:* Quoted in Pervez Hoodbhoy, *Islam and Science: Religious Orthodoxy and the Battle for Rationality* (London: Zed Books, 1991), p. 98.

107 *"We confess that God":* Ibid.

110 *"The connection between what" et. seq.:* Al-Ghazzalli, *Philosophers,* 17, 1–34.

113 *"The meaning of the world":* Hao Wang, *Reflections on Kurt Gödel* (Cambridge, Massachusetts: MIT Press, 1987), p. 236.

CHAPTER SEVEN

115 *Sometime in the year 1184 A.D.:* The best account of the conjunction and panic of 1186 can be found in Theodore Wedel, *The Mediaeval Attitude Towards Astrology* (New Haven: Yale University Press, 1920), pp. 90–94; for Roger of Hoveden, see *Chronica Magistri Roger de Houedene,* 2.297, edited by William Stubbs (London: Longmans, Green, 1869).

115 *The Spanish astrologer Corumphiza offered a few pertinent details:* Roger of Hoveden, *Chronica Magistri,* 2.290–2, but see also the text of the letter offered online [cited August 18, 2003] at http://academics.hamilton.edu/religious_studies/rseager/re336.00/ text_medieval.html

115 *A letter written by:* Wedel, *Mediaeval Attitude,* p. 93.

116 *"This is something that the writer":* Nicolas Whyte, *Astronomy and Astrology in the 12th Century,* published online [cited August 18, 2003] at http://explorers.whyte.com/astrol.htm.

120 *Alone among the scholastics:* My discussion of action at a distance in the work of Albertus Magnus owes much to Francis Kovach. See Francis Kovach, "The Enduring Question of Action at a Distance in Saint Albert the Great," in *Albert the Great:*

Commemorative Essays, edited by Francis Kovach and Robert Shahan (Norman: University of Oklahoma, 1980), pp. 161–235.

118 *"A menstruating woman," he wrote:* Albertus Magnus, *Summa de Creaturis,* II, q. 45 a.4, quoted in Kovach, *Albert the Great,* p. 173.

118 *With lunatic assurance, Aristotle:* Aristotle, *De insomniis,* 459b24ff.

120 *Some men, Albertus observed:* Albertus Magnus, *De Animalibus,* XXII, tr.1 c.5, quoted in Kovach, *Albert the Great,* p. 204.

121 *In a wonderfully suggestive image:* Albertus Magnus, *Summa de Creaturis,* I, tr. 4 q.60 a.2, quoted in Kovach, *Albert the Great,* p. 172.

122 *The life of Michael Scot:* The best account of the life of Michael Scot is Lynn Thorndike, *Michael Scot* (London: Nelson, 1965).

123 *The chronicler Jacques de Vitry:* Jacobus de Vitriaco: *Hist. occid.* II.7, *Translations and Reprints from the Original Sources of European History,* published for the Department of History of the University of Pennsylvania. Philadelphia: University of Pennsylvania Press [1897?–1907?], vol. II:3, pp. 19–20. This is online [cited August 18, 2003] at http://www.fordham.edu/halsall/source/vitry1.html.

124 *Pope Honorius III described Michael Scot:* Thorndike, *Michael Scot,* p. 11.

124 *"Nor is there an instrument,":* Ibid., p. 12.

125 *When it is in a fire or air sign:* Michael Scot, *Liber Introductorius,* M 118ra, quoted in Lynn Thorndike, *Michael Scot,* p. 94.

125 *It follows, Scot argues, that those:* Ibid., M 52rb, p. 97.

125 *Saturn, when found in a certain position,:* Ibid., pp. 105–106.

126 *"I began, as the custom is,":* Ibid.

127 *The tenements of Lucy Mills et. seq.:* F. W. Maitland, ed., *Select Pleas in Manorial and Other Seignorial Courts: Volume 1—Reigns of Henry III and Edward I* (London: Bernard Quaritch, 1889), online [cited August 18, 2003] at http://www.fordham.edu/halsall/seth/bec1280.html.

127 *"Even in Bracton's day":* Frederick Pollock and Frederic Mait-

land, *History of English Law,* vol. I (Cambridge: Cambridge University Press, 1968), p. 526.

128 *"Whether divination by the stars is unlawful?" et. seq.:* Thomas Aquinas, *Summa Theologica,* II.II.95.5, translated by the Fathers of the English Dominican Province (New York: Benzinger Brothers, 1922).

135 *Marcilio Ficino, the Renaissance:* Plotinus, *Enneads,* II.3.7, translated by S. MacKenna (New York: Pantheon, 1957).

138 *Like so many of:* Thorndike, *Michael Scot,* pp. 54–55.

139 *"Michael is said to have forseen":* See the Web site [cited August 18, 2003] http://www.brown.edu/Departments/Italian_Studies/ dweb/history/characters/michael_scot.shtml for the complete text, in both the original Latin and English translation.

141 *When Saturn is in Libra:* Abu Mashar, *On Historical Astrology: The Book of Religions and Dynasties,* 1.12, translated by Charles Burnett and Keiji Yamamato (Boston: Brill, 1999).

141 *If Jupiter or the moon:* Ibid., III.10.

141 *If Mars is near Saturn:* Ibid., III.9.

142 *Venus in Libra:* Ibid., IV.10.

142 *And Mercury?:* Ibid., V.9.

142 *The moon in Libra:* Ibid., VI.10.

142 *And finally the sun:* Ibid., VII.9.

CHAPTER EIGHT

For an excellent discussion, see:
Norman Cantor, *In the Wake of the Plague: The Black Death and the World It Made* (New York: Perennial, 2002).

146 *"But see with what":* Rosemary Horrox, *The Black Death* (Manchester: Manchester University Press, 1994), p. 250.

146 *It is his autopsy report et. seq.:* Edward Grant, *A Sourcebook in Medieval Science* (Cambridge, Massachusetts: Harvard University Press, 1973), pp. 740–742.

148 *"In the year of our Lord":* Jean Ganivet, *Amicus Medicorum,* translated by Robert Zoller (London: New Library Limited, 1979); available online [cited August 18, 2003] at http://www. new-library.com/zoller/library/ganivet/rz-ganivet-medicorum.pdf.

150 *In 1555, more than:* Andrew Dygges, *A Prognostication, Manuscript on Medical Astrology* (London, 1555); quoted online [cited August 18, 2003] at http://www.homeoint.org/morrell/astrology/medical.htm.

151 *"The heart and the liver":* Grant, *Medieval Science,* p. 745.

151 *Living and working in:* Roger French, "Astrology in Medical Practice," in *Practical Medicine from Salerno to the Black Death,* edited by Luis Garcia-Ballester, Roger French, *et al.* (Cambridge: Cambridge University Press, 1994), pp. 44–47.

153 *In his* Historia de Morbo *(History of the illness):* Horrox, *Black Death,* pp. 14–26.

153 *The physician and surgeon Guy de Chauliac:* Grant, *Medieval Science,* pp. 773–774.

154 *The medical faculty complied, issuing their report:* Horrox, *Black Death,* pp. 158–163.

158 *Galen was born in roughly 130* A.D.: See Owsei Temkin, *Galenism: Rise and Decline of a Medical Philosophy* (Ithaca, New York: Cornell University Press, 1973).

161 *"Although major pestilential illnesses" et. seq.:* Horrox, *Black Death,* p. 160.

162 *For many years, the explanation:* See Cantor, *Wake of the Plague,* for an interesting discussion.

165 *Andronikous Palealogous, a librarian:* Horrox, *Black Death,* p. 8.

166 *In letters to his friend:* Ibid., pp. 248–249.

CHAPTER NINE

169 *The Imperial Mathematician:* See Victor Thoren, *The Lord of Uraniborg: A Biography of Tycho Brahe* (Cambridge: Cambridge University Press, 1990).

171 *At roughly the same historical moment:* For a complete account

of the destruction of the Istanbul observatory, and an excellent discussion of the history of the observatory in the Islamic world, see Aydin Sayili, *The Observatory in Islam* (New York: Arno Press, 1981), pp. 289–300; for the poem, see Aydin Sayili, "Alâ al dîn al Manṣûr's Poems on the Istanbul Observatory," *Belleten* 20 (1956): pp. 429–484.

172 *Johannes Kepler had come:* For the life of Kepler, see Max Caspar, *Kepler,* translated by C. Doris Hellman (New York: Dover, 1993).

174 *"I like to be on the side of the majority":* Quoted in Owen Gingerich, "Kepler," *Dictionary of Scientific Biography,* vol. 9 (New York: Scribner, 1981), p. 307.

174 *When skeptics challenged Kepler's willingness:* "There is much therein which must be deliberately pardoned or else it injures my reputation with you. The thing is this: I write not for the large masses, nor for learned people, but rather for noblemen and prelates, who claim a knowledge of things they do not understand. No more than four hundred to six hundred copies will be distributed, none goes beyond the boundaries of these lands. With all prognostications, I see to it that I give my above-described circle of readers a happy enjoyment of the vastness of nature with sentences which happen to occur to me and appear true, in the hope that the readers might be tempted thereby to raise my salary." Caspar, *Kepler,* p. 60.

175 *He was indifferently disposed toward numbers:* Ibid., p. 93.

176 *An armillary sphere:* The armillary sphere is today in the National Maritime Museum in Greenwich. A reproduction of the sphere can be found in Elly Dekker, *Globes from Greenwich* (London: Zwemmer, 1993), p. 65.

180 *"Almost a whole summer," et. seq.:* Gingerich, "Kepler," in *Dictionary of Scientific Biography,* p. 290.

185 *"In the case of Jupiter first":* J. V. Field, "Astrology in Kepler's Cosmology," in *Astrology, Science, and Society: Historical Essays,* edited by Patrick Curry (Woodbridge, Suffolk: Boydell Press, 1987), p. 147.

187 *Kepler answered Röslinus:* See Franz Hammer, "Die Astrologie des Johannes Kepler," *Zeitschrift Fuer Wissenschaftsgeschichte* (Wiesbaden: Band 55, 1971). No English translation is available. Excerpts from Kepler's *Tertius Interveniens* have been published by Kenneth G. Negus, *Kepler's Astrology* (Princeton, New Jersey: Eucopia Publications, 1987). Kepler's original work, *Tertius Interveniens* (Frankfurt: Gottfried Tampachs, 1610), remains available only in German and in German gothic script.

189 *The* **Harmonicum Mundi** *(Harmony of the World):* My account of the *Harmonicum Mundi* owes much to J. V. Field, "A Lutheran Astrologer: Johannes Kepler," *Archive for the History of the Exact Sciences,* 31, 1984, pp. 229–268; and Owen Gingerich, *The Eye of Heaven: Ptolemy, Copernicus, and Kepler* (New York: American Institute of Physics, 1993).

CHAPTER TEN

200 *The men were "discoursing on many things," et. seq.:* William Lilly, *The Last of the Astrologers: Mr. William Lilly's History of His Life and Times from the Year 1602 to 1681,* edited by Katherine M. Briggs (London: Folklore Society, 1974), p. 21.

203 *Whatever his afflictions:* Ibid., p. 35.

204 *Lilly's intelligence, while sensitive, was not large:* Ibid., pp. 25–28.

206 *The battle of Alresford et. seq.:* William Lilly, *Christian Astrology,* available online [cited August 18, 2003] at http://ourworld. compuserve.com/homepages/mcmcann/alresfor.htm.

209 *The historian A. L. Rowse:* A. L. Rowse, *Simon Forman: Sex and Society in Shakespeare's Age* (London: Weidenfeld & Nicolson, 1974), p. 7.

210 *The social historian Ann Geneva:* Ann Geneva, *Astrology and the Seventeenth Century Mind: William Lilly and the Language of the Stars* (Manchester: Manchester University Press, 1995), p. 9.

212 *A young woman "had permitted a Lord to have the Use of her Body.":* Lilly, *Last of the Astrologers,* p. 32.

213 *On occasion, he used his art:* Lilly, *Christian Astrology,* pp. 397–399.

215 *In 1684, Dr. Halley came:* See David Berlinski, *Newton's Gift* (New York: Free Press, 2000), p. 91.

216 *"Amidst other discourse":* Berlinski, *Newton's Gift,* p. 2.

218 *The problem is built into the very notion:* Consider two closed regions of space S and S* with boundaries B and B*. Either the distance between them is greater than 0 or 0. If greater than 0, there is no *contact.* If 0, this means that at some common point P on B and B*, S and S* are occupying the same region of space at the same time. This is physically impossible. No two physically distinct objects can be in the same place at the same time. This issue is, in fact, not soluble within Newtonian mechanics and is glossed over even in sophisticated texts. The point dissolves as a problem within quantum mechanics in view of the uncertainty principle, which places a limit on the degree to which an object's position and momentum may simultaneously be measured. But quantum mechanics resolves one conceptual difficulty only by introducing another. If there is contact in a world explained by quantum theory, there is no longer distinctness in identity.

221 *"Does this really involve a considerable":* Max Jammer, *Concepts of Force: A Study of the Foundations of Dynamics* (Cambridge, Massachusetts: Harvard University Press, 1957), p. 12.

222 *In the years before the restoration of 1652:* See Patrick Curry, *Prophecy and Power: Astrology in Early Modern England* (Princeton, New Jersey: Princeton University Press, 1989), pp. 40–42.

CHAPTER ELEVEN

225 *"Acceptance of astrology pervades modern society":* From "Objections to Astrology: A Statement by 186 Leading Scientists," *The Humanist* (September 1975). Available online [cited August 18, 2003] at http://www.americanhumanist.org/about/astrology.html.

227 *"For the anti-scientific astrologers":* Paul Choisnard, *Essaie d'astrologie Expérimentale* (Paris: Chacornac, 1913), p. 31.

227 *Consider, for example, Jan Erik Hanussen:* Details are drawn from Mel Gordon, *Hanussen: Hitler's Jewish Clairvoyant* (Los Angeles: Feral House, 2001). I have measured Gordon's account against the recollection of my parents, both of whom remembered Hanussen very well.

230 *Like Augustus, high Nazi officials:* There is not yet a definitive account of astrology in the Third Reich. I have assembled my account from a variety of sources on the Internet—sources whose reliability it is often difficult to assess. For further details, see Wullf, Wilhelm, *Zodiac & Swastika: How Astrology guided Hitler's Germany* (London: Barker, 1973); [cited August 18, 2003] http://www.service-asp.de/horoskope/geschichten/krafft.htm; [cited August 18, 2003] http://www.geocities.com/karlkrafft/; [cited August 18, 2003] http://www.meta-religion.com/Esoterism/Astrology/into_the_twentieth_century.htm.

233 *"Earthquakes will occur":* This and subsequent quotations available online [cited August 18, 2003] at http://www.astrology-and-science.com/intv2p8.htm.

236 *Choisnard died in "his famous sixty third climateric year":* See Patrice Guinard, *French Astrology in the 20th Century,* available online [cited August 18, 2003] at http://cura.free.fr/docum/16afr-en.html.

237 *"At the age of twenty":* Michel Gauquelin, *The Truth About Astrology* (New York: Random House, 1984).

237 *"From year to year":* Michel Gauquelin, *The Scientific Basis for Astrology* (New York: Stein & Day, 1973), p. 163.

240 *In L'influence des astres:* See M. Gauquelin, Francoise Gauquelin, and S. B. G. Eysenck, "Personality and position of the planets at birth: An empirical study," *British Journal of Social and Clinical Psychology* 18 (1979), pp. 71–75.

241 *The Mars effect has, of course:* For a complete account of the controversy, see Suitbert Ertel and Kenneth Irving, *The Tenacious Mars Effect* (London: Urania Trust, 1996).

CHAPTER TWELVE

247 ***Within mathematical physics:*** My ideas in this chapter were first expressed (and expressed in greater detail) in a number of separate essays: "The Soul of Man under Physics," *Commentary* (1995); "The Deniable Darwin," *Commentary* (1996); "The End of Materialist Science," *Forbes ASAP* (1996); "What Brings a World into Being?", *Commentary* (2001); "Einstein and Goedel: Friendship between Equals," *Discover* (2002); "Has Darwin Met His Match?" *Commentary* (2002).

248 ***Pierre-Simon Laplace was born:*** There are any number of sources in which the life and work of Laplace are discussed. See, for example, the entry under Laplace in the *Dictionary of Scientific Biography* (New York: Scribner, 1990), whence the Napoleon anecdote.

The idea that time is unreal or that change is by no means a clear or a simple thesis. It would require a treatment of book length to make the case I have presented in this chapter in a philosophically compelling way. See Berlinski, "Einstein and Goedel," for further details.

253 ***Samuelson was nonetheless able to demonstrate:*** See David Berlinski, *Black Mischief: Language, Life, Logic and Luck* (San Diego: Harcourt, 1986).

255 ***The explanation's pivot is Darwin's theory:*** See Berlinski, "The Deniable Darwin."

259 ***Darwinists do not think:*** Quoted in Shiochi Habu, "Religion, Group Affiliation at Root of Conflicts," *The Yomiuri Shimbun Online,* online [cited August 18, 2003] at http://www.yomiuri.co.jp/dy/civil/civil010.htm.

259 ***Genes do not determine:*** Cosma Shalizi, *Bactra Review,* online [cited August 18, 2003] at http://www.cscs.umich.edu/~crshalizi/reviews/extended-phenotype/.

261 ***"Perhaps we should think of socio-biology":*** Tom Bethell, "Against Sociobiology," *First Things* 109 (2001), pp. 18–24.

262 ***The biochemistry of living systems is based on carbon:*** See Berlinski, "Has Darwin Met His Match?" for details.

INDEX